HOW
BAD
DO YOU
WANT IT?

HOW BAD

DO YOU

WANT IT?

MASTERING

THE PSYCHOLOGY OF

MIND OVER MUSCLE

MATT FITZGERALD

FOREWORD BY SAMUELE MARCORA, PHD

BOULDER, COLORADO

velopress®

3002 Sterling Circle, Suite 100
Boulder, CO 80301-2338 USA

VeloPress is the leading publisher of books on endurance sports. Focused on cycling, triathlon, running, swimming, and nutrition/diet, VeloPress books help athletes achieve their goals of going faster and farther. Preview books and contact us at velopress.com.

Distributed in the United States and Canada by Ingram Publisher Services

Library of Congress Cataloging-in-Publication Data
Names: Fitzgerald, Matt, author.
Title: How bad do you want it?: mastering the psychology of mind over muscle /
    Matt Fitzgerald; foreword by Samuele Marcora, PhD.
Description: Boulder, Colorado: VeloPress, [2016] | Includes bibliographical
    references and index.
Identifiers: LCCN 2015048381 | ISBN 9781937715410 (pbk: alk. paper)
Subjects: LCSH: Endurance sports. | Endurance sports—Psychological aspects. |
    Endurance sports—Physiological aspects.
Classification: LCC GV749.5 .F55 2016 | DDC 612/.044—dc23
LC record available at https://lccn.loc.gov/2015048381

This paper meets the requirements of ANSI/NISO Z39.48-1992 (Permanence of Paper).

Cover design by Kevin Roberson
Cover photograph by Jeff Johnson
Interior design by Jane Raese

Text set in Lino Letter

18/ 10 9 8 7 6 5

THE MIND IS THE ATHLETE.

—Bryce Courtenay, *The Power of One*

CONTENTS

FOREWORD

Doing research to understand what limits endurance performance is not just an academic exercise. It also affects the way endurance athletes are tested, the way they train, and how they prepare for competitions. For the first 100 years in the history of exercise physiology, endurance was thought to be limited by muscle fatigue caused by energy depletion or inadequate oxygen delivery and consequent acidification of the locomotor muscles. As a result, endurance athletes wear heart rate monitors during training and have their ears pierced to measure blood lactate, erythropoietin use has plagued cycling and other endurance sports, and tons of pasta and rice have been consumed before competitions. These are only some examples of how exercise physiology has had an impact on the lives of endurance athletes.

Then, in the late 1990s, Professor Tim Noakes came up with the Central Governor Model (CGM). This model proposes that endurance performance is limited by a subconscious intelligent system in the brain (the central governor) that regulates locomotor muscle recruitment so that the speed/power output sustained over a race never exceeds the capacity of the body to cope with the stress of endurance exercise. The hypothesis is that if this safety system didn't exist, a highly motivated endurance athlete might exercise beyond his/her physiological capacity and threaten his/her own life with heat shock, myocardial ischemia, and rigor mortis.

The CGM was revolutionary because it convinced many exercise physiologists that the organ that limits endurance performance is the brain, not the cardiovascular system and fatigued locomotor muscles. Subsequent research, including our 2010 study that inspired the subtitle of this book, confirmed this no longer controversial idea. There is a big problem, however: If endurance performance was limited by a subconscious and intelligent safety system in the brain, what could endurance athletes do about it? The answer would be nothing apart from training the way they have always done to increase the capacity of their bodies to cope with the stress of endurance exercise. Indeed, the CGM has not had any significant impact on the way endurance athletes train and prepare for competitions.

Fortunately, there is no evidence to indicate that a central governor exists inside our brains, and endurance athletes have considerable control over their performance. This alternative model of how the brain regulates endurance performance is called the Psychobiological Model. Its core principles are that decisions about pacing or quitting during endurance competitions are taken by the conscious brain and that these decisions are primarily based on the conscious sensation of how hard, heavy, and strenuous exercise is, a feeling we call perception of effort.

Many of my colleagues in exercise physiology find it difficult to accept the Psychobiological Model; how can something ephemeral and subjective like a perception have such a great influence on endurance performance? Surely things that can be objectively measured (e.g., heart size and how much glycogen is inside the locomotor muscles) are more influential. This conclusion may be justified if one considers endurance performance simply as the output of a biological machine with no thoughts and feelings. However, I consider endurance performance to be a self-regulated behavior on which thoughts and feelings can have profound influences. The pain of torture (a perception) can force soldiers to betray the country they dedicated their lives to. Intense hunger (a perception) can turn civilized people into cannibals. Thoughts and feelings can also lead to the ultimate catastrophic failure of homeostasis: death by suicide. Therefore, we shouldn't be surprised that perception of effort (and thoughts related to it) can limit endurance performance. Perceptions are powerful.

Matt Fitzgerald was one of the first sportswriters to recognize the potential implications of this Psychobiological Model for endurance athletes. I still remember our first chat over a cranky mobile-phone connection in 2009 after we published our seminal study on the effects of mental fatigue on perception of effort and endurance performance. I was at a track and field meeting in Italy, and Matt was in his house in the United States. We talked for well over an hour, fueled by my passion about interdisciplinary research (and a natural tendency of Italians to talk a lot!) and Matt's thirst for the latest scientific developments that may have a positive impact on his many readers. Our "long-distance relationship" has continued over the years with me producing more research on the psychobiology of endurance performance and Matt translating it for the general public via his articles and books.

In this book, Matt has put together an impressive collection of real-life examples of how perception of effort and other psychological factors affect endurance performance. These examples from the lives of elite athletes from a variety of endurance sports are skillfully mixed with summaries of the most relevant scientific research. The result is quite remarkable: a book that can be read as a sports biography but, at the same time, provides suggestions on how to improve endurance performance by becoming your own "sport psychologist." I hope this will lead to a more widespread application of psychological principles and techniques by endurance athletes and their coaches. Indeed, the power of psychology has not been fully exploited in endurance sports, and to use it deliberately and systematically is one of the main practical suggestions derived from the Psychobiological Model.

However, as Matt points out, this does not mean that winning endurance competitions is simply a matter of "willpower." Conscious self-regulation of thoughts, emotions, and behavior can have a dramatic influence on endurance performance, as beautifully illustrated by the real-life examples provided in this book. But genetics, physical training, and nutrition (e.g., carb intake and caffeine) also play a big role because they have profound influences on perception of effort. The subconscious brain can also influence perception of effort, as we recently demonstrated using subliminal visual messages. How to avoid the negative effects of some subconscious stimuli and harness the power of the subconscious to improve endurance performance is going to be one of the future developments of psychology applied to endurance sports.

We are also working on a novel kind of training, called Brain Endurance Training, that combines physical training with mentally demanding tasks to stimulate the brain areas involved in self-regulation and to increase resistance to mental fatigue. It is an exciting time because the Psychobiological Model is inspiring innovative performance-enhancing strategies that work over and above those developed on the basis of the traditional cardiovascular/muscle fatigue model.

So keep an eye on Matt. I am sure this book is only the first of a series of successful books on this very promising area of development for endurance athletes.

—*Samuele Marcora*, PhD

ACKNOWLEDGMENTS

The process of researching and writing this book was a rewarding test of endurance, one that I could not have completed and would not have enjoyed without the help of a great many talented and generous people. In particular, I wish to acknowledge and thank Bob Babbitt, Kevin Beck, Chris Bednarek and Team Unlimited, Greg Benning, John Bingham, Casey Blaine, Serena Burla, Walt Chadwick, Nathan Cohen, Ted Costantino, Louis Delahaije, Chris Derrick, Adam Elder, David Epstein, Nataki Fitzgerald, Robert Gary, Elliott Heath, Elena Ivanova, David Jankowksi, Renee Jardine, Jeff Johnson, Hunter Kemper, Linda Konner, Siri Lindley, Bobby Mack, Samuele Marcora, Alissa McKaig, Greg Meyer, T. J. Murphy, Connie Oehring, Ned Overend, Beth Partin, Linda Prefontaine, Pete and Zika Rae, Toni Reavis, Stephen Roth, Josh Sandeman, Jenny Simpson, Neely Spence, Willie Stewart, Joseph Sullivan, Fritz Taylor, and Ryan Vail.

INTRODUCTION

MY FIRST ENDURANCE RACE was a two-lap run around the athletic fields at Oyster River Elementary School in Durham, New Hampshire. The contest was one of many that made up the program for Field Day, a sort of graduation rite for fifth graders. Like most 11-year-olds, I had run plenty of neighborhood races, but they'd all been short sprints. Children do not compete over long distances except under the direction of adults. On Field Day, I found out why.

Knowing no better, we all took off from the start line at full speed. After 60 or 70 yards, a flu-like weakness invaded my legs. I seemed to grow 2 pounds heavier with each stride. My esophagus burned like an open wound dunked in saltwater. A tingling sensation crept into my head, and my consciousness became a weak flame guttering in a malevolent wind. The few thoughts I was able to form were fragmentary and panicked: *What the hell is happening to me? Is this normal? Are the other kids hurting this much?*

I completed the first lap and, shaking off a powerful temptation to quit, started the second. One boy remained in front of me—Jeff Burton, the only kid in my class as skinny as I was. I understood my situation. I could either push harder to catch Jeff at the cost of intensifying my misery or cap my misery and let Jeff go. But a third option materialized: Jeff faltered. Buoyed by the sight of his unraveling, I passed him on the approach to the last turn and crossed the finish line victorious, though too weary to celebrate except inwardly.

I came away from this experience having learned a fundamental truth about endurance sports. While my legs and lungs had put me in a position to win, it was my mind—particularly my ability to absorb the shock of the novel sensations I felt and my willingness to suffer a bit for the sake of winning—that had carried me over the top. The essential challenge of long-distance racing, I understood, was mental.

Three years after my Field Day triumph, I blew out my left knee on a soccer pitch. The surgeon who stapled it back together advised me to find another sport. I'd been moonlighting as a miler for the Oyster River Middle School track team and having some success with it at the time of my injury. So I decided to put all my chips on running.

This was 1985, medieval times in the evolution of post–knee reconstruction recovery and rehabilitation. I wore a full-leg cast for six weeks after surgery and then graduated to a brace, which stayed on for another six months. That Kevlar-and-Velcro albatross circled the track with me throughout my first season of high school indoor track. When the brace came off in the spring, I felt reborn. I raced the mile seven times in the outdoor season and set personal bests six times.

In the fall, I led our cross country team to a state championship title in one of New Hampshire's three interscholastic athletic divisions. A week later, I took 10th place individually at the "Meet of Champions," where the top teams and individuals from all three divisions went head-to-head. I was the second-highest finisher among sophomores and the highest-placing first-year runner. I was on a path to become the best high school runner in the Granite State before I graduated.

It never happened. The first indication that it wasn't to be came at the very moment of my big breakthrough at the divisional state cross country championship. The race was held at Derryfield Park in Manchester, the toughest high school cross country course in America. It starts at the bottom of a ski slope, goes right to the top, and comes

2

back down. I summited the mountain in second place behind Sean Livingston, a senior who was on a completely different plane of talent. I didn't think much of it until we came out of the woods, and my girlfriend saw me and squealed at the person standing next to her, "Oh, my God! He's second!" Then I realized I was killing it.

Moments later, though, I was passed by Todd Geil of rival Stevens Academy, a fellow sophomore. At the base of the hill, he had 10 or 15 meters on me. But the course made one last diabolical turn upward before flattening out for the finish. I was a better uphill runner than Todd (that was how I'd gotten ahead of him in the first place), and I started to reel him in.

We rounded the final turn together. Todd got up on his toes and charged. I did the same. We sprinted in virtual lockstep down the homestretch as our parents and coaches and teammates screamed in our ears.

Then I just gave up. Threw in the towel. Quit. It happened as Todd ratcheted up his pace one more notch—his final ante. I will never know if I could have matched his quickening and perhaps raised him a notch of my own, because I didn't even try. The reason was simple: It hurt too much. A part of me seemed to ask, *How bad do you really want this?*, and another part answered, *Not as much as that guy.* I don't think Todd was more talented or fitter than I was—indeed, I would defeat him in two of the five championship cross country races remaining in our high school careers. What separated us that day was that he was willing to try harder.

The shock of my first exposure at age 11 to the suffering that comes with endurance racing had never left me. I loved running, loved getting fitter and faster, but I hated suffering the way I did in races. My aversion to the dark side of the sport I'd chosen had been manageable when I was new to it and my expectations were low. But when I reached the level of the contenders, I discovered that I could hurt even more than I had, and that I would have to hurt more in order to become a champion. Only then did I realize that I had previously operated inside a sort of comfort zone within discomfort, an illusory "100 percent" that I had no choice but to move beyond if I was ever going to be *the* best.

But I did not make that choice. Instead I became a classic head case. An all-consuming dread possessed me on race days. My stomach churned, my heart raced, and my thoughts circled obsessively around the agony to come. If the race fell on a Tuesday, I sat through my classes in a fugue state, hearing nothing the teachers said. If it was on a Saturday, I could barely force down my Honey Nut Cheerios before I left home to meet up with my teammates for the bus ride to the slaughterhouse.

In my junior year, I began to mail in my races, my false 100 percent efforts becoming an inwardly acknowledged 95 percent. I ran just hard enough that no one else knew I was sandbagging. Even so, I still had some good days—I finished sixth in the Meet of Champions in 1987—but more often I left the racecourse disgusted with myself, knowing I hadn't left it all out there.

Things got worse. At an outdoor track meet in Boston, I faked an ankle sprain halfway through a 2-mile race and fell to the ground writhing in phony pain. Weeks later, I pretended to miss the call to the start line of another 2-mile race, and the field went off without me. After my senior cross country season (which I capped with a pathetic 17th place finish in the Meet of Champions, a race in which my nemesis, Todd Geil, took second), I quit running. The wimp in me had prevailed.

In 1995, two years out of college and still believing I was through with running, I moved to San Francisco. My goal was to take the first decent writing job I was offered. As it turned out, that offer came from Bill Katovsky, who had founded *Triathlete* 12 years earlier and was then launching a new endurance magazine called *Multisport*. I would just as gladly have taken a gig with *High Times*, but fate chose to immerse me neck-deep in an environment filled with people who loved working out and getting fitter and faster, as I once had.

The inevitable happened. I got sucked back into training and racing, first as a runner and then as a triathlete. It was a slippery slope.

I became increasingly devoted to these pastimes and more and more ambitious. Two overlapping desires fueled this second act of my life as an endurance athlete. Above all, I wanted to become the athlete I might have been if I hadn't quit. But to do this, I understood, I needed to overcome the mental weakness that had kept me from becoming the athlete I might have been the first time around, and I wanted to get that monkey off my back for its own sake.

I never did become the athlete I might have been. My true Achilles heel proved to be a mutinously fragile body that caused me to pull up lame if I so much as uttered the words *plantar fasciitis*. (There were portents of this weakness in my youth, among them my left-knee blowout at age 14.) But if I failed to become the athlete I might have been, I succeeded at least in becoming the best athlete I could be given the flawed body I was stuck with. I got the monkey off my back.

If the moment I let Todd Geil go in the homestretch of the divisional state cross country championship marked the symbolic loss of my integrity as an athlete, a moment during the 2008 Silicon Valley Marathon signaled my redemption. I was about 3 miles from the finish line and suffering mightily when I passed a young couple standing at the roadside, probably waiting for a friend to come by. I'd gone about a dozen paces beyond them when I heard the woman speak one word.

"Wow."

This word might have meant any of a number of things. Perhaps the young lady was impressed by how fast I was running. But the leader of the race (I would finish third) had come through 4 minutes ahead of me. So it wasn't that. Or maybe she was admiring my beautiful running style. But I do not have a beautiful running style, and my stride probably never looked worse than it did in that moment.

Indeed, I believe the woman who said "wow" was actually awed by how *terrible* I looked, by the hideous strain in my movements. I must have appeared to her like a man slogging through invisible waist-deep liquid. That's certainly what the effort felt like to me. I was drooling too, I'm pretty sure. The stranger's monosyllabic utterance was a nod of respect to how hard I was trying, how much I was willing to suffer in pursuit of my meaningless goal of finishing in a certain amount of time.

I did not, in fact, achieve my personal time goal in that race, yet another injury having curtailed my training just enough to put it out of reach. But I achieved something greater—the satisfaction of knowing that for once I had truly left it all out there on the racecourse.

Mile 23 of the 2008 Silicon Valley Marathon remains my most treasured moment as an athlete. More than that, I regard it as one of the finer moments of my entire life. Sure, it was just a race, but sports are not really separate from life, nor is the athlete distinct from the person. In mastering my fear of suffering in races, I acquired a greater level of respect for myself, a sense of inner strength that has helped me tackle other challenges, both inside and outside sports.

I might never have redeemed myself in this way if not for a certain advantage I gained from my work as an endurance sports writer: frequent contact with world-class athletes. Through these interactions I discovered that the most gifted .001 percent have the same psychological vulnerabilities that the rest of us have, and must overcome them to achieve things we do not. Talent alone doesn't cut it. This realization filled me with a mix of healthy shame and inspiration that moved me to try harder.

At a relatively early point in the second act of my life as an endurance athlete, I had a long telephone conversation with Hunter Kemper, who had competed in the 1998 USA Triathlon Elite National Championship in Oceanside, California, two days earlier. I'd seen the event in person as a reporter for *Triathlete*. Halfway through the closing 10K run, Hunter and Australian Greg Welch shook themselves loose from the lead pack. Welch had won the 1990 Triathlon World Championship, the 1993 Duathlon World Championship, the 1994 Ironman World Championship, and the 1996 Long-Distance Triathlon World Championship. Hunter was a 22-year-old rookie pro whose greatest athletic feat was a second-place finish in the Atlantic

Coast Conference Championship 10000 meters. The two men came into the last half mile still running side by side. I asked Hunter what that was like.

"I was freaking out," he told me.

Hunter's fuller explanation made it clear to me that he felt as intimidated, as terrified, and as surreally out of place as I would have felt in his shoes. He suffered a soul-twisting crisis of confidence as he ran down the long final stretch toward the finish line with Welch right beside him. Something within Hunter seemed to ask, *How bad do you want it?* There was a moment of uncertainty, of wavering. But in the next moment, Hunter recognized that he wanted to win the race more than he feared his legendary challenger, and enough to suffer for it. He took a blind leap into the abyss and discovered the possibility of a whole new level of effort. His sudden acceleration snapped Welch's neck—figuratively—and the rookie sped to the finish line alone, winning the first of an eventual seven national championship titles.

Later in the same phone conversation, I learned from Hunter that his best high school time for 2 miles was 2 seconds slower than mine. Experiences like this one—and there were many more—deflated my fear of suffering in races. They strengthened my determination to become a tougher racer, and my belief that I could.

While this personal evolution was ongoing, a revolution was taking place in sports science. New technologies such as functional magnetic resonance imaging had opened the first narrow window into the brain, allowing exercise physiologists to learn more about that sodden, 3-pound electrified organ's role in relation to endurance performance, a process that has culminated in the development of a new "psychobiological" model of endurance performance. Named by Samuele Marcora, an Italian exercise physiologist who lives and works in England, this new model views mind and body as interconnected, with the body distinctly subordinate. Given my lifelong fascination with the mental dimension of endurance racing, I followed this research keenly and eventually I began to share what I was learning in magazine articles and in books such as *Brain Training for Runners*. What excited me most about the brain revolution in endurance sports, and about the psychobiological model that issued from it, was that they resoundingly validated the lesson I had taken away from my fifth-grade initiation into the experience of endurance racing. It turns out the essential challenge of endurance sports really is psychological.

Many aspects of endurance performance that were always presumed to be biological in nature are now known to be mind-based. To give one example, studies by Paul Laursen of Australia's Edith Cowen University and other researchers have demonstrated that, except in extreme cases, dehydration, which is biological, does not cause athletes to slow down in races; instead, the psychological condition of *feeling thirsty* does.

As a "hard" science, the field of exercise physiology is peopled by men and women who have strong materialist leanings, and who are therefore dispositionally disinclined to value the role of the mind in endurance performance. This bias has made them generally dismissive of champion athletes' frequent insistence that the mind, in fact, is running the show. But the brain revolution has turned many of these scientists against their materialist bent. These enlightened researchers are now willing to concede that the great Finnish runner Paavo Nurmi had it right when he said almost a century ago, "Mind is everything. Muscle—pieces of rubber. All that I am, I am because of my mind."

A more rigorous if less poetic way of expressing Nurmi's belief is this: From a psychobiological perspective, endurance performance is determined solely by the mind's output; biology is no more than an external input to the mind, influencing its output. The British neuroscientist Vincent Walsh has even suggested that sports competition is the single most challenging thing the human brain ever does—more challenging even than "purely" mental tasks like solving differential equations and also more challenging to the brain than it is to the body.

If you think that's a stretch, consider this: Muscles are not needed at all for endurance racing, or for any other form of movement, for that matter. They are entirely expendable and replaceable. Today quadriplegics can control robotic limbs *with their thoughts* through electrodes attached to the scalp. Soon it will be possible for victims of full paralysis to compete in endurance races while strapped inside a mechanical body, or remotely. Will these cybernetic athletes be able to go forever? No. Their performance will be limited by the mind, just as the performance of able-bodied endurance athletes has always been.

Controlling a robotic body with one's thoughts is not easy, even though the robotic body is doing all of the work—because it's *not* doing all of the work. After 30 minutes or so of feeding herself with a robotic arm, the user hits a wall of fatigue that renders her powerless to continue. There is no practical difference between this phenomenon and the case of a mountain biker bonking on the last hill of a race. In both scenarios, the breakdown occurs in the brain as a result of the mental effort of pushing the body—be it flesh or metal—to do work.

If science has only recently recognized that endurance is fundamentally psychological, common language has always known. When we say that a person has *endured* something, what do we mean? We mean that the person has gone through a challenging *experience*. A hiker might endure 36 hours of wandering lost on a cold mountain, or a naval officer might endure seven days of sleep deprivation during the SEAL training program's Hell Week (as my father did during the war in Vietnam). But it's the experience, not the biological effects of cold exposure or sleep deprivation, that must be endured. If the hiker did not feel the cold, or if the naval officer did not feel his tiredness, there would be no basis for congratulating him on surviving the ordeal.

Endurance athletes, by definition, endure. They endure long hours of training, the privations of a monastic lifestyle, and all manner of aches and pains. But what endurance athletes must endure above all is not actual effort, but *perception of effort*. This is the phrase that scientists now use to refer to what athletes normally describe as "how hard" exercise feels in a given moment, and it represents the central concept of the psychobiological model of endurance performance. It was perceived effort that so shocked me on Field Day in 1982 and that I later recoiled from as a high school runner. And it is perceived effort, according to the latest science, that causes the mountain biker to hit the wall on the last hill of a race, makes the paralytic woman manipulating a robotic arm with her thoughts bonk after 30 minutes of self-feeding, and constrains endurance performance in all circumstances. The most important discovery of the brain revolution in endurance sports, and the most important truth you can know as an endurance athlete, is this: *One cannot improve as an endurance athlete except by changing one's relationship with perception of effort.*

Even something as seemingly physical as training conforms to this principle. The training process increases an athlete's physical capacity, but at the same time it changes her relationship with perception of effort. The fitter the athlete becomes, the easier it feels for her to swim, bike, run, or whatever at any given speed, and *that* is why her performance improves. If the athlete's physical capacity increased but her relationship with perception of effort did not change accordingly, her race times would not get any better because she would be psychologically unable to access that increased physical capacity.

In reality, the scenario I've just described could never happen. Perceived effort is essentially the body's resistance to the mind's will. The fitter an athlete becomes, the less resistance the body puts up. Therefore increased physical capacity is always *felt*.

A variety of factors that affect the mind directly may also change an athlete's relationship to perception of effort and thereby enhance performance. Some of these factors increase the amount of output (i.e., speed) that results from a given level of effort, just as training does. One such factor is *inhibitory control*, or the ability to stay focused on task-relevant stimuli (such as a competitor up ahead) in the presence of distracting stimuli (such as a memory of losing to that same competitor in a previous race). A 2014 study conducted by Samuele Marcora and published in the *European Journal of Applied Psychology* showed that a cognitive test designed to fatigue the brain's inhibitory control mechanism increased perceived effort and reduced performance in a subsequent 5-km run. One year later, researchers at the University of Padua reported in *PLOS ONE* that runners who achieved higher scores on a measurement scale for inhibitory control performed better in an ultramarathon.

Other factors increase the amount of perceived effort an athlete can (or will) tolerate. An obvious example of this sort is motivation. It was mainly through heightened motivation that I developed a greater tolerance for perceived effort and moved beyond being a head case as an endurance athlete.

Not all endurance athletes are head cases, but given the nature of the sports in which they participate, all endurance athletes face psychological challenges, and all such challenges are either directly or indirectly related to perception of effort. If racing wasn't as hard as hell, athletes would not experience moments of self-doubt, or pre-race apprehension, or post-race regret, or mental burnout, or intimidation. Even most training errors, such as overtraining, originate in the fear of suffering.

Psychologists use the term *coping* to refer to a person's behavioral, emotional, and cognitive responses to discomfort and stress. Endurance sports are largely about discomfort and stress; hence they are largely about coping. In a race, the job of the muscles is to perform. The job of the mind is to cope. But here's the hitch: The muscles can only perform to the degree that the mind is able to cope. Endurance sports are therefore a game of "mind over muscle."

In endurance sports, successful coping is any behavior, emotion, thought, or combination thereof that yields better performance. Phrased another way, successful coping in endurance sports is any response to discomfort and stress that favorably changes an athlete's relationship to perception of effort, either by increasing the amount of effort the athlete is able to give or by enhancing what the athlete gets out of her best effort.

Some methods of coping are more effective than others. Faking an injury to avoid the discomfort of completing a race, as I did in high school, is one example of an ineffective coping method. Drawing inspiration from elite athletes to embrace greater levels of discomfort, as I did in the second act of my life as an endurance athlete, is an example of a more effective coping method.

To become the best athlete you can be, you need to become really good at coping with the characteristic forms of discomfort and stress that the endurance sports experience dishes out, beginning with perceived effort and extending to the many challenges that are secondary to it, such as fear of failure. You must discover, practice, and perfect the coping skills that conquer these challenges most effectively. My own term for a highly developed overall coping capacity in endurance sports is *mental fitness*.

Traditional sports psychology is of limited use in developing mental fitness. Before the brain revolution, when mind and body were treated as separate and when biology explained almost everything (except it didn't), the discipline of sports psychology was confined to a small space in the margins of the athletic sphere. It consisted of a hodgepodge of techniques that were overtly nonphysical, such as visualization and goal setting, and almost always practiced outside the context of the sport itself. These same tricks were foisted upon athletes in all sports, from those in which perception of effort plays a small role, such as baseball, to those in which perception of effort is everything: endurance sports.

The brain revolution has caused a new sports psychology to begin to emerge, one that is grounded in the psychobiological model of endurance performance and hence is specific to these disciplines. The new psychology differs from the old in two key ways. First, it focuses squarely on the development of mental fitness, or of coping skills that directly and indirectly alter an athlete's relationship to perceived effort in ways that improve performance. It is a psychology of mind over muscle.

Second, in the new endurance sports psychology, the role of sports psychologist is taken on by you—the athlete. Why? Because the only way to become really good at coping with the discomforts and stresses of endurance sports is to experience them. Visualization sessions and goal-setting exercises alone won't help your mind quell your body's rebellion in the toughest moments of a race. Developing mental fitness requires exposure to these challenges no less than the development of physical fitness requires exposure to workouts. Nobody can do this work for you, or even guide you through it. Coping is a *response* to discomfort and stress, after all.

Being your own sports psychologist means more than learning the hard way from experience, however. There is a crucial difference between muddling blindly through athletic challenges and encountering them with prior knowledge of their nature and of the methods of coping with them that have proven most effective for other athletes. The overarching mission of the new psychology of endurance sports is to equip athletes with this knowledge so that they do not have to "reinvent the wheel" in their attempts to master the discomfort and stress of their sport but can function successfully as their own sports psychologist.

The best source of knowledge concerning the most effective methods of coping with the challenges of endurance sports is the example set by elite endurance athletes. The methods that the greatest athletes rely on to overcome the toughest and most common mental barriers to better performance are practically by definition the most effective coping methods for all athletes. Champions are the ultimate role models for sports psychology no less than they are for training and nutrition. It is not possible to succeed at the highest level of any major endurance sport with a B+ mental game. No athlete, no matter how talented, can win on the international stage today without harnessing the full power of his mind to maximize both the amount of effort he is able to give and the amount of performance he gets out of his best effort. Consider how much more Hunter Kemper achieved than I did with perhaps only slightly greater raw physical talent.

To learn from the champions, it is not enough to be exposed to their stories of overcoming. We must also know how to interpret these examples. What is the essential nature of the challenges the most successful racers face and overcome? How do we understand the coping skills they use to master these challenges in a way that allows us to replicate them in our own experience? These are the questions we have to answer in order to benefit from the example set by the best of the best. The psychobiological model of endurance performance helps us here. By applying this new science to elite-athlete case studies we can tease out practical lessons that can then be applied to our own athletic journeys.

It was this combination of vicarious experience and scientific interpretation that directed my path to redemption in the second act of my life as an endurance athlete. As a high school runner I lacked even the vaguest scientific understanding of the fears that held me back. Nor did I realize that elite athletes faced and overcame the same fears. As an adult runner-triathlete I tackled these fears head-on in the role of sports psychologist to myself, armed with knowledge of their neuropsychological essence and with inspiration taken from the examples of elite athletes who demonstrated the most effective ways to cope with them. This wisdom did not itself conquer the challenge I sought to master, but it gave me the wherewithal to actively exploit my athletic experiences to gain mental fitness.

The job of this book is to help you become your own sports psychologist—a competent and ever-improving practitioner of the new psychology of endurance sports. You will find no techniques or exercises in the pages ahead. That's traditional sports psychology. Instead you will encounter true stories of overcoming, drawn mainly from the elite stratum of endurance sports, which become "teachable moments" when viewed from the perspective of the psychobiological model of endurance performance.

In every race, something within each athlete (something we may now specify as perception of effort) poses a simple question: *How bad do you want it?* To realize your potential as an athlete, you must respond with some version of this answer: *More.* And then you have to prove it. It's easy in principle, hard in practice—much harder than figuring out how to train, what to eat, and which shoes to wear. Here's my promise to you: After you've read this book, your answer to the most important question in endurance sports will never be the same.

CHAPTER ONE

A RACE IS LIKE A FIRE WALK

AT A PRESS CONFERENCE held the day before the 2010 Chicago Marathon, returning champion Sammy Wanjiru confessed that he was only 75 percent fit for the race. He wasn't bluffing. Three weeks earlier, Sammy had contracted a stomach virus that caused him to miss several critical days of training. While he was laid up in bed, he contemplated pulling out of Chicago and running the following month's New York City Marathon instead.

Had the flu been his only complaint, Sammy would not have considered such a drastic step. But 2010 had been a tough year all around for the 23-year-old hero of Kenya. While training for April's London Marathon, where he was also the defending champion, Sammy had tumbled and whacked his right knee. He started the race anyway, but the injury flared up and he was forced to drop out 10 miles from the finish line. Ethiopia's Tsegaye Kebede went on to win the race.

If Sammy had a rival, it was this man. Kebede had finished second to Sammy in the prior year's London Marathon and had taken the bronze medal to Sammy's gold in the 2008 Olympic Marathon in Beijing. Kebede was on the start list of the 2010 Chicago Marathon, and this may have been why Sammy chose not to withdraw despite his lack of fitness. The two men were ranked first and second in the World Marathon Majors competition, a two-year series that awarded a half-million-dollar prize (equivalent to $26.5 million in Kenya) to the runner who accumulated the most points in the participating events. The 2009–2010 competition was set to conclude at New York. None of the other contenders for the prize was racing there, though, so whoever finished ahead in Chicago—Sammy or Kebede—would have the thing sewn up.

After dropping out of London, Sammy flew with his coach, Federico Rosa, to Italy, where the athlete received intensive treatment on his damaged joint. In June, he started a half marathon in Sicily, but the knee gave him more trouble and Sammy bailed out again. The next race on his calendar was September's Berlin Marathon. He withdrew from it and shifted his sights to Chicago. Even with an extra four weeks to prepare, there was no room for any more setbacks.

Then came more setbacks. No sooner had the knee finally healed than Sammy's low back turned cranky. He trained through the pain as best he could and was just beginning to round into form when the stomach virus hit.

Upon regaining his health, Sammy realized that he still wanted to race despite his spotty preparation, if only to keep Kebede from stealing his half-million-dollar payday. Rosa reluctantly supported the decision, but insisted that Sammy race cautiously, sitting behind the leaders in an effort to slow the race and conserve what strength he had for a late attack.

Cautious race tactics did not come naturally to Sammy. His normal racing style was best described as savagely aggressive. At the Olympics, he had launched a surprise attack *from the start line*. Olympic marathons are notoriously tactical and slow, even when they don't begin in 84 degrees of Beijing summer heat. Sammy scorched the first mile in 4:41—a world-record pace. Only 19 runners managed to stay with him even that far. At the 10K mark, the lead pack was down to eight. Sammy did not relent. One by one his chasers fell off. He ran the last several miles utterly alone and crossed the finish line in 2:06:39 to shatter the Olympic record by nearly 3 minutes. Some observers called it the greatest marathon performance ever. Sammy was 21 years old.

October 10, 2010, was not a hot day in Chicago, but it was warm. The temperature had already reached 67 degrees when the race started at 7:30 in the morning. Sammy dutifully tucked himself at the back of the lead bunch. Shadrack Kosgei, one of two hired pacesetters, led a 12-man all-African group through 5 km in 15:03—a slowish pace. Kebede, clad in purple and black, hovered close to Sammy.

Watching from a VIP vehicle at the front of the race, Federico Rosa could see right away that Sammy was restless. The gap-toothed Olympic champion was easy to pick out of the crowd with his childlike, scampering stride, arms unbent and spread wide from his body, splayed-fingered hands sweeping the air at hip level. He kept inching toward the front, then remembering himself and sheepishly fading back to the caboose.

Don't do it, Rosa thought.

It was no use. Nine miles into the race, Sammy took a flier. Shouldering past the pacesetters, he dropped the pace from 4:50 per mile to below 4:40. All but one of the runners near him answered the acceleration with relative ease. It was still fairly early. Only Robert Cheruiyot, the reigning champion of the Boston Marathon, was put under pressure. He clung to the rear of the group briefly before coming unhitched.

Sammy, despite being the instigator, didn't feel much better than the man he'd just thrown under the bus. He felt a spasm of fear as he realized that his legs were not equal to his instincts on this day. The young Kenyan eased up and handed the reins over to the pacesetters. The pace slowed and Cheruiyot clawed his way back into the pack.

Kebede, perhaps reading his rival's weakness, now moved forward. He did not attack right away, but his opponents knew it was only a matter of time before he did. The first major assault came at 18 miles. Cheruiyot was dislodged again, this time for good. Then the real carnage began.

At 20 miles, Kebede pounced a second time and the shrunken lead group immediately splintered. Five of the remaining eight—including 2:05 marathoner Vincent Kipruto and 59-minute half-marathoner Deriba Merga—vanished as if through trap doors. Whoosh! Gone.

The only survivors were Sammy and a 20-year-old Ethiopian named Feyisa Lelisa, who had run 2:05:23 at Rotterdam in the spring. These men pursued Kebede like evacuees racing after the last train out, lips peeled back in distress. Unlike the previous assault, this one was sustained. There was something almost taunting in the way the Ethiopian dragged his frozen-faced pursuers along in his wake, matching every slight acceleration of theirs with another of his own so that the distance between them, about two paces, never decreased.

Approaching 23 miles, the three runners, now in a strung-out single file, made a sweeping left turn off Wentworth Avenue and onto 33rd Street. Kebede punched the accelerator again. Lelisa had no response. Sammy opened up his stride in a frantic effort to hang on. His head teetered back and his shoulders cinched toward his ears, signaling imminent implosion. He wore the doomed expression of a rock climber dangling from the end of a fraying rope. His attention was entirely on the 6 feet between him and Kebede and not at all on the 3 miles left to the finish line. Everything depended on *now*. But 6 feet became 12 feet, and 12 became 24. The rope had snapped. Sammy began to lose hope.

Also losing hope were Sammy's many fans around the world, who were watching the race live on television and the Internet. Some of those participating in online message boards as they watched now declared the race over, mourning the Kenyan's uncharacteristic lack of fight.

"Kebede wins . . . damn!" wrote one dejected Wanjiru partisan on letsrun.com.

Nobody watching what was happening at that moment on the streets of Chicago could be faulted for chiseling Sammy's epitaph so hastily. After all, Kenyans do not "run within themselves" or "run their own race" as runners from other places do. These concepts are foreign to them. When a Kenyan runner enters a race to win, he either leads or stays with whoever is leading as long as he possibly can. He will answer every surge, regardless of how close he is to his own limit already. Even if responding to an attack virtually guarantees he blows up and loses 5 minutes in the last 6 miles to finish eighth, he will do it. Because if you don't win, you might as well be eighth.

An American runner conceding 20 meters to a surging leader with 3 miles left in a marathon might be seen as shrewdly preserving his last bit of strength. But Sammy was Kenyan, and his failed pursuit could mean only one thing: He had no strength left to preserve.

Sammy knew this better than anyone. As Kebede continued to glide away in front of him, the Olympic champion's thoughts turned toward the man three steps behind. His goal abruptly shifted from winning the race (and a massive check) to holding on to second place and the still-substantial money that would come with that. But just then, Kebede's tempo slackened a bit. If Sammy couldn't sustain the ferocious pace of Kebede's surge, neither could the Ethiopian himself. Heartened, Sammy searched inside himself and found the spirit to close the gap, and Lelisa regained contact as well. It was a three-man race again.

Not for long. Knowing the confidence Sammy derived from being in front, Kebede sped up, forcing his rival back into his shadow. Lelisa exited stage rear, permanently. An intense battle of wills was now waged between the old rivals. Sammy was determined to have the lead, if only by a centimeter. Kebede was determined not to allow Sammy to gain that centimeter. Sammy forced his way into a nominal lead nevertheless. It lasted all of 2 seconds before Kebede grabbed an equal share. For the next quarter-mile, the foes ran elbow to elbow, shoulders rolling and heads bobbing in perfect synchrony.

Both men were now visibly suffering, but the aura of control still hovered around the Ethiopian. As they came upon a timing mat at 40 km (24.8 miles), Kebede found himself a step ahead of Sammy, so he pressed. Within seconds, Sammy was once again 20 meters behind, in freefall. His hopes sank to a new low.

But then he saw something: Kebede kept looking back. Not once, not twice, but three times. Each time it was over the left shoulder. Sammy quietly drifted over to the right side of the road. When Kebede looked again, Sammy was no longer in sight.

Thinking he'd finally delivered the coup de grace, Kebede eased up a tiny bit. Sammy did not. He crept up on his rival once more. With less than a mile to go, Kebede began to hear screaming from spectators on the right side of the road just after he'd passed them. He looked over his right shoulder—and there was Sammy. Kebede put his eyes back on the road ahead, lowered his chin, and prepared to break the Kenyan's will. A moment later Sammy rocketed past his *left* shoulder.

The challenger reacted quickly, matching Sammy's near sprint. For all its craftiness, Sammy's bid had failed. He had no choice but to downshift. The moment he did so, Kebede counterattacked, demonstrating his own wiliness. Somehow the Ethiopian's hobbled stride became beautiful again. He flew down Michigan Avenue with the confidence of a man who knew he had taken his opponent's last best shot and survived it. Sammy was suddenly three strides back. This time—at last—it was over.

It was not over. With no juice left in his legs, Sammy drove his arms wildly as if using them to jumpstart his depleted lower extremities. It wasn't pretty, but it served. He charged ahead. Feeling him, Kebede looked back and saw his thrice-dead enemy risen and coming for him yet again. Kebede got up on his toes just in time to keep Sammy a half-step behind him. For a fraction of a second, time seemed to stand still, with Sammy frozen just off Kebede's shoulder. An unfocused look in Sammy's eyes signaled an inner calculation. In the next instant, Sammy launched his body into a full sprint—the kind of absolute, nothing-held-back effort that no man can sustain longer than 10 or 12 seconds even on fresh legs. It was crazy. But Kebede did not think so. He sprinted too. The two men ran full-throttle, hip to hip, as though they were mere yards away from the finish line, when in fact they still had nearly half a mile of running ahead of them.

Sammy Wanjiru fans around the world screamed at their televisions and computer screens. Toni Reavis, one of the commentators providing TV coverage locally, had already shouted himself hoarse.

It could not last, and it did not. When the murder-suicide sprint petered out, Kebede was back in the lead. Despite Sammy's almost unimaginable grit, it was clear at every step that Kebede was the stronger man. Kebede held pole position when the runners made the next-to-last turn of the race, a right bend onto Roosevelt Road.

There is only one hill in the Chicago Marathon and it falls right here, at the 26-mile mark. Before the race, Sammy and his coach had decided that Sammy would make his decisive move at this point, if the opportunity existed. Rosa did not expect the opportunity to exist. In the privacy of his mind, he judged that even a third-place finish would be a terrific result, all things considered.

Sammy trailed Kebede through the first 10 meters of the steeply pitched ascent. Taking advantage of his invisibility, he catapulted his ravaged body into one last sprint. He blasted past Kebede's right side. Kebede fought back with everything he had, but he couldn't match his rival's power. With a terror that belied this power, Sammy stole three quick glances backward as he sped away from Kebede, who had already packed it in. Sammy broke the finish tape 19 seconds ahead of the shattered Ethiopian and collapsed to the pavement in the awkward pose of a battlefield casualty.

"IT WAS THE GREATEST surprise I have ever seen in my life," said Federico Rosa to reporters later in the day.

What Rosa knew that his audience did not was that a knee injury and a stomach virus had been the least of the problems Sammy had overcome to defend his Chicago Marathon title. The bigger problem was the self-destructive lifestyle he'd fallen into after his Olympic triumph made him a minor deity and a de facto billionaire in his homeland. As recently as June, Sammy had been drinking every night and getting most of his exercise in the beds of groupies. In July,

Sammy had been 10 pounds over his racing weight. In August, he was still unable to keep up with lesser runners in training. In September, Sammy's Kenya-based coach, Claudio Berardelli, had told Rosa that if Sammy was foolish enough to start the Chicago Marathon, he would never finish.

How, then, did Sammy manage not only to finish the race but to win it? Chicago Marathon race director Carey Pinkowski had a theory.

"Sammy proved his heart today," he said at a post-race press gathering.

In sports, "heart" is a metaphor for mental fitness. Pinkowski's theory was that Sammy had overcome physical weakness with psychological fortitude. That's certainly how it appeared. If the race had been judged like a boxing match, Kebede would have won every round except the one that counted, the last, where Sammy scored a one-punch knockout. In past marathon duels with similar dynamics, the runner in Kebede's shoes—looking more comfortable, absorbing the other's attacks more readily than the other did his—always won. It was just plain obvious to any knowledgeable observer that Sammy was closer to the limit of his physical capacity than was Kebede.

The physiological factors that limit performance in a marathon are well known. One of these factors is depletion of glycogen fuel stores in the working muscles. If Pinkowski's theory was correct, muscle biopsies taken from the legs of Sammy and Kebede at the finish line would have revealed lower levels of glycogen in the winner.

Is this even possible? Can the weaker, more fatigued man really win such a hard-fought, high-stakes competition? Until fairly recently, exercise scientists would have said that a physically weaker athlete could not defeat a stronger rival by virtue of greater mental fitness. From the 1920s through the 1990s, the field of exercise science was dominated by a strict biological model of endurance performance that completely excluded the mind and the brain from consideration. According to this model, endurance performance was determined entirely by physiology below the neck and was limited by hard constraints such as the maximum speed a runner could sustain over a given distance before glycogen depletion occurred.

A newer model of endurance performance integrates the body and the mind through the brain. This alternative theory was dubbed the "psychobiological model" by its primary developer, Samuele Marcora. According to the model, exhaustion occurs during real-world endurance competition not when the body encounters a hard physical limit such as total glycogen depletion but rather when the athlete experiences the maximum level of perceived effort he is willing or able to tolerate. Hard physical limits do exist, of course, but no athlete ever reaches them because the purely psychological limit of perceived effort tolerance is always encountered first. The seemingly inexorable slowing that occurs at the approach to exhaustion is not mechanistic, like a car running out of gas, but voluntary.

Proof that athletes always have some reserve physical capacity at the point of exhaustion comes from a variety of studies, including some in which subjects are required to exercise to exhaustion and then their muscles are electrically stimulated to determine whether they could continue to work if only the athlete were willing to make them continue—and every time it is discovered that they could.

In plain English, perception of effort is an athlete's sense of how hard she is working. It is distinct from pain, fatigue, proprioception, and other perceptions that athletes experience when racing, and it is the primary source of the discomfort that causes athletes to slow down or quit when they hit the wall in races. Athletes commonly label this feeling "fatigue," but fatigue is a separate perception, and much weaker than effort. When you reach the finish line of a hard race and stop, you immediately feel a lot better even though stopping has no immediate effect on your fatigue level. Why do you feel better? Because your *effort* has ceased.

If you want to get a sense of what a very high level of perceived effort feels like in isolation from fatigue, find a steep hill and run up it as fast as you can. (You should probably warm up first.) That feeling of trying as hard as you can that hits you immediately, before fatigue sets in, is the feeling of a very high level of perceived effort.

Now compare the experience of being a few strides into an all-out uphill sprint to that of being 1 mile from the finish line of a marathon. The two experiences are different in many ways. In the uphill sprint your leg muscles are straining but not painful, whereas in the marathon they are more pained than strained. But there is something about the two experiences that is the same: a powerful feeling of general resistance to your will to move, of being at your limit, which exists nowhere in particular yet also everywhere in your body (much like fatigue, actually, when it is experienced at rest, for example, when you have the flu). If asked in each of these circumstances how hard you were working, you would probably say, "As hard as I can!" and mean the same thing in both instances.

What makes the last mile of a marathon feel hard in the same way as the third or fourth stride of a short uphill sprint is the effect of fatigue on perception of effort. The neurophysiology of perception of effort is complex and not yet fully understood, but it appears to be closely linked to the intensity of activity in parts of the brain that drive the muscles to contract. Those brain areas are intensely active from the very start of an all-out uphill sprint, so the effort feels hard right away. Those same brain areas are much less active in the early miles of a marathon, but they become increasingly active as the race goes on and the muscles become fatigued, hence less responsive to the crack of the brain's whip, requiring the brain to work harder in order to get the same level of output from the muscles.

There's a twist, though. The brain itself becomes fatigued during prolonged exercise, and brain fatigue also increases perceived effort. Samuele Marcora proved this in a 2009 study published in the *Journal of Applied Physiology*, in which he tired out the brains of subjects with a mental task before they performed an endurance test. The subjects reported higher levels of perceived effort and bonked sooner than they did when they performed the same endurance test without preexisting brain fatigue. I've referred to endurance racing as a game of mind over muscle, but it might be more accurate to call it a game of mind over brain and muscle.

The fact that perception of effort comes from the brain and not from the body explains why there is a long list of factors that increase endurance performance without increasing physical capacity. If I asked you to complete a 10-mile simulated time trial on a stationary bike, and five days later I asked you to do the same thing a second time after ingesting caffeine, you would almost certainly perform better in the second time trial. If I asked you to run as far as you could in 30 minutes, and five days later I asked you to do the same thing a second time while listening to up-tempo music, you would again perform better in the second test. And if I asked you to complete 3,000 kilojoules of work on a rowing machine in as little time as possible, and five days later I asked you to do the same thing a second time after receiving electrical stimulation to the insular and temporal lobes of your brain, you would once again very likely perform better in the second bout.

Caffeine, music, and transcranial electrical stimulation do not conserve glycogen or neutralize lactic acid or enhance physical capacity in any other way. Yet they *do* enhance endurance performance. Acting on the brain instead of the muscles, these things work by making exercise *feel* easier. When cycling or running or rowing at race intensity feels easier, athletes are able to push closer to their true physical limit before they max out their tolerance for suffering. But even if you took caffeine *and* received electrical brain stimulation before an endurance test *and* listened to your favorite high-energy music during it, you still would not be able to realize 100 percent of your physical potential. No matter what you do, you will always have reserve physical capacity at the end of any race or time trial that lasts longer than 30 seconds, give or take. (I'll explain that 30-second threshold in Chapter 3.)

Yet while no athlete ever reaches his absolute physical limit in a race, some athletes get closer to their personal limit than others do. An athlete who gets just a bit closer to his physical limit in comparison to another athlete who is somewhat stronger may indeed defeat the stronger athlete in head-to-head competition (so to speak).

There are two ways to win a race. You can win by bringing greater physical capacity to the race, or you can win by utilizing a greater portion of a slightly lesser physical capacity within the race. Rarely do champion endurance athletes credit their physical capacity for their success. More often, they insist that their advantage lies not in having more to give but rather in being able to give more of what they have. Past generations of exercise scientists dismissed such talk as magical thinking. But the psychobiological model of endurance performance gives credence to the wisdom of the champions and suggests that the ability to actuate physical capacity is no less important than physical capacity itself.

A race is like a fire walk. When you start a race, you are standing before a bed of hot coals, at the far end of which stands a wall. The wall represents your ultimate physical limit. You will never reach it. Your goal is merely to get as close to the wall as possible, for the closer you get, the better you perform. As the race progresses, your bare feet press into the searing coals again and again. Each step is more painful than the one before. (Don't forget: Pain is different from perceived effort. This is a metaphor.) Eventually, you come to the limit of your pain tolerance and you are compelled to leap off the glowing embers. The distance between this point and the wall is a measure of how well you performed relative to your full potential.

Physical fitness determines where the wall that represents your physical limit is placed. Mental fitness determines how close you are able to get to that limit in competition. Mental fitness is a collection of coping skills—behaviors, thoughts, and emotions that help athletes master the discomfort and stress of the athletic experience, mainly by increasing tolerance for perceived effort and by reducing the amount of effort that is perceived at any given intensity of exercise. What I call the new psychology of endurance sports aims to cultivate mental fitness by helping athletes understand the challenges they face from a psychobiological perspective and by showing them how to emulate the ways in which the most successful athletes cope with these challenges.

The new psychology of endurance sports cannot offer a complete taxonomy of effective coping skills for endurance athletes. *Any* behavior, thought, or emotion that enables an athlete to perform better qualifies as an effective coping skill. That's a mighty long—indeed infinite—list. There is, however, a handful of salient coping skills that the most successful racers rely on consistently to master the biggest challenges endurance athletes face. These skills and those challenges are the focus of the following chapters.

We know that physical fitness comes only partly from training—the rest comes from natural inheritance. Sammy Wanjiru trained hard to get fit enough to win marathons, but thanks to his genetic makeup, he was fitter without training than most runners can become with any amount of hard work. Mental fitness is also partly innate. Some athletes are natural fire walkers. Sammy Wanjiru was one of them. He had an inborn ability to cope with extremely high levels of perceived effort. This ability appears to have been woven into the very fabric of his personality.

Sammy had a reckless streak. He exhibited this quality in his everyday life by doing things like threatening his wife with an AK-47 assault rifle and falling to his death from a balcony in a drunken stupor just seven months after the 2010 Chicago Marathon. He exhibited the same recklessness on the racecourse by doing things like running the first mile of the Olympic Marathon in 4:41 on a hot day. It was this hardwired recklessness that made Sammy mentally fitter than runners of equal talent.

From a psychobiological perspective, endurance performance is a species of self-regulation, or the process by which organisms control their internal states and behavior in the pursuit of their goals. In the study of self-regulation, the concept of personality is replaced by that of *coping style*. This alternative concept captures the idea that what we call personality exists not only in humans but in other animals and serves a practical purpose. A coping style is a characteristic set of individual behaviors, emotions, and (in the case of humans) thought patterns that are called upon to respond to life's challenges. Put another way, a coping style is the sum of an individual person's characteristic coping skills (or traits). As any parent can attest, coping styles are largely innate. Distinct personality traits begin to show themselves in infants from the moment of birth, sometimes even earlier. A natural fire walker is someone who was fortunate enough to have been born with a coping style that manifests as a high level of mental fitness in the athletic sphere.

"Fortunate" isn't always the right word, however. A coping style that is advantageous in the athletic sphere may be maladaptive in everyday life, as was the case with Sammy Wanjiru's fatal recklessness, a trait that, according to recent findings in the field of neuropsychology, may have resulted from abnormal wiring in the serotonergic system of his brain. Other coping styles are beneficial both on the racecourse and off. For example, the unbridled optimism at the center of Louis Zamperini's personality enabled him to win the 1936 U.S. Olympic trials 5000 meters at age 19. It later helped him survive 47 days lost at sea and more than two years of torture, starvation, and sickness as a prisoner of war in the hands of the Japanese. Zamperini's natural sanguinity may also have been the reason he still rode a skateboard in his 80s and lived to be 97.

It is impossible to become a champion endurance athlete without a very high level of inherited physical fitness. Does the same rule apply to mental fitness? If it did, there would be little point in trying to emulate the coping skills—or styles—of the champions. Indeed, it is self-evident that the recklessness of a Sammy Wanjiru and the unchecked optimism of a Louis Zamperini are nonreplicable. Fortunately, natural fire walkers are exceptional even at the elite level. There are many great endurance athletes with "normal" innate coping styles who develop mental fitness as they go, charting a course that the rest of us *can* replicate to some degree in our own athletic journeys.

NINE MONTHS AFTER SAMMY Wanjiru's heart lifted him to victory at the Chicago Marathon, I saw another elite runner's heart fail her at the USA Track and Field Outdoor Championships in Eugene, Oregon.

With two and a half laps to go in the women's 5000 meters, Alissa McKaig was clinging to ninth position as American record holder Molly Huddle executed a punishing surge at the front. Alissa's teammate David "Janko" Jankowski stood in a throng of spectators just beyond a chain-link fence outside turn four. When Alissa hit the turn, Janko cupped his hands to his mouth.

"Get on your horse!" he shouted. *"How bad do you want it?"*

That was precisely the problem. Alissa did not want it just then—not as much as Molly Huddle did, anyway. If she could have paused to answer Janko's question, Alissa would have insisted she wanted desperately to finish in the top three and punch her ticket to the world championships, and she would have meant what she said. But her running told a different story. The only proof of wanting it more is suffering more, and with less than 1,000 meters left in the biggest race she had ever run, Alissa had already taken one foot off the hot coals. And she hated herself for it.

At the start of the second-to-last lap, Huddle smoothly shifted into her next gear—a gear that two of the three women closest behind her lacked. They dropped away like dragsters with blown engines. The only runner now left on Huddle's heels was Angela Bizzarri, an unheralded twenty-three-year-old who was having the race of her life—the race Alissa McKaig should have been having. When the bell rang for the last lap, Huddle showed all her cards. She pulled away from Bizzarri with ease and streaked to victory.

More than 20 meters back, Alissa's charge toward the finish was fueled not so much by competitive fire as it was by a desire to end her misery. She caught and passed Elizabeth Maloy, but only because the latter was tanking. Then Lauren Fleshman subjected Alissa to the same treatment. Beyond caring, Alissa made no effort to respond and remained in ninth place until, mercifully, she hit the line.

Head down, she scuttled off the track and collected her bag from a holding area underneath Hayward Field's west grandstand and then walked over to the practice track behind it. Janko soon found her there. The moment their eyes met, Alissa broke down. Janko did little to console her. He knew she didn't want him to. Silent except for her sniffles, Alissa pulled on a pair of tights and a long-sleeve warm-up top and started jogging, Janko falling in beside her. As she shuffled along, Alissa discovered that her body felt surprisingly fresh, as though she hadn't even raced. Her self-loathing intensified.

Alissa was a talented and hardworking runner. Within the past year alone, she had finished sixth at the USA Cross Country Championships and fifth at the USA Women's Marathon Championships. But she had a history of choking in some of the bigger races. Hours before this latest episode, Alissa had been receiving final tactical instructions from her coach, Pete Rea, when she suddenly burst into tears. Rea recounted the episode for me later.

"Alissa, what's wrong?" he asked.

"I don't know!" she said. "I guess it's the stage. So much pressure!"

On the flight home, Alissa made a decision. She had choked for the last time. The regret and self-directed anger she felt were nothing new, but something else was different. This time she was *sick and tired* of choking.

Alissa's next big race was even bigger: the Olympic trials marathon. Held in Houston on January 14, 2012, it featured the strongest field of American marathon runners ever assembled. Alissa's primary goal was not to make the Olympic team or to finish among the top 10 or to set a new personal best time (though, of course, she wanted all of those things) but rather to run bravely and let the rest take care of itself. At 10 miles, Alissa was mired in 13th place. Instead of losing heart and falling back, she reminded herself how much worse she would feel after the race if she backed off than she would feel during the remainder of the race if she kept pressing, so she pressed on as others crumbled around her. Alissa passed five runners within the final 10 miles to finish eighth. Her time of 2:31:56 obliterated her previous best by almost 6 minutes. Had she run the same time four years earlier, she would have gone to the Olympics.

Afterward, Alissa was interviewed on camera for Flotrack. Throughout the five-and-a-half-minute Q&A she couldn't stop smiling.

"It makes me so excited for the future," she said of her performance. "I had a lot of confidence issues in the past. Now I can let go of all of that."

So, yes, athletes can learn to become better fire walkers. Alissa McKaig's story proves it. It also offers a window into how the process works. The standard formula is as follows: Underdeveloped coping skills cause an athlete to struggle in some way; the experience of struggle provokes an adaptive response from the athlete; this response gives rise, sooner or later, to a more effective coping skill. In Alissa's case, lack of confidence caused her to choke in an important race, her choking inspired her to vow "never again," and this vow pushed her to discover the helpful trick of comparing her present physical suffering in crucial moments of a race against the future emotional suffering that would await her if she allowed herself to choke again. This particular coping skill is a specific manifestation of a broader skill of *angry resolve*, which I will discuss in much greater depth in Chapter 6.

Because coping skills make up a person's coping style, or personality, it is not inaccurate to say that the Alissa McKaig who finished strong in the 2012 Olympic trials marathon was not the same person who had choked in the 2011 USA Track and Field Outdoor Championships. The "confidence issues" she overcame had not been confined to the athletic domain but had affected her in all spheres of life. These issues just happened to cause the most harm in the sporting context because the pursuit of her athletic dreams tested her confidence more severely than anything else that she did in life. For the same reason, though, running gave Alissa the best opportunity to become a more confident person generally. When you listen to her speak in that interview after the Olympic trials, you hear something more than a woman who has learned a helpful new trick; you hear a woman who has changed on a deep level, who sees herself differently than before.

Some coping skills are context specific and can be acquired without any disruption to a person's overall coping style. One example of an endurance sports–specific coping skill is using accumulated race experience to refine one's sense of pacing, which is the art of finding the most aggressive pace that can be sustained to the finish line without exceeding one's maximum tolerance for perceived effort. But an athlete cannot truly maximize her mental fitness without going beyond the acquisition of context-specific coping skills and improving her overall coping style—by changing as a person—to some degree.

Psychologists make a distinction between skills and traits. A trait is essentially a generalized, or non-context-specific, coping skill. Examples of coping traits are general self-efficacy, or belief in one's overall competence, and internal locus of control, or belief that one is the captain of one's ship rather than a mere puppet of fate. No athlete can maximize her mental fitness without enhancing traits like general self-efficacy and internal locus of control in addition to gaining context-specific skills such as a refined sense of pace.

Experimental research confirms what Alissa McKaig proved in the real world: that it is possible for people to develop generalized coping traits through the process of acquiring context-specific coping skills. One of the leaders in this area of research is Ronald Smith, a sports psychologist at the University of Washington. In a 1989 study conducted as part of the Women's Self-Defense Project and published in *Personality and Social Psychology Bulletin*, Smith found that self-defense training improved not only self-defense skills in women but also "more global aspects of personality, including physical self-efficacy and assertiveness." It works the same way in endurance sports. Sometimes the only way to work through an obstacle to further progress as an athlete is to acquire a specific skill that demands an evolution of the self—a trait-level step forward.

Merely participating in sports does not guarantee that an athlete will develop a more mature and effective coping style, however. This only happens to the degree that the individual athlete invests herself in the sport, consciously recognizing her struggles as challenges to her very self. Six-time Ironman winner Mark Allen hit the nail on the head when he described endurance racing as "a test of you *as a person* on top of a test of you as an athlete." But he did not always possess this wisdom. Allen lost Ironman six times as a result of mental self-sabotage before he allowed his struggles to change him and he began to win.

The question that one part of you asks another in the crucial moments of a race—*How bad do you want it?*—is really an invitation to self-exploration. Not all athletes accept this invitation. If you want to become the best "fire walker" you can be—and more than that, if you want to get the most you can get as a person out of the athletic experience—you will accept it. The journey toward becoming a mentally fit athlete is very much a journey of personal development.

We see this especially clearly in the example of Alissa McKaig. She had worked on her confidence issues with a sports psychologist for two years before the crisis that precipitated her breakthrough. The tools she learned from him were of little use until she had that experience. The techniques that sports psychologists have traditionally taught just don't go deep enough on their own to rescue athletes in critical moments when their very soul is challenged to respond. No type of mental training or therapy that is conducted in street clothes can match the power of lived experience to spur the development of effective coping skills.

Alissa's technique of reminding herself how much she preferred the suffering of running hard all the way to the finish line to the shame of giving up could not have worked for her if she hadn't lived through the experience of choking on many occasions and become sick and tired of it. Yet as focused and specific as this coping skill was, its acquisition and use transformed Alissa on a trait level, branding her with a more confident overall coping style.

There will never be a five-step method that makes enhanced mental fitness a predictable outcome in the way that enhanced physical capacity is a predictable outcome of proper training. Mental fitness must be earned within the messy context of an athlete's life. The one thing an athlete can control is how she deals with what life gives her. One way or another, the athlete who wishes to gain mental fitness must somehow make use of those experiences that have the potential to propel her through barriers.

All athletes face challenges that present opportunities to increase their mental fitness in some specific way. In the coming chapters we will look at examples of athletes who increased their mental fitness in the process of overcoming problems such as underperforming or choking in races, suffering a severe injury, repeatedly failing to attain an important goal, and facing physically superior competition. Whether an athlete is able to find a solution to such a challenge and become mentally fitter in the process depends on his overall mindset toward the sport. Athletes who consciously *intend* to use their experiences to develop their mental fitness tend to acquire better coping skills more quickly than do athletes for whom becoming a better fire walker is not an explicit goal. Again, I point to the example of Alissa McKaig, whose breakthrough began with and was made possible by a conscious commitment to becoming more mentally fit.

The power of intention in endurance sports is well documented. For example, a study conducted by Jacob Havenar of the University of San Francisco and presented at the 2006 annual meeting of the American College of Sports Medicine reported that the likelihood of first-time marathoners bailing out of a group training program varied significantly by goal type. Those who were most motivated by personal goal achievement, self-esteem, or finding meaning in life were far less likely to quit than were those whose primary goal was weight loss or social recognition. All of the runners were facing the same challenge—whether they overcame it depended largely on the intention they brought to the experience.

The overarching intention that all competitive endurance athletes share is improved performance. But maximizing one's mental fitness is instrumental to this goal. Therefore the intention of maximizing mental fitness should be as consciously held as that of getting faster.

If you believe that you cannot improve as an endurance athlete except by changing your relationship to perceived effort, you will be more successful in doing so. If you buy into the idea that you should be your own sports psychologist, and that your objective in this capacity is to engage the full power of your mind to increase the amount of effort you are able to give and to enhance what you get out of your best effort, you will build mental fitness more quickly. If you accept as fact that the only limitations you ever encounter in your sport are mental, then you will become a better fire walker, creeping closer to your unreachable physical limit than you would otherwise. In short, if you embrace the new psychology of endurance sports, your performance will improve more than it would if you did not.

While there will never be a five-step program for building mental fitness, there is a sensible first step, and perhaps you've just taken it.

CHAPTER TWO

BRACE YOURSELF

ON NOVEMBER 20, 2009, competitor.com associate editor Sean McKeon sat down at his desk amid a maze of cubicles stretching across a warehouse-like office building in San Diego, opened a Word file, and began to write a preview of the NCAA Cross Country Championships, then three days away. He had no trouble picking a winner for the women's race.

"Why don't we just give Jenny Barringer the trophy, spare the field the embarrassment, and let the other women race for the lesser positions?" he wrote. "All right, that may be an exaggeration," McKeon amended, "but in my mind it's not a matter of *if* the Colorado senior is going to win, it's by how much."

McKeon's confidence in Jenny was well placed. She was already the most decorated female college runner in history. She'd come to the University of Colorado on a full athletic scholarship after having won eight high school state championship titles and set state records at four distances in her native Florida. As a freshman, Jenny won an NCAA championship title in the 3000-meter steeplechase. The next year, competing against professionals, she won the same event at the U.S. national championships and qualified for the world championships in Osaka. After her junior season, Jenny earned a spot on the

U.S. Olympic team and finished ninth in the steeplechase at the 2008 Summer Games in Beijing.

If Jenny had achieved no more than all of this before the 2009 NCAA Cross Country Championships, she would have come into the race as a prohibitive favorite. But she was just getting started. After redshirting her senior cross country season, Jenny returned to competition in the winter, setting new NCAA records for 3000 meters and 5000 meters indoors. In the spring, she broke three more records, for 1500 meters, the 3000-meter steeplechase, and 5000 meters. In June, Jenny won her second elite national title in the steeplechase. Her momentum continued through the summer, during which she set an American record of 9:12.50 in the steeplechase at the world championships in Berlin, where she finished fifth.

Having skipped her senior cross country season, Jenny was eligible to return to Boulder and compete for the Lady Buffaloes in the fall of 2009. Despite the big payday awaiting her when she turned pro, she chose to exercise the option, citing grounds of loyalty.

"I cannot repay this university what they've given me, the resources and just the gift of the four years here," Jenny said when she announced her decision. "The closest I can come is to fulfill the promise I made four years ago [to exhaust my eligibility]. I'm definitely staying."

Besides, she had unfinished business. When Jenny had first arrived at the University of Colorado as an 18-year-old, she had told coach Mark Wetmore that her top ambition for her collegiate career was to win an NCAA title in cross country. Five years later, this ambition remained unfulfilled, despite everything else she had achieved. She'd come close in 2007, finishing second to Kenya's Sally Kipyego, who had since graduated. Jenny didn't mind letting her professional career wait a few more months while she completed her mission.

She opened her final season of collegiate running on the third of October at the Rocky Mountain Shootout, a large meet held on the Buffaloes' home course. Jenny won the 5.8-km race by 58 seconds, smashing a nine-year-old course record in the process. Jenny's next race was pre-nationals, held October 14 in Terre Haute, Indiana, site of the following month's national championships. There Jenny went head-to-head against Florida State's Susan Kuijken (pronounced *kykin*), considered Jenny's biggest threat for the NCAA title. Jenny beat her by 30 seconds.

Two weeks later, Jenny traveled with her teammates to Columbia, Missouri, for the Big 12 Championship. An almost apologetic smile spread across her face as she glided away from the 96 overmatched runners trailing behind her to win by 46 seconds. Afterward, coach Mark Wetmore admitted the obvious to CU's assistant sports information director, Linda Sprouse. "She was cruising," he said. "It was an easy run for her and she was having fun the whole way."

On November 14, Jenny got in one last competitive tune-up at the NCAA Mountain West Conference Championships in Albuquerque. This time, for kicks, Jenny paced her teammate Allie McLaughlin through the first 4 km and then eased ahead to win by 12 seconds.

With all of this information as background, Sean McKeon was merely stating a fact when, in his NCAA Cross Country Championships preview, he wrote, "If she doesn't win, it will be the biggest upset in NCAA history, bar none." He was also right—more right than he knew—to add that nothing short of an "epic collapse" would prevent her from winning the title she coveted.

THE LAVERN GIBSON CHAMPIONSHIP Cross Country course is enfolded in 280 grassy acres east of Terre Haute. Race day brought nearly ideal running weather to the site—mild and dry. The sun emerged from behind a layer of clouds at half past noon, as the men's race was wrapping up and Jenny and her teammates were getting ready for their turn on the course. The air temperature climbed into the mid-50s, above average for late November, prompting runners to peel off gloves and arm sleeves and stuff them into gear bags.

While jogging around the perimeter of the grounds with her teammates, Jenny became lightheaded. The feeling persisted as she completed her warm-up with mobility exercises and stride-outs. The team then gathered with their coaches to hear a few final words of instruction. Jenny thought about mentioning her wooziness to assistant coach Heather Burroughs, but decided against it. She knew it was probably a symptom of nerves, nothing more, and already it had begun to dissipate.

At 12:35, the racers were called to the start line. They arranged themselves three deep along a chalk line stretching seemingly forever across a vast expanse of freshly mowed turf. A pistol popped and the last vestiges of Jenny's nerves vanished instantly as she broke from the line. Two hundred and fifty-four women rumbled across a 900-meter opening straightaway, gradually coming together in the shape of a squat teardrop with Jenny (who else?) at its pointy end. Susan Kuijken, who had started 25 feet to the left of Jenny, quickly found her shoulder. Despite the beatdown Jenny had laid on her at pre-nationals, the Florida State senior still hoped to win. Her plan was to hang with Jenny if she could and otherwise to keep her in range and try to chase her down at the end.

As she settled into a rhythm, Jenny checked in on her body and discovered that she felt good—strong and relaxed—as indeed she had all season long. There was no reason she should have felt otherwise. Her training in recent weeks had gone almost perfectly. In the lead-up to the Mountain West Conference Championships, she had notched her best times ever in benchmark workouts. After that race, Mark Wetmore had dialed her training way back and her legs had responded with a whole new bounce. Jenny had also managed to avoid the cold virus that had been making its way around the CU campus. She had never been more physically ready to race, and her body's inner gauges confirmed it. That brief dizzy spell was just a blip.

Jenny drifted toward the right edge of the straightaway, close to the fencing that kept spectators out of the way, in anticipation of making the first bend on the circuitous course. The field remained closely bunched behind her, with Kuijken, Kendra Schaff of Washington, and Angela Bizzarri of Illinois marking her closest.

Rounding the bend, Jenny subtly increased her speed, gaining immediate separation from her chasers. Kuijken made a split-second decision to respond and quickly closed the gap. She stayed a deferential half-step behind Jenny, however, lest she tempt the odds-on favorite to pick up the pace even more. The Norwegian's long, golden ponytail bounced in synchrony with Jenny's honey-colored mane as the pair put more and more empty grass between themselves and the other racers. They passed the 1-km mark of the 6-km race at 3:04. Jenny noted the split with approval. She had come to Terre Haute with a secondary goal of eclipsing Sally Kipyego's course record of 19:28, and she was on track to do so.

Jenny charged up the first hill. She ran with her trademark gladiatorial style, her jutting chin, forward-tilted torso, wide elbows, and fisted hands communicating confidence and aggression. Yet something in her eyes seemed to express impatience also, as Kuijken, who had claimed to have no fear of Jenny in pre-race interviews, continued to tailgate her.

After topping the hill, the leaders negotiated a tight bend to the left, passing within inches of shouting spectators pressed against the chain-link boundary fencing. A plurality of the cheers were for Jenny, who in addition to having many schoolmates, friends, and family members present, had a national fan base.

Jenny and her flaxen shadow hit the 1-mile mark at 5:02. Kipyego had recorded the same split in her record-setting run two years before. Jenny still looked in charge, but her brow was uncharacteristically furrowed.

Six strides back, Kendra Schaff ran alone, having pulled away from the lead chase pack in a bid to hunt down the leaders. She'd committed to the gamble after recognizing that Jenny's pace wasn't quite as severe as she'd expected. Ten meters behind Schaff, Angela Bizzarri was making a slightly different calculation at the head of the main field. Her plan had been to run her own race and hope that anyone who tried to run with Jenny—if not Jenny herself—would wear herself out and come back to her eventually. That plan still felt right.

Jenny spotted another time clock ahead, this one at the 2-km mark, and locked her eyes on it: 6:15, 6:16, 6:17. . . She had slowed a little, but not much, and the pace was still a lot faster than Kuijken had ever run for a race of this distance. All Jenny had to do was hold steady and her pesky challenger would eventually crack.

They started up another hill. Kuijken remained glued to Jenny's right shoulder. The distance between the two women and Schaff, and between Schaff and Bizzarri's group, had ceased to expand. A pleading tone entered the shouts directed Jenny's way by fans lining the course.

At the midpoint of the race, which was reached at 9:38, Kuijken noticed that she no longer felt Jenny pulling her along. In fact, she was coasting a bit, running slightly slower than she might be if she were alone. So she put a little more juice in her stride and immediately drew even with Jenny, who flinchingly sped up to reassert a half-step advantage. Moments later, Kuijken was again crowding Jenny from the back, getting increasingly antsy.

Jenny's head began to bob. It was subtle at first, then not so subtle. The bob turned into a wobble. The wobble descended into her shoulders, trunk, and hips, until Jenny was lurching like a swollen-eyed prizefighter fumbling for his corner. Her speed dropped precipitously and Kuijken pranced away, hardly believing her luck. Jenny now appeared to be speaking to herself, her mouth making sloppy movements as she stumbled ahead. Her eyelids drooped to half-mast.

Kendra Schaff, Angela Bizzarri, and Sheila Reid of Villanova passed Jenny in a merciless single file. Seconds later, the main field caught her. Villanova's Amanda Marino overtook Jenny with ease. Then came Florida State's Pasca Cheruiyot and Jenny's own freshman teammate Allie McLaughlin, who offered Jenny a baffled word of encouragement.

Jenny was a lost calf caught in a stampede of angry steer. She dropped to 10th place, 20th, 30th. Jenny's former high school rival Erin Bedell, now a senior at Baylor, came upon her and was moved to help.

"Run with me!" Bedell called.

Jenny obeyed, but another crushing wave of heaviness quickly overwhelmed her. The wobble returned. With each successive stride, Jenny's movements became more inexact, less integrated. Her head bent forward and stayed there, as though she were looking for a lost ring. She felt oddly distant from the sights and sounds around her. *Am I dreaming?* she wondered. Her jog became a shuffle, her shuffle a walk. She took three last tottering steps and dropped to the ground like a sniper's target. Spectators watched in stunned silence as runners passed Jenny's crumpled body by the dozen.

The stillness of Jenny's prostrate form suggested she would rise neither soon nor without assistance. But after just a few seconds, Jenny stirred, as if trying to beat a 10-count. She got back on her feet in three slow stages—all fours to half-kneel to loosely vertical—steadied herself, and broke into a stiff jog. Runners continued to overtake her, but not as whizzingly as before. Emma Coburn, another of Jenny's teammates, came up beside her and Jenny, now fully lucid and mortified, thought ("insanely," she told Flotrack afterward), *I hope she doesn't see me!*

Little by little, Jenny's stride smoothed out and her pace quickened. The trickle of runners overtaking her became a drip. By the time Jenny rounded a wide bend that dumped her onto a 400-meter straightaway to the finish line, she was matching the pace of the thickly bunched runners around her.

Before the race, Jenny had told her teammates to keep an eye out for runners wearing the uniforms of Villanova, Washington, and West Virginia. These were the schools most likely to stand in the way of Colorado's winning the team title. Jenny now saw a runner in the purple and gold of Washington ahead of her. She picked up her pace and reeled her in, passing a number of other runners along the way.

With the finish banner looming, Jenny spied another Washington runner in front of her. She got up onto her toes, drove her arms, and rocketed ahead, slaloming expertly between runners who had only recently passed her, eyes fixed on her prey. Her form looked beautiful. There was absolutely nothing wrong with her. Six feet from the finish, Jenny blasted by Washington's Kayla Evans, a freshman whose best 3000-meter time was 93 seconds slower than Jenny's. The greatest female college runner in history crossed the finish line 163rd in her last collegiate race.

THE 2009 NCAA CROSS COUNTRY Championships were covered live on the Versus cable television network. A camera crew awaited Jenny Barringer 30 feet beyond the finish line. She was still recovering her breath when reporter Cat Andersen stuck a microphone in her face and asked her what had happened.

"I didn't feel so good halfway into it," she answered tearfully.

The next day, Jenny recorded a 24-minute video interview for Flotrack from her hotel room in Terre Haute. Very little was added to her understated first explanation of the meltdown.

"It was a wave," she said. "It was all of a sudden: 'I don't know if I can run. I don't know if I can stand up.'"

More revealing, perhaps, than what Jenny *did* say about her unraveling was what she did *not* say. She did not say that she had pulled a hamstring, or suffered an asthma attack, or was struck by an agonizing abdominal cramp caused by a floating rib jabbing her diaphragm (which is what happened to Susan Kuijken, who finished in third place). Rather, Jenny's terse description of her implosion seemed to suggest she had been brought down not by anything physical but by a *feeling*.

Is this explanation even plausible? According to the psychobiological model of endurance performance, it is.

In endurance races, athletes pace themselves largely by feel. External feedback in the form of time splits and the relative positions of other racers may influence pacing, but it's an internal sense of the appropriateness of one's pace from moment to moment that has the first and final say in determining whether an athlete chooses to speed up, hold steady, slow down, or collapse into a lifeless heap. The scientific name for this pacing mechanism is *anticipatory regulation*. Its output is a continuously refreshed, intuition-like feeling for how to adjust one's effort in order to get to the finish line as quickly as possible. Its inputs are perception of effort, motivation, knowledge of the distance left to be covered, and past experience.

In an overview of Samuele Marcora's psychobiological model of endurance performance published in 2013, Brazilian exercise physiologists wrote that "perception of effort is the conscious awareness of the central motor command sent to the active muscles." In other words, perception of effort is the feeling of activity in the brain that stimulates muscle work; it is not the feeling of muscle work itself. Except in the case of reflex actions, all muscle work begins with an act of conscious willing. This command originates in the brain's motor cortex and supplementary motor area. Scientists are able to measure the intensity of these commands, and this measurement is referred to as movement-related cortical potential (MRCP). Marcora has shown that MRCP and perception of effort are high when subjects exercise at maximum intensity and also that they increase covariantly when exercise of lower intensity is performed for a long period of time. This is compelling evidence that perceived effort is indeed related to brain activity, not muscle activity.

When experienced endurance athletes race at a familiar distance, perceived effort tends to increase linearly until it reaches a maximal level near the finish line. But perceived effort is subjective, and for this reason, what is considered maximal changes by circumstance. When athletes really want it, they are able to tolerate a higher level of perceived effort than when they are comparatively unmotivated. As a consequence, their pacing strategy changes. The same level of perceived effort that causes them to hold steady at a given point in a race for which they are unmotivated might cause them to speed up at an equivalent point in a race that matters more to them.

The athlete's conscious awareness of how far away the finish line sits also affects how a given level of perceived effort is interpreted and used. A runner who experiences a certain level of effort at the

4-km mark of a 10-km race might panic and slow down, whereas a runner who experiences the same effort level at the 7-km point of a 10-km race might get a shot of confidence and speed up.

These calculations, in turn, are strongly influenced by past experience. Through experience, athletes learn how they *should* feel at various points in a race of a given distance. An experienced athlete enters each race with preprogrammed expectations about how she can expect to feel at various points. Any mismatch between how she expects to feel and how she actually feels will cause her to adjust her pace accordingly. For example, an athlete who consumes dietary nitrates before a time trial is likely to feel better than expected and thus go faster than normal, while an athlete who is infused with Interleuken-6 (a cell-signaling compound linked to fatigue) before a time trial is likely to feel worse than expected and consequently go slower than normal.

Perceived effort actually has two layers. The first layer is how the athlete feels. The second layer is how the athlete feels *about* how she feels. The first layer is strictly physiological, whereas the second is emotional, or affective. Crudely put, an athlete can have either a good attitude or a bad attitude about any given level of discomfort. If she has a good attitude, she will be less bothered by the feeling and will likely push harder. Research has shown that when athletes feel worse than expected during a race, they tend to develop a bad attitude about their discomfort and as a result they slow down even more than they need to. (Of course, from a strictly physiological perspective, they don't need to slow down at all.)

In 2005, Alan St. Clair Gibson studied the effect of thwarted expectations on perception of effort in a group of 16 well-trained runners. The experiment had two parts. In one part the subjects were required to run at a steady pace for 20 minutes on a treadmill. At the end of each minute, they were asked to rate their perception of effort as well as their "positive affect," or enjoyment level. In the other part of the experiment, the subjects were asked to run for just 10 minutes at the same pace, but at the end of the 10th minute they were told they had to run 10 minutes longer. So the second run was in fact identical to the first, but the subjects expected it to be shorter and hence easier. (The actual order of the two runs was randomized.)

When he reviewed the data he'd collected, St. Clair Gibson found that the runners' perceived effort ratings spiked and their positive affect scores nosedived right after they were informed that they would have to run 10 minutes longer than they'd expected to. The runners did not feel worse on a purely physical level, but they developed a bad attitude about how they felt, so in effect they did feel worse.

Research on the psychology of pain has produced similar findings. A number of studies have compared the effects of two contrasting anticipatory attitudes—acceptance and suppression—on pain perception. Some people have a natural tendency to look ahead to the repetition of a familiar pain stimulus with acceptance. They tell themselves, "This is going to hurt, but no worse than before." Other people try to cope with the same situation through suppression, a form of denial. They tell themselves, in effect, "I really hope this doesn't hurt as much as it did the last time." Psychologists have generally found that, compared to suppression, acceptance reduces the unpleasantness of pain without reducing the pain itself. For this reason, it is a more effective coping skill.

The same skill also reduces perceived effort. In a 2014 study published in *Medicine and Science in Sports and Exercise*, psychologist Elena Ivanova looked at the effects of a certain type of psychotherapy called acceptance and commitment therapy on endurance performance in a group of nonathletic women. Acceptance and commitment therapy entails learning to accept unpleasant feelings as unavoidable features of certain experiences—in this case exercise. Ivanova found that the therapy reduced perceived effort at a high intensity of exercise by 55 percent and increased time to exhaustion at that same intensity by 15 percent.

In common language, this attitude of acceptance toward an impending disagreeable experience is called "bracing yourself." Many of us use this coping skill instinctively to reduce the unpleasantness of everyday trials such as a trip to the dentist's office. "Indeed," observed psychologists Jeff Galak and Tom Meyvis in a 2011 paper published in the *Journal of Experimental Psychology*, "people often choose to expect the worst of an upcoming experience in hopes of creating a more favorable contrast between their expectations and reality."

In the context of endurance competition, this "favorable contrast" can enhance performance. The more discomfort an athlete expects, the more she can tolerate, and the more discomfort she can tolerate, the faster she can go. It's no wonder, then, that champion endurance athletes habitually brace themselves for important races. The great British runner Mo Farah told a reporter for *The Daily Mirror* ahead of his first marathon, "This will be the hardest race of my life." He wasn't being negative; he was bracing himself.

You never know how much your next race is going to hurt. Perception of effort is mysterious. You can push yourself equally hard in two separate races and yet somehow feel "on top of" your suffering in one race and overwhelmed by it in the other. Because you never know exactly what you'll find inside that black box until you open it, there is a temptation to hope—perhaps not quite consciously—that your next race won't be one of those grinding affairs. This hope is a poor coping skill. Bracing yourself—always expecting your next race to be your hardest yet—is a much more mature and effective way to prepare mentally for competition.

Jenny Barringer failed to brace herself for the discomfort she should have anticipated in the 2009 NCAA Cross Country Championships, and it doomed her. Her first mistake was looking past the race to the future. The meet in Terre Haute was to be her final encore as an amateur runner. Soon afterward, she would hire an agent, sign a big shoe contract, and embark on a career as a professional athlete. Although Jenny had chosen to return to Colorado for the 2009 cross country season to fulfill a promise and a dream, she was ready to move on—and in a crucial sense she already had moved on before her nightmarish last competition in a Buffaloes uniform.

She told Flotrack's Ryan Fenton the day after the catastrophe, "A month or two before the race, I started saying, 'I can't wait for nationals to be over.' I've never been like that before. I've always really looked forward to these events."

In addition to looking past the race itself, Jenny looked past her competition. "That's another mistake," she said to Fenton. "I didn't go out yesterday just to win. I had to break Sally's course record and win by 30 seconds."

No matter how much an athlete pushes herself in a race, to win by 30 seconds is to win *easily*. Jenny's goals reflected an expectation of winning the race comfortably, in both senses of the word. This expectation was not unreasonable, as she had won every preceding event of the season without being challenged. But as a consequence of all this cakewalking, Jenny not only stopped expecting to suffer against college competition, but she also fell a bit out of practice with it.

It's easy for experienced athletes to lose their appreciation for just how intense the suffering felt in races really is. They get used to it, which is a good thing, because getting used to suffering calluses them to it. But this tolerance only holds up when an athlete is properly braced. Any athlete who experienced race-level effort completely out of context would instantly regain full respect for its awfulness. If a runner were to suddenly experience the same level of effort she felt during the last mile of her hardest marathon while climbing a flight of steps at home, for example, she would probably fall to the floor and call for help, believing she was dying.

Granted, Jenny Barringer was not caught quite so off guard by the suffering she experienced in the 2009 NCAA Cross Country Championships. But Susan Kuijken's challenge and the discomfort that it provoked in Jenny were surprising enough to make her panic. To be sure, certain elements of her "epic collapse" (to borrow Sean McKeon's prophetic phrase) were bizarre. The suddenness of her "feeling not so good" and the completeness of her post-collapse recovery had no precedent. We may never understand fully why it all went down the way it did. Nevertheless, the only explanation that makes any sense is Jenny's own.

"It's something I set myself up for," she said.

ON DECEMBER 3, 2009, just a few weeks after Terre Haute, Jenny Barringer hired track and field super agent Ray Flynn to represent her professional interests. Flynn quickly orchestrated an intense bidding war among the major running shoe brands. Jenny's crumbling at the NCAAs had not dulled her luster in the eyes of their marketing executives. In January, Jenny signed a multiyear endorsement contract with New Balance. Three weeks later, she hired a new coach, entrusting her fitness to Juli Benson, a former Olympic middle-distance runner now coaching cross country and track at the U.S. Air Force Academy in Colorado Springs.

Benson and Jenny agreed that she should take an extended break from competition to recharge her mental and physical batteries and focus on training. Her first race as a professional was the Payton Jordan Invitational 1500 meters, held at Stanford University on May 1, 2010. She had sworn emphatically in her morning-after interview for Flotrack that nothing like her debacle in Terre Haute would ever happen again, but as her pro debut approached, the memory weighed heavily on her mind. Despite her anxiety, she won handily. After she crossed the finish line, Jenny celebrated as though she had just won an Olympic gold medal. A few days later, I had an opportunity to ask Jenny if her elation had anything to do with the trauma of her last race.

"The excitement I expressed at the end of my race was really a triumph over that," she told me. "Just getting through the first race was a mental victory."

With the monkey off her back, Jenny was able to focus on her greater ambition of winning on the world stage. In February 2011, now married and bearing the last name Simpson, she won the mile and the 3000 meters at the USA Track and Field Indoor Championships.

Four months later, she finished second to Morgan Uceny in the 1500 meters at the USA Track and Field Outdoor Championships, qualifying for the world championships in Daegu, South Korea. In Daegu, Jenny successfully advanced from the first round to the semifinal to the final.

The 12-woman final was staged under the lights of Daegu Stadium on the night of September 1. At 8:55 p.m., the world's best female milers crouched over a curvilinear mark, Jenny standing farthest from the inside rail. She looked nervous, and she was—as nervous as she had been on the start line of the 2009 NCAA Cross Country Championship some 21 months ago. But her thoughts were of a different nature.

Jenny's first thought was that 25 percent of the women in this race would take home a medal—pretty good odds. Her next thought was that she really didn't want to rely on chance; she wanted to fight for a place in the top three. Her last thought was that if she won the race, the national anthem of the United States would be played in her honor and the ceremony would later be seen and heard by her sister Emily, who had just joined the Army. Beating all 11 of the women to her left would be harder than anything Jenny had done before—it would demand her absolute best effort, and perhaps even that would not be enough. But she was determined to try for nothing less.

The gun cracked and the runners dashed ahead over the Smurf-blue track surface in search of a tactically advantageous position, everyone wanting to be near but not at the front. Jenny was slow off the mark and hit the first turn with only one runner behind her.

As so often happens in championship 1500-meter finals, the field bogged down quickly after the initial mad dash for position. Exploiting the slackening pace, Jenny swung wide and charged to the head of the field, settling on the right hip of early leader Mimi Belete of Bahrain. Maryam Jamal, also of Bahrain, thought Jenny had a pretty good idea and replicated it. She moved up, placed herself directly in front of Jenny, and then slowed down, forcing the rookie pro back one place.

Moments later, Kenya's Hellen Obiri executed the same maneuver. Turkey's Tugba Karakaya followed suit. One by one, runners at the back slung themselves to the front until the field had inverted itself, with Jenny relegated again to the rear.

Belete held onto pole position, however, and led the field through 400 meters in a very slow time of 1:08.78. The strong kickers in the race, especially Spain's Natalia Rodriguez, could not have been happier. If the dawdling continued, these fast closers would be well set up to steal the race in the last half-lap.

It was in everyone else's interest to make the race honest, yet no one dared to seize the burden of leading from Belete, who herself lifted the pace modestly but not enough to put anyone under pressure. The tight bunching of the racers brought many elbows into contact with ribs, and spikes with shins.

Belete hit 800 meters at 2:13.94. With only 300 meters left before the bell lap, the athletes' jockeying intensified. Runners caught behind pressed forward. Those boxed in at the rail forced their way outside. Women already in good position fought to hold their ground. Jenny gained one place, sliding up from 12th to 11th, where she was at least out of range of the elbows and spikes.

Rodriguez was first to challenge Belete's lead. Her move set off a chain reaction. Everyone vaulted ahead at once in an effort to ride the Spaniard's coattails. Obiri clipped Rodriguez's heel from behind and the Kenyan sprawled to the track. Morgan Uceny could not react in time and went down as well. Jenny found a narrow pathway between the felled runners. The melee among the surviving athletes only worsened, with athletes moving into the third and fourth lanes in their panic to reach the front, while those trapped inside tried to run over those in front of them.

As the bell lap started, Jenny held the rearmost position in a lead pack of eight with a struggling Jamal—who had nearly fallen—immediately to her right. Jenny had to move up, and to move up she had to get away from the rail. She slowed down just enough to put Jamal a stride ahead of her, shifted right, and surged past Jamal and

Karakaya, while the new leader, Rodriguez, led the pack out of turn two and onto the back straight.

The pace continued to wind up on the approach to turn three. Jenny was now only a stride back from Rodriguez but, stuck behind Norway's Ingvill Bovim in lane 2, had to cover extra distance.

Entering the final straightaway, Jenny strayed even wider, into lane 3. Rodriguez now had separation from her closest pursuer, Ethiopia's Kalkidan Gezahegne.

Driving her arms, Jenny bulleted past Bovim. Each galloping stride swallowed up twice as much track, it seemed, as Rodriguez's tightening steps. Forty meters from the finish line, Jenny burst into the lead.

Great Britain's Hannah England was charging hard behind her, but with 20 meters left in the race, she stopped gaining ground. Jenny hit the line first at 4:05.40. She was the new 1500-meter world champion.

Jenny placed her hands on top of her head and shook it from side to side in ecstatic disbelief. She laughed and wept simultaneously. She jumped up and down with her fists in the air, tucking her knees like a cheerleader at the apex of each leap. In an interview conducted minutes later, Jenny would confess to the truth that this sequence of peculiar behavior had already made plain: She truly had not expected this. She had expected only to run harder than ever and to face the fight of her life in her bid to stand where she now stood— which is precisely what had gotten her there.

Jenny was rescued from her immediate post-race delirium by the arrival of a big American flag, which she wrapped around herself like a cape as she set out on a victory lap.

In less than two years, Jenny Barringer (Simpson) had gone from 163rd place in a collegiate championship race to first place in a world championship final. She had fallen. But she'd gotten back up—and learned that, no matter how gifted and successful an athlete may be, she must always brace for the worst to race her best.

CHAPTER THREE

TIME IS ON YOUR SIDE

GREG LEMOND WOKE UP in a strange bed. For a second or two he knew nothing more, his mind hovering in that narrative-free state of animal consciousness that greets each of us at the threshold of wakefulness. Then it all came back to him. He was in a hotel room in Versailles, France. The date was Sunday, July 23, 1989. At 4:14 that afternoon, he would compete in the final stage of the Tour de France. It was going to be the most important race of his life.

He dressed in a yellow T-shirt and baggy blue shorts and made his way down to the ground floor, where he sat at a long table and ate a hearty breakfast of pasta, bread, cereal, eggs, and coffee with his teammates on the ADR cycling team. An hour later, they were on their bikes, just cruising, loosening up their legs for later. Overcast skies loomed above them as they pedaled away from the hotel, but by the time the ride was complete the clouds had burned off and the air temperature had risen into the low 80s. Greg later told writer Sam Abt what he told his trainer, Otto Jácome, when he returned to his lodgings.

"My legs are good. I'm going to have a very good day."

There was plenty of time left to kill. As the second-place rider in the General Classification (G.C.), or overall race standings, Greg would start the conclusive 24.5-km individual time trial next to last among the Tour's 134 surviving competitors, 2 minutes before Frenchman Laurent Fignon, the race leader. A two-time winner of the Tour de France, Fignon stood merely 50 seconds ahead of Greg after 20 stages and more than 2,000 miles of riding. Greg was the stronger time trialist, but he would have to make up an improbable 2 seconds per kilometer between Versailles and Paris to overtake Fignon in the G.C. and claim his own second Tour de France victory. Whichever way it went, it promised to be the closest finish in the event's 76-year history.

Greg's many fans in America and around the world considered it victory enough that he was even in this position. Two years earlier, Greg's brother-in-law Pat Blades had plugged him in the back with a shotgun from a distance of 30 yards. The accident happened on April 20, 1987, on Greg's uncle Rod LeMond's property in Lincoln, California. Greg should have been in Europe, racing with the La Vie Claire team and preparing to defend the Tour title he had won the previous July, but a crash in Italy had left him with a broken bone in his left hand and he was sent back to the States to convalesce. Near the end of the six-week recuperative stint, Greg's uncle talked him into taking a short break from training to hunt wild turkey. Greg remembers every detail of that life-altering morning, and has recounted it publicly many times in interviews and speeches.

Greg and Rod LeMond were both experienced hunters. Pat Blades was not. They set out at 7:30 in the morning, splitting up to cover more territory. Greg went to the left, Uncle Rod to the right, and Blades up the middle, all three men wearing camouflage gear. Greg crouched under a berry bush to wait. After some time had passed, he heard Blades whistle. Wary of alerting nearby game to their presence, Greg elected not to respond. Instead he stood up, intending to creep forward to a new hiding spot. His movements caused the berry bush to quiver. Seeing this, Blades took quick aim and fired, spraying his brother-in-law with buckshot.

Greg found himself on the ground without knowing how he'd gotten there. He saw blood on the ring finger of his left hand, but felt no pain. In fact, his whole body was numb. He tried to stand up, became lightheaded, and fell back to the dirt. He tried to speak but could only croak, a collapsed lung making it a struggle for him just to breathe, let alone call for help. Only now did Greg realize, with cold terror, that he'd been shot.

"What happened?" Blades shouted from his hiding spot.

Greg couldn't answer. He heard crashing footsteps and then saw his brother-in-law looming above him. Blades's face showed no surprise, the effect of a reflexive effort to conceal his horror lest he send his accidental victim into a panic. No such luck. Greg began to babble.

"I'm going to die! I won't see my wife anymore! I won't be able to race anymore!"

Soon Blades was shouting too. Rod LeMond heard the ruckus and came running. The sight of his nephew's blood-soaked, crumpled body hit him like a sucker punch. Blades and Uncle Rod conferred in tight voices, quickly agreeing that they had to get Greg onto his feet and out of the woods ASAP. But they disagreed on how to go about it. Greg pictured sand draining from the hourglass of his life while the two men debated.

"Just go get the ambulance!" he interjected.

Uncle Rod ran down to the house and dialed 9-1-1. Minutes later, he was back at the scene of the mishap. No ambulance could reach Greg where he lay, so Blades and Uncle Rod tried to lift him, but the movement stirred up an inferno of pain in Greg's right shoulder, which had taken the brunt of the blast.

"Go get your truck," Greg said.

Uncle Rod ran down to the house a second time and rumbled back in his pickup. With grunting help from the others, Greg hauled himself into the truck, where he waited for help to arrive. Ten minutes passed. No ambulance. Fifteen minutes. Greg's shirt was now drenched in blood. Twenty minutes. He was running out of time.

After 25 minutes had gone by, Uncle Rod started up the truck and drove to the edge of the property. They came to a gate, closed and padlocked, with an ambulance, a fire truck, and a police car sitting idly on the other side, as though staging for a small-town Independence Day parade.

A team of paramedics got Greg onto a stretcher, cut his shirt off, and set to work on him. The nearest hospital was 35 minutes away over bumpy roads. Greg knew he'd probably bleed out before he got there. As he reeled from this dark thought, he heard the unmistakable sound of a helicopter. A chopper from the California Highway Patrol that just happened to have been passing through the area had caught the radio chatter and made a beeline for Rod LeMond's property. Greg was hastily loaded in and taken to the hospital at the University of California–Davis, which specialized in the treatment of gunshot wounds and other traumas. The flight took 11 minutes.

He spent five hours in the operating room. The surgeon was able to remove only half of the 60 pellets that had struck him; most of the rest would remain inside Greg for the rest of his life, two of them nestled against the lining of his heart.

When he woke up, Greg was told that he would indeed have bled to death—at age 26—if not for the miracle of the passing copter, but he could now expect to make a full recovery. It would take a very long time, however, and in the interim he was destined to lose nearly all of the fitness he had built up through 12 years of competitive cycling. His comeback would start at zero.

Greg lost 10 pounds in the first 10 days of his recuperation. His longest workout during that period was a 20-foot walk. Not until six weeks after his release from the hospital did he mount a bike. He started at 5 kilometers and went a little farther in each subsequent ride. Two months after the accident, Greg's blood volume had finally returned to normal.

By September, Greg was racing again. His results were less than spectacular (he finished 44th in the Tour of Ireland), but this was only to be expected at such an early stage in his return to competition. The point of mixing it up in these late-season events was merely to get his racing legs back and set himself up for an ascension to top form in the 1988 season. Alarmingly, though, Greg's form was no better in November than it had been two months earlier. He abandoned his last event of the season, the Tour of Mexico, because he couldn't get up the hills.

Greg's first race of 1988, the Ruta del Sol in Spain, didn't go any better. This time his teammates had to push him—literally, with hands placed on the small of his back—up the climbs. A few weeks later, Greg crashed again. He suffered only a minor injury to a muscle in his right lower leg, but when he jumped back into training too aggressively after two weeks off the bike, the problem became chronic. Instead of riding the Tour de France in July, he got an operation.

By the fall, Greg was racing once more, but poorly, and he was straining to maintain his customary rosy outlook. "I'm feeling better but starting over again," he told the *New York Times*. "I'm always starting over."

Greg's lack of results caused his relationship with his new employer, the PDM team, to sour. The tension became a breach when team management pressured their struggling star rider to receive injections of testosterone, a banned performance enhancer, and he refused. In one form or another, doping had always been a part of cycling, but in 1988 it was on the brink of getting out of control. The previous year, Laurent Fignon had failed a drug test for amphetamines. Weeks later, during that year's Tour de France, Spaniard Pedro Delgado was caught with a steroid masking agent in his system but was allowed to complete the race—which he won—because the substance had not yet been formally banned. Greg believed, perhaps naively, that such cheating was rare, but it was becoming increasingly common, and the methods more sophisticated.

After Greg's break with PDM, his lawyer, Ron Stanko, told a *Los Angeles Times* reporter, "I explained to them that we were not interested in using chemicals to improve performances. That is Greg's position, 100 percent." This stance was based not only on Greg's distaste for cheating but also on his conviction that he was talented enough to win without shortcuts. After all, he had done it before.

On New Year's Eve, 1988, Greg signed with a new team, ADR. He had previously derided ADR as second rate, claiming its roster was too weak to support a Tour de France contender. But it was now the only team willing to compensate him as a still-young past Tour winner rather than as a cyclist whose own recent performances were second rate.

Greg opened the 1989 season with some promising results, finishing sixth overall in the Tirreno-Adriatico race in Italy and taking second place in a stage of the Criterium Internationale. But the promise of these performances was not fulfilled. In May, Greg competed in the inaugural Tour de Trump in the United States, an event that, owing to its namesake's knack for spectacle, attracted extraordinary public attention by the standards of American bicycle racing. It would have been an ideal showcase for the talents of the first American winner of the Tour de France—if only he hadn't finished 27th.

The next stop for Greg and his ADR teammates was the Giro d'Italia, a three-week "Grand Tour" like the Tour de France. Greg continued to feel not quite right on the bike, and it showed in his results. On the very first big climb of the race, he lost 8 minutes to the leaders. As he slid farther and farther behind in the succeeding days, Greg began to despair. After one stage, he sat on his bed in a crummy hotel room and wept, bitterness and frustration pouring out of him like steam from a burst pipe. He told his roommate, Johan Lammerts, that he was finished as a cyclist. He could not continue to suffer so much to achieve so little in the shadow of what he once was. It was time to quit and move on.

Lammerts urged Greg to at least finish the Giro before he made any sweeping decisions about his future. Greg relented, and the next morning he was back in the saddle and once again bringing up the rear of the peloton. He came into the last day of the Giro more than 55 minutes behind the race leader, Laurent Fignon, who was making a comeback of his own after three consecutive years marred by injuries and other setbacks. But something had changed since Greg's hotel room crisis: He had been diagnosed with severe anemia—probably a lasting effect of his accident—and had started a course of (perfectly legal, and indeed medically necessary) iron injections. He felt better immediately. The final stage of the Giro was a 53-km individual time trial. From the moment he left the starting gate, Greg knew he was back—or mostly back. Six kilometers into the ride, he caught and passed a rider who had started 90 seconds ahead of him. Fifteen kilometers farther along, he overtook a second competitor, this one having begun with a 3-minute head start. Greg finished with the second-best time of the day, outpacing Fignon, who held on for the overall tour victory, by 78 seconds.

Greg had been so far down for so long that this performance did little to alter appraisals of his prospects for the Tour de France, which would begin three weeks later. All eyes were on defending champion Pedro Delgado and the newly resurgent Fignon. Greg himself said he would consider a top-20 finish a success, as his body was still a bit of a question mark. His mind, however, was not.

The Tour began on Saturday, July 1, in Luxembourg, with a prologue in the form of a 7.8-km individual time trial. Greg stopped the clock at 10 minutes flat, a time bettered by just one rider and matched by two others, including Fignon. Greg's fine result was overshadowed by a debacle involving the defending champion, who missed his start time and lost 2:40 to the rest of the 198-man field before he'd even left the gate. But while the media overlooked Greg in all the hullabaloo over Pedro Delgado's inexplicable self-sabotage, at least one of his rivals did not. Upon seeing the results of the prologue, Fignon marked the American as the man most likely to stand in the way of his third Tour victory.

Greg himself was ecstatic about his performance, but he tried hard to tamp down the emotion. For two long years, hope had never amounted to anything more than a setup for crushing disappointment. "I have to be careful not to get too confident too quickly," he told the press.

The first big test for the ADR team as a collective came two days later with a 48-km team time trial. Greg and the eight nobodies who wore the same uniform surpassed low expectations with a fifth-place finish, losing 51 seconds to Fignon's Super U team. Greg came away from the stage in 14th place in the General Classification, 11 spots behind the French favorite.

Stage five pitted each man against all in an unusually long, 73-km time trial contested in wet conditions. Greg had felt strong enough in the preceding stages that he dared to dream of winning this one. To better his chances, he tried a new piece of equipment: aero handlebars, or triathlon bars, as they were more often called in those days. More functionally than technically innovative, the device consisted of an elongated U-shaped piece of metal tubing upon which the rider rested his forearms, a position that flattened the back and narrowed the front profile, reducing wind drag. Aerobars had debuted at the Tour de Trump, where they were used by a handful of American riders. The Europeans scorned them, but Greg judged them worth a try.

They were. Greg won the time trial, beating Delgado by 24 seconds and Fignon by 56. The latter margin was sufficient to lift Greg to first place in the G.C. At a ceremony held after the race, he donned the yellow jersey of the race leader for the first time since he had won the Tour in 1986. He told the crowd, "This is the most wonderful moment of my life," and he meant it. Being on top, he discovered, was that much sweeter when you'd come up from the very bottom.

When the Tour entered the mountains in stage 9, Delgado, still paying for his late start in the prologue, had little choice but to go on the attack. On the first of two tough days in the Pyrenees, the

Spaniard gained back 29 seconds on Fignon and Greg, who were more concerned with marking each other. The next day, Delgado took fuller advantage of his rivals' distraction, crossing the finish line at the summit of the Superbagnères ski resort nearly 3.5 minutes ahead of Fignon, who used a late attack to beat Greg by 12 seconds and reclaim the yellow jersey.

The next few stages were uneventful. Mostly flat, they featured bunch sprints to the finish line and breakaways by cyclists who were not threats to the top riders in the General Classification. Then came stage 15, another individual time trial. Greg again used the triathlon bars, but he spent little time in them because the 39-km course was largely uphill, removing aerodynamics from the performance equation. He finished fifth, losing 7 seconds to Delgado and gaining 47 on Fignon. Greg was back in yellow.

After a rest day, which Greg spent with his family, the Tour entered the Alps. By this time, three of Greg's teammates had abandoned the race. The remaining ADR riders were not strong climbers. This left Greg exposed on the major climbs of stage 16, a vulnerability that the other contenders exploited by taking turns attacking him. As the wearer of the *maillot jaune*, Greg had to answer each new assault, and he did so successfully, finishing the stage with Delgado and 13 seconds ahead of Fignon to increase his overall lead on the Frenchman to 53 seconds. Afterward, Greg spoke openly to reporters for the first time about the possibility of winning the Tour.

"If I have another good day tomorrow," he allowed, "I'd say I was in a strong position to win."

Alas, he did not have another good day. Greg cracked on the final climb of stage 17, hitting a wall on the fabled switchbacks of L'Alpe d'Huez. Delgado and Fignon pedaled away to steal 69 seconds from the American. The yellow jersey belonged once again to Fignon. In stage 18, the new leader dropped Greg and Delgado on the approach to another summit finish, padding his lead by 24 seconds.

The mountains had taught Greg that, despite his high hopes, he was not quite as strong as he'd been when he won the Tour in 1986, nor—as he would confess after his retirement—would he ever be. He was riding with 30 shotgun pellets in his body, after all. What's more, he was up against two past Tour winners who'd been caught doping and perhaps were cheating still. If Greg was to beat them, his mind would have to find a way to do more with less—to become stronger to the same degree that his body was weaker.

There was one more mountain stage left to survive. Greg knew that he could not afford to lose any more time to Fignon, or all hope of overtaking him in the final showdown of stage 21 would be gone. Fignon, Delgado, and Greg showed all their cards in stage 19, a 125-km race from Villard de Lans to Aix les Bains that passed over three major climbs. The three rivals formed a "royal breakaway" with the fourth- and seventh-place riders in the General Classification, leaving the rest of the field far behind as they traded attacks. Greg won the stage in a sprint with Fignon. He recovered no time, but gained a moral victory.

Stage 20 was flat and relatively easy, leaving the overall rankings unaffected. It ended at L'Isle d'Abeau, where the competitors boarded a train bound for Versailles, site of the start of stage 21. The following afternoon, Greg would have one last chance to make up 50 seconds on Fignon. If he fell short in the 24.5-km individual time trial—and if he did, it would likely be by a few ticks—he would be crushed. He was no longer the same man who had said he would be happy to crack the top 20.

Despite the daunting challenge he faced, Greg was his usual congenial self during the train ride to Versailles, chatting casually with journalists the whole way. Meanwhile, Fignon, also true to form, cursed and spat at a Spanish camera crew that tried to approach him. Perhaps both men felt, in their heart of hearts, that what seemed impossible was not.

A 24.5-KM CYCLING TIME TRIAL is an exercise in pacing. So are all races that last longer than 30 seconds. In races that last less than

30 seconds, competitors go all-out, pedaling, striding, or stroking at absolute maximum intensity from start to finish. They hold nothing back and utilize their full physical capacity. In races that last longer than 30 seconds, competitors do hold back. They pedal, stride, or stroke at less than maximum intensity at all points of the race except perhaps the very end. Instead of going all-out, they maintain the highest intensity they feel capable of sustaining through the full race distance.

Why 30 seconds? Because humans cannot sustain maximum-intensity exercise longer than about 30 seconds without exceeding the highest level of perceived effort they can tolerate. Athletes are conscious of their effort in shorter races, of course, but because they know their suffering will end quickly they do not use this perception to control their pace, which is constrained only by their physical capacity. But when an athlete starts a race that he knows will last longer than 30 seconds, he holds back just enough that his perceived effort limit is not reached until he is at the finish line. That is the art of pacing.

What happens when an athlete tries to sustain a maximum intensity of exercise longer than 30 seconds? Anna Wittekind of the University of Essex answered this question in a 2009 study published in the *British Journal of Sports Medicine*. Nine subjects were asked to ride stationary bikes outfitted with power meters as hard as they could for 5 seconds, 15 seconds, 30 seconds, and 45 seconds on separate occasions. When she reviewed the results, Wittekind found that the subjects had generated slightly less power during the *first* 15 seconds of the 45-second test than they had in the 15-second test. In other words, they had *not* pedaled as hard as they could at the start of the longest test ride, even though they had been instructed to do so. Instead, they had unconsciously paced themselves.

Wittekind speculated that, on the basis of past experience, the subjects recognized that they could not sustain a true maximal effort for 45 seconds without exceeding their maximum tolerance for perceived effort, so they held back just a little without even realizing it.

These results suggest that the limit of maximum perceived effort tolerance is so impenetrable that athletes are not psychologically capable of even *trying* to sustain a maximum exercise intensity longer than approximately 30 seconds.

The fact that pacing is required to maximize performance in all races lasting longer than half a minute has some interesting implications. A sprinter finishes every race knowing he went as fast as he could (technical errors notwithstanding). Longer races are different. Because it is necessary to hold back to some degree at almost every point in these races, it is impossible for the athlete to know upon finishing whether he might have gone faster—if only by a second or two—if he'd held back just a bit less somewhere along the way.

Many automobiles have a "range" feature that displays the number of miles the vehicle can travel before it runs out of gasoline. This number is not open to interpretation. If the range display says 29 miles, you'd better find a gas station within the next 29 miles. The mechanism of regulatory anticipation that athletes use to control their pace in races is different. It's not a number but a feeling, and like all feelings it is open to interpretation. One of the most important and valuable coping skills in endurance sports is the ability to interpret the perceptions that influence pacing decisions in a performance-maximizing way. As an endurance athlete, you want to get better and better at reading these perceptions in such a way that your internal pacing mechanism functions more and more like an automobile's range display. You want to be as correct as you can possibly be when determining the swiftest pace you can sustain to the finish line without exceeding your perceived effort tolerance.

Setting and pursuing time-based race goals is very helpful in the process of calibrating anticipatory regulation. This practice enables athletes to interpret their effort perceptions in a more performance-enhancing way by transforming the racing experience from an effort to go as fast as possible into an effort to go faster than ever before. Validation of this approach comes from a 1997 study done by researchers at Israel's Ben-Gurion University and published

in the *Journal of Sports Science.* High school students were subjected
to a test of muscular endurance and then spent eight weeks training
to increase their time to exhaustion. Some of the students were given
a nonquantitative goal to "do their best." Others were given a quantitative goal to better their performance in the initial test by a certain
percentage. Even though all of the students did the same training,
those who pursued quantitative goals improved their performance
significantly more when the muscular endurance test was repeated
after eight weeks.

More recently, a team of researchers led by Eric Allen of the University of California found that finish times in marathons tend to
cluster near the round numbers (such as 4:30 and 4:00) that runners
typically pursue as goals. This pattern would have carried little sig-
nificance if Allen and his colleagues had not also noted that those
runners who end up closest to these round numbers at the finish line
slow down less than other runners in the final miles of a marathon—
evidence that the pursuit of these round-number goals enhances
performance. Regardless of how an athlete chooses to train, her
training will yield greater improvement in race times if improving
race times is the explicit goal of the training process.

Paying attention to the clock reduces the uncertainty associated
with reaching beyond past limits and in this way facilitates effective
pacing. While it may be impossible for an athlete who completes a
race of a certain distance to know if he could have tried harder, it's
relatively easy for an athlete who completes a race of a certain distance in a certain time to aim to cover the next race of the same distance a second or two faster than he did the last time.

According to Samuele Marcora's psychobiological model of
endurance performance, the amount of effort that an athlete puts
into a race is influenced by her perception of the attainability of her
goal, a concept borrowed from Jack Brehm's theory of motivational
intensity. If the goal seems to fall out of reach at any point during
the race, the athlete is likely to back off her effort. If the goal seems
attainable, but only with increased effort, the athlete is likely to

increase her effort, provided she's not already at her limit. By keeping track of, and aiming to improve, personal best times for specific race distances, athletes can exploit this phenomenon to try harder than they would otherwise be able to. The goal of improving your time for a certain distance by 1 measly second almost always seems attainable. And if that goal is attainable, then the very slightly greater level of perceived effort that an athlete must endure to achieve it is likely to seem more endurable than it would seem if the athlete were going entirely by feel. It's not the time goal itself that enhances performance but the effect that the goal has on how the athlete interprets her perception of effort.

Setting time-based goals that stretch you just beyond past limits is like setting a flag next to a bed of hot coals to mark the furthest point reached in your best fire walk. That flag says to you, "This is possible, and you know it. So why wouldn't it be possible for you to make it just one step farther the next time?"

A real-world example of this process of using time-based goals to recalibrate perceived effort in a performance-enhancing way is South African runner Elana Meyer's career progression at the half-marathon distance. In 1980, when she was 13 years old, Meyer took her first shot at 13.1 miles, winning the Foot of Africa half-marathon in a mind-boggling time of 1:27:10. Nine years later, Meyer made her professional debut at the same distance, running 1:09:26 in Durban. In 1991, she smashed the half-marathon world record in London, clocking 1:07:59. Between 1997 and 1999, Meyer broke the record thrice more, running 1:07:36, 1:07:29, and finally 1:06:44 in Tokyo at age 32.

Obviously, Meyer's development as an athlete was responsible for much of this improvement. But her pursuit of time goals also played a role. It is interesting to note that her margins of improvement tended to get smaller as her career advanced. Her big leaps from 1:27 to 1:09 and from 1:09 to 1:07 were undoubtedly fueled principally by gains in fitness. Meyer probably wasn't even thinking about her first half-marathon when she made her pro debut, so much stronger was she by then. But her last two world records were set on familiar courses on which she had already posted fast times, and in each of these cases she set out deliberately to run faster than ever before. It's likely that Meyer was not any fitter at the 1999 Tokyo Half Marathon, where she ran 1:06:44, than she had been a year earlier in Kyoto, where she ran 1:07:29, but she had the crucial advantage of having run 1:07:29 already.

But wait: If Meyer was just as fit (not to mention a year younger) when she ran the slower time, then can it not be said that timekeeping *held her back* in the 1998 Kyoto Half Marathon, even as it pulled her beyond the world record of 1:07:36 she had set on the same course in 1997? There is indeed evidence that the influence of clock watching on endurance performance is two-sided. The same time goal that enhances performance when it is perceived as a target constrains performance when it is perceived as a limit.

The potential for time standards to become performance limiters is most apparent at the elite level of endurance sports. There have been many noteworthy cases in which a performance breakthrough by one athlete triggered a widespread revolution in performance and thereby revealed that previous standards had been holding the sport back. Between 1994 and 2008, for example, the women's world record for triathlon's Ironman distance was stuck at 8:50:53. Only seven women recorded times under 9 hours in that 14-year span. When Yvonne van Vlerken finally lowered the Ironman world record to 8:45:48 in July 2008, the floodgates were opened. Six other women dipped under the 9-hour barrier in the next few months. Van Vlerken's mark lasted only one year, as did the subsequent record. By the end of the 2011 season, the Ironman world record for women stood at 8:18:13, and sub-8:50 performances had become commonplace. Was the new generation of female triathletes that much more talented than the previous one? No. These women just weren't held back by a tendency to regard the time of 8:50:53 as an unsurpassable human limit.

In consideration of the two-sided nature of time's effect on endurance performance, it is tempting to ask what sort of time goal would have the best possible effect on performance. Such a goal would need to seem reachable, but barely so. (Indeed, in the Ben-Gurion University study I mentioned above, students given a "difficult/realistic" goal improved more than those given either an "easy" goal or an "improbable/unattainable" goal.) This ideal goal would also need to be sufficiently well defined to pull the athlete beyond past limits, yet somehow vague enough that it did not place an artificial ceiling on the athlete's performance.

Greg LeMond's situation at the start of stage 21 of the 1989 Tour de France met these requirements perfectly. Greg had to beat Laurent Fignon's time in the 24.5-km time trial by 50 seconds. But Fignon would start *behind* him, so Greg could not approach the race with a specific time in mind, such as the 27:30 clocking that Thierry Marie posted early in the day, which stood as the best time in the field when Greg started his ride. Instead, Greg knew only that he had to ride 50 seconds faster than the best time Fignon—one of the world's best time trialists besides Greg himself—could conceivably achieve on his best day.

Greg told reporters before the race that he believed the task facing him lay at the very outer limits of the achievable. He was not certain that he could pull it off even if he gave more than he had ever given before on a day when he had more to give than ever before. Nor was he certain that he couldn't. It is hard to imagine a goal construct that would have elicited a better performance from Greg LeMond in the most important race of his life.

AFTER LUNCH, GREG CHECKED OUT of the hotel and made his way toward the Palace of Versailles, a Vatican-like architectural colossus in front of which a comparatively flimsy temporary starting platform had been erected under a white canopy. A massive crowd had gathered there to witness the showdown between the two men at the top of the General Classification. Behind the start line was a small warm-up area. Within its narrow confines a handful of riders traced tight loops. Greg joined them and soon met Fignon head on. Greg averted his gaze. Despite this demurral, Fignon thought the American looked relaxed. In fact, Greg was terrified, his stomach knotted with dread of the suffering he was about to inflict on himself.

At 4:12, Pedro Delgado, who stood 1:38 behind Greg in the G.C., rolled off the starting ramp and accelerated down the broad Avenue de Paris. It was now Greg's turn to mount the platform. Television cameras rolled as a silver-haired race official with black-framed glasses held Greg's bright red Bottechia time trial bike upright and a countdown was intoned over loudspeakers.

"Cinq … quatre … troix … deux … un … Allez!"

Greg stood on the pedals and began a hard windup, his feet churning like the steel wheels of an accelerating locomotive. When he hit 100 revolutions per minute, he dropped his butt onto the saddle and settled his forearms into the aero bars. A pair of police motorcycles guided him down the runway-wide boulevard as a flotilla of vehicles, including a white Peugeot containing ADR team manager José de Cauwer, followed behind.

Greg's plan was simple: to ride just a bit faster than he ever had, holding back a little less than he had ever dared in similar circumstances. Greg lowered his head and rode with his eyes cast straight downward, as though indifferent to where he was going, looking up only briefly every few seconds to check his line. His meaty quadriceps billowed with every downstroke.

Greg was already more than a mile down the road toward the Parisian suburb of Viroflay when Fignon set off behind him. With his granny glasses and blond ponytail, he looked more like a high school drama teacher than a professional cyclist as he sprinted away from the starting gate. Fignon had been seen fiddling around with a set of triathlon bars earlier in the day, but he'd elected to leave them behind. His bike did have the advantage of being outfitted with two aerodynamic disk wheels, however, whereas Greg, expecting more crosswinds than he actually would encounter on the course, had gone with spokes in the front.

Just over 2 miles into his race, Greg suddenly swerved, his bike wobbling precariously from left to right for a fraction of a second. On looking up from the road he had discovered that he was taking the long way around an S-curve, started, and gone squirrely. Swerving is not something a cyclist ever wants to do with his arms stuck in aero-bars, where the slightest flinch at high speed translates into a sharp veering of the front wheel. But Greg was one of the sport's greatest bike handlers and most audacious daredevils, who sometimes showed off by riding down steep descents with his hands clasped behind his back like a ski jumper. In the blink of an eye he controlled his reflex and transformed the close call into an efficient course correction. The near disaster was instantly forgotten as Greg put his head back down and continued to spin a huge gear on a 55-tooth chainring that would have felt like lifting weights to most cyclists.

Behind him, Fignon felt strong and confident. He zipped through Viroflay and approached Chaville, the crowds thinning as he went. After he passed 5 kilometers, his team manager, Cyrille Guimard, shouted from the trailing car, his words captured by a nearby cameraman's mic.

"Six secondes!" he called out. "Vous avez perdu six secondes!"

He had already lost 6 seconds to LeMond. Fignon turned his head and stared incredulously at Guimard. Greg was not yet gaining the 2 seconds per kilometer he needed to overtake the Frenchman, but given how well Fignon himself was riding, he couldn't believe the American was going that much faster.

Up the road, Greg received the same news from José de Cauwer. Before the race, Greg had asked Cauwer not to supply any such information, and he tersely reminded his manager of that wish now. For the remainder of the time trial, his mind would be focused entirely on the image of creating distance between himself and the man behind him, and on the only number that mattered: 50 seconds.

Passing through Sèvres, on the west bank of the River Seine, Greg came to an overpass. He moved his hands to the outer bars and pedaled from a standing position to avoid losing speed as he climbed. If the policeman on a motorcycle cruising close behind him had checked his speed gauge at this moment, he would have seen the needle fixed at 54 kilometers per hour.

Minutes later, Greg crossed the Pont de Sèvres, a bridge over the River Seine, at the far end of which he made a sharp right turn onto the Quai Georges Gorse, carving the corner with such bold precision that his right shoulder came within centimeters of clipping spectators leaning against a barrier on the inside of the turn.

At 11.5 kilometers, Greg passed an official time check. His split of 12:08 was the fastest of the day by 20 seconds. Fignon reached the same point 2 minutes and 21 seconds later, having now lost 21 seconds to Greg since the start. If Fignon continued to lose time at the same rate, he would complete the time trial 45 seconds slower than Greg and would win the Tour de France by 5 seconds.

The Quai was as flat and straight as a drag strip. Greg took full advantage, settling into a chugging rhythm that nudged his speed even higher. The drivers of any trailing cars with manual transmission would have been forced to shift into fourth gear to keep up.

As Greg approached 14 kilometers, the Eiffel Tower rose into view ahead. Fignon's deficit had risen to 24 seconds. Greg still was not gaining time quite fast enough, but as hard as he was pushing himself, he still felt strong, whereas Fignon's shoulders had begun to rock, a telltale sign of encroaching weariness. A clear difference in the relative speeds of the two men became apparent to cycling fans watching the battle on television at home. Every 10 or 15 seconds, the coverage jumped from Fignon to Greg, and when it did, the passing scenery accelerated noticeably.

The last part of the course skirted the famous Jardin des Tuileries—Paris's Central Park—and dumped riders onto the Champs-Élysées for the homestretch to the finish line. Tens of thousands of spectators lining the streets there erupted when Greg came into view. (His French surname, French language skills, and all-American charm had won him many admirers in the Tour's host nation.) He passed under a banner marking 4 kilometers to the finish line. His advantage was now 35 seconds. Greg had stolen exactly 2 seconds per kilometer from Fignon over the last 6.5 kilometers; he would have to nearly double that rate of separation on the Champs-Élysées to win the Tour.

Greg's last best chance to gain that separation lay just ahead of him, at 3 kilometers to go, where a false flat rose gently from the Place de la Concorde to the Arc de Triomphe. It wasn't much of a hill by Tour standards, but to an exhausted rider—as Fignon was quickly becoming—it would feel like a Pyrenean switchback. Greg attacked it hard, telling himself that his career depended on it. As he neared the top, his torso began to pump up and down like an oil horse. Any consideration of good form had gone out the window—all that mattered now was effort at any cost.

At the Arc de Triomphe, Greg made a hairpin right turn and entered the final straight to the finish line. Moving down the same false flat he had just ascended, he hit 40 mph, approaching the motor vehicle speed limit on the Champs-Élysées. He passed under the 1-km banner. Over the race radio came word that Greg still needed 10 seconds.

Ahead on the road, Greg saw the rocking posterior of Pedro Delgado, who had started 2 minutes before him. Greg felt a magnetic pull, and he used it to raise his effort level one more excruciating notch for the final drive to the finish line. He crossed at 26:57, beating the previous best time of the day by 33 seconds. Greg hung his head like a recipient of bad news as he coasted to a stop. A moment earlier his legs had felt as though they were going to explode. Now they suddenly felt capable of going another 10 miles. Had he done enough?

The waiting began. Greg dismounted and turned back toward the racecourse and the finish line clock, understanding that if it displayed the number 27:47 before Fignon finished, he had won the Tour de France. The anticipation was unbearable. When Fignon came into sight, Greg reflexively shaded his eyes and looked away—but only briefly.

Fignon was shattered with fatigue, no longer able to hold a straight line and nearly drifting into a barrier of scaffolding at the outer edge of the 70-meter-wide road in his flailing efforts to drive his machine toward the line. The seconds ticked by with surreal slowness. But the magic number finally appeared, and when it did, Fignon was still 100 meters from the finish. He stopped the clock at 27:55. Greg LeMond had won the Tour by 8 seconds.

Greg's average speed for the 24.5-km time trial was 33.89 mph—an all-time record for Tour de France time trials, by a long shot. Greg (who would win his third and last Tour de France in 1990) could not have known it, but at that moment his sport was on the threshold of an era of unprecedented technological advancement. In the coming years, bikes would be completely transformed with stiffer, lighter materials, computer- and wind tunnel–assisted aerodynamics, and more efficient and reliable components and accessories. The sport was also entering an era of rampant and sophisticated doping. Most of the top riders of the 1990s and 2000s would gain a tremendous performance advantage from drugs such as erythropoietin (EPO). Yet none of these pharmaceutically enhanced athletes on space-age bikes was able to better Greg LeMond's time trial speed record until 2005. And to this day, no Tour rider has ridden faster than Greg except in shorter time trials undertaken on fresh legs on the first day of the race instead of the last.

It would seem that, in the right circumstances, an old-fashioned stopwatch—properly used—can affect endurance performance more powerfully than either the finest equipment or the most potent chemicals—not to mention lift an athlete to his finest hour even after his best days are behind him.

CHAPTER FOUR

THE ART OF
LETTING GO

WHEN SIRI LINDLEY WAS 23 years old, she did not know how to swim, she did not own a bike, and she had never run farther than a mile. One year later, in the summer of 1994, the International Olympic Committee announced that the sport of triathlon had been awarded full medal status and would make its Olympic debut at the 2000 Summer Games in Sydney. Upon learning of this announcement, Siri immediately resolved to do everything in her power to become a member of the first U.S. Olympic triathlon team. She had six years to turn herself into one of the best combined swimmer-cyclist-runners in the world.

Siri was not alone in this dream. Hundreds, if not thousands, of men and women on all five inhabited continents reacted similarly to the IOC's declaration. But few of them faced longer odds than Siri. She had by that time completed only a couple of short triathlons, and her prior athletic background was entirely in team sports—field hockey, ice hockey, and lacrosse. While she had been talented enough to play all three at the college level, swinging sticks at balls and pucks is not exactly ideal preparation for endurance races consisting of

1.5 km of swimming, 40 km of cycling, and 10 km of running (the official Olympic triathlon format).

The seed of Siri's unlikely triathlon dream was planted one weekend when she watched her friend Lynn Oski compete in a small triathlon in Worcester, Massachusetts, where Siri had taken a job at a YMCA after graduating from Brown University in 1992. Something about it grabbed her. The very next day, Siri visited the Y's pool to tackle her fear of putting her face in the water. Soon thereafter she bought some running shoes and a rusted old 10-speed bike with a basket on the front. She was bound and determined to become a triathlete.

She showed no immediate promise. Even after she was no longer a drowning risk, Siri could barely keep up with the elderly breast-strokers in the pool, and on group bike rides with Oski and others she invariably got left behind on the hills. So fearful was Siri of humiliating herself in front of friends and acquaintances in her triathlon debut that she chose a low-key sprint race some 2,000 miles from home in Colorado, where she was able to humiliate herself in front of strangers.

The race started with a pool swim. As the participants gathered on deck, the event's organizer went around asking them for their "100 times" so that athletes of similar ability could be grouped together in the same lane. Siri did not even know what a 100 time was. She picked a number at random and ended up in a lane with eight young men built like torpedoes. They mauled her in the process of completing the 800-yard swim in half the time it took her. Things went downhill from there.

Despite it all, Siri was hooked—so much so that a year later she returned to Colorado to take up full-time residence and pursue triathlon with total devotion in one of its major hotbeds. The intensity of her desire to master the sport seemed strange even to her, yet she wholly trusted the instinct that was leading her.

Siri's parents had divorced when she was four. The split left her saddled with deep feelings of inadequacy. To her child's way of thinking, her mother and father would not have broken up if Siri had been important enough to them. Both parents soon remarried, causing Siri to feel even more cast off. Her dad exited her life almost entirely, while her mom gave more time and attention to her new husband than to her youngest child. And, naturally, Siri's big sis, Lisa, wanted nothing to do with her. Siri would eventually become closer to her father, her sister, and her mother, Astrid, especially, but the inner doubts stayed with her.

In athletics Siri sought the validation that she wasn't getting at home. But she always fell just short of achieving enough to fill the gaping hole inside her. She won a Coach's Award but was passed over for the MVP trophy. She was invited to try out for the World Cup lacrosse team but didn't make the cut. Triathlon appealed to Siri first of all because it was an individual sport in which she did not have to depend on a coach's judgment for awards or selection. And though initially she was terrible at it, somehow she just knew she could be good. A deep intuition assured Siri that if she gave her heart and soul to triathlon she would achieve something truly special by her own standards for the first time in her life, something that would make her feel good about herself in a way she never had.

Indeed, she was not terrible for long. Siri finished third in her division at the 1994 age-group triathlon world championships and then turned professional. She continued to improve, her swim becoming less and less of a liability and her run an ever-more-dangerous weapon. In 1998, Siri won the U.S. pro national championship in Oceanside, California. Afterward, beaming the winsome smile that would help her become one of the sport's most popular and marketable personalities, she told reporters, "This is the happiest moment of my life!"

Siri could picture an even happier moment, though, and she still yearned after it: the Sydney Olympics. Her first taste of major success in triathlon served only to intensify her hunger, like a light appetizer after a long fast.

The year 1999 was a critical one for aspiring Olympic triathletes. Their performance in the seven-race World Cup triathlon series would determine whether they were invited to Olympic selection races to be held the following spring. Siri racked up five top-five finishes in these events, more than any other American. The former long shot now looked like a sure bet.

At the conclusion of the 1999 triathlon season, Siri took a big step: She packed some bags, crated her bike, and moved to Sydney, Australia. Her plan was to live and train there for the four months leading up to the Sydney World Cup on April 16, when the top American finisher would claim the first of three Olympic berths reserved for U.S. women. Sydney offered several advantages. For starters, Siri would arrive there just in time for the beginning of the subequatorial summer. In addition, her coach, Jack Ralston, lived close by. And no less important, Sydney was far away from her friends, family, and other "distractions." Siri had resolved to make her dream of Olympic qualification not just the center of her life but the whole of her life until she achieved it.

She rented a one-bedroom apartment in the sparkling beachside suburb of Cronulla. Each morning she ate a solitary breakfast before heading to the pool for swim practice. She then returned home for lunch before heading out again for her afternoon workouts—a bike ride and a run—which she did alone whenever possible. She ate an early dinner at the apartment and then climbed inside a bubble-like high-altitude simulation chamber to read until bedtime. Before she fell asleep, she imagined herself competing in the Olympic triathlon. Her vision followed the same ideal script every time: a perfectly executed start followed by a smooth middle leading to a triumphant ending. Siri had initiated the nightly practice on September 16, 1999, exactly one year before the actual event would take place, and she intended to keep it up through September 15, 2000—provided she qualified.

Siri explained her mindset in a column she wrote for *Triathlete* after her self-imposed quarantine. "I had many opportunities for a more social way of life," she wrote, "but I felt that I had to do things differently now, in order to achieve my goals. I tried to be solitary as much as possible. This would give me a better chance to be one with myself and really pay attention to my needs and my progress. In some ways, it was as though I was trying to dehumanize my very human nature. Trying to become impervious to pain, warmth, love, and flattery. Deep down I missed my family, my friends, my pets, my home and my normal 'full-of-life' life but I ignored all of this, hardened myself and reminded myself how I needed to do this on my own. This would make me stronger, this would be a true accomplishment, this would fulfill the ultimate requirement of proving myself to myself. I felt as though I was on a spiritual mission, out to find the very secret, the very essence of my being. My faith being a great companion, I didn't feel alone. I became personally empowered and derived great strength and comfort in knowing that I was doing everything 'right.'"

So focused was Siri on her quasi-spiritual quest that she didn't realize it was draining all the fun out of being a triathlete. At home in Boulder, she had two dogs, a St. Bernard named Billy and a mutt named Whoopi. Siri did all of her running with Whoopi, even track workouts. It was Whoopi's insatiable enthusiasm for running that had made Siri herself fall in love with the activity and discover her gift for it. Whoopi was always up for a run and never gave any indication of wanting to stop. Her slobbering zeal for the simple act of running was infectious, and Siri caught the bug.

In Sydney, Siri lacked Whoopi's cheerful influence, among others. She had given it all up intentionally, open-eyed, thinking it a great idea. Her most nourishing relationship in Australia was with a beat-up 1980 Mitsubishi Colt that she had bought for $400 to get around in.

Nevertheless, her training went well, and when the fateful date of April 16 arrived, Siri woke up feeling fitter than ever. At 10 in the morning, she found herself standing shoulder to shoulder with 40 of the world's best female short-course triathletes on a pontoon floating atop the briny waters of Farm Cove, with Sydney's famed Opera House as the backdrop. Siri felt confident—at least she thought she did. But she kept forgetting to breathe, and she stood with marmoreal rigidity on the start platform while the women around her shook their arms and legs to stay loose. A gun sounded and Siri dived into the choppy water, where she quickly found the heels of two-time world champion Michellie Jones, exactly as she had done every night in her bedtime visualizations.

A buoy marked the halfway point of the 1500-meter course. The racers bunched together as they negotiated this hairpin bend, the race suddenly becoming a full-contact affair. Siri got dunked by a competitor who swam right over the top of her. When she came up, she was gasping and—much worse—she was 2 meters behind Jones's pack. Panicked, Siri thrashed through the waves in a furious effort to catch the group, but they were swimming as hard as they could too, and they were better swimmers. Siri staggered out of the ocean 10 crucial seconds behind the Jones cabal. She sprinted to her bike, strapped on her helmet, wheeled the bike to the end of a spongy blue mat that carpeted the transition area, mounted, and continued her desperate chase.

Siri did not need to win. All she had to do was beat the four other American women in the race and she'd have punched her ticket to return to the very same course for the Olympics. The problem was that her countrywoman Barb Lindquist was leading the race more than a minute up the road, well ahead of Jones and company. Siri pushed herself to the limit to catch Lindquist's pursuers, aware that if she reached them in time she could then ride in their draft to save her legs for the run, where she held the advantage over Lindquist. But to her infinite dismay, Siri discovered that her legs felt like jelly, almost inert, as though she were riding through mud after completing five sets of heavy barbell squats and an hour-long tennis match. Unable to generate her accustomed power, Siri not only failed to catch Jones's group but was herself caught and passed by a cluster of slower swimmers.

The bike course was a loop of just under 7 km that the racers would complete six times. By the start of lap 2, Siri was almost dead last. As she finished the third circuit, rain began to fall. It seemed like a signal. She braked, unclipped her shoes from the pedals, dismounted. She quit.

In a self-lacerating postmortem penned for *Triathlete*, Siri diagnosed the cause of her nightmarish meltdown in frank terms. "I was fully responsible for my actions and had absolutely no excuse for my horrible performance except that I choked," she wrote.

All was not lost, though. Two positions on the U.S. Olympic triathlon team remained open. (Jennifer Gutierrez had snatched the first one after Barb Lindquist wrecked her bike on the rain-slickened streets of Sydney.) These last slots would be awarded to the top two American finishers at a second qualification race to be held on May 27 in Dallas.

Siri's greatest fear was a hot day, and she got one. When the race started at 9 in the morning, the air temperature was 81 degrees and rising. As expected, former Olympic swimmer Sheila Taormina swam clear of the rest of the 27-woman field with Barb Lindquist on her feet. The pair splashed out of Lake Carolyn 40 seconds ahead of a chase group containing Siri and the other strong runners in the field, including Joanna Zeiger and Laura Reback.

On the five-loop, 40-km bike course, Taormina and Lindquist worked together to extend their lead. With their superior numbers, the chasers should have held the advantage, but nobody wanted to do the work. Frustratingly disorganized, they lost ground with each lap. When they arrived at the bike-run transition, they were more than 3 minutes behind the leading duo.

Siri burst out of the transition area as though it were dynamite on a 10-second fuse. Only Zeiger and Reback could equal her frenzied pace. The sun had shrugged off its morning robe of cloud cover and now hung naked overhead. Siri sliced through the soupy heat with a singular focus on catching at least one of the two women ahead of her. Unfortunately for her, taking fluid from aid stations along the course fell outside of that focus, and as a consequence Siri became increasingly dehydrated.

When Zeiger surged, Siri could not go with her. Still, she pressed hard, hopeful that Zeiger would hit a wall, as indeed Barb Lindquist had already done, staggering to a hyperthermic collapse up the road. With 2 miles to go, Siri was locked in third place, just seconds out of position to qualify for the Olympic Games. But it was already over, Siri's body having entered a state of crisis. As she pushed through ever-worsening depletion, her consciousness shrank to a point and then winked out entirely. Siri ran the last lap in a blackout, having no idea where she was or what she was doing, knowing only that she was supposed to keep running as hard as she could.

Siri crossed the finish line still in third place and fell to the ground, her dream dead. Medical personnel rushed her into a tent and emptied three bags of saline solution into her veins to revive her. When she came to, her dream died a second time.

THE SCIENTIFIC TERM for choking is "choking." Psychologists haven't come up with anything that sounds more clinical. Sian Beilock, a psychologist and leading expert on choking, defined the phenomenon in her book *Choke* as "poor performance that occurs in response to the perceived stress of a situation." The source of perceived stress is one's sense of the importance of the performance in question—specifically, the importance of achieving a certain outcome from it. Choking is therefore a kind of ironic self-sabotage. The desire to maximize performance and achieve a particular outcome creates a feeling of pressure. This feeling of pressure compromises performance and ensures that the wanted outcome is *not* achieved.

Some people are more susceptible to choking than others, but everyone is susceptible to some degree. The universality of this weakness suggests that choking serves a practical purpose—that it is an evolved coping skill with benefits for survival. But what survival advantage could possibly be conferred by a tendency to underperform in important situations?

Choking is probably useful in much the same way that acrophobia (fear of heights) and glossophobia (fear of public speaking) are believed to be useful. Like the propensity for choking, fear of heights is stronger in some individuals than it is in others but exists in all humans. One of the symptoms of acrophobia is dizziness, which increases the likelihood that a person will fall when standing at the edge of a long drop. It seems a rather backward instinct, but this symptom keeps us from getting too close to the edge in the first place, and thereby aids survival.

Fear of public speaking is also helpful in an ironic sort of way. At the root of glossophobia is dread of being socially judged. Although fear of public speaking today seems absurdly out of proportion to the worst-case outcome of making a fool of oneself, sociobiologists believe that in the ancient past, the social ostracization that followed failure in front of an audience was often fatal. In any case, this fear only increases the likelihood that a person will perform poorly when speaking publically and become the target of a negative judgment, but its true purpose is to prevent us from taking the risk of putting ourselves out there to begin with.

Choking is similar. Most likely, the phenomenon originated in situations of high-stakes (i.e., life-or-death) competition. It serves us by discouraging us from entering into competitive situations in which we are likely to come up short. But it is far less helpful as a coping skill when we cannot avoid competition or we choose to enter into it despite the risks. Psychologist Abraham Maslow referred to choking as the "Jonah complex," which he understood to be essentially a fear of success. In the athletic context, this description hits the nail on the head.

The recent revolution in brain science has revealed that it is not pressure per se that causes people to perform poorly in important competitions. Rather, it is self-consciousness. Sian Beilock's research has shown that impaired performance in high-pressure athletic situations is associated with heightened activity in parts of the brain that are linked to self-awareness. What happens is that the athlete's feeling of being under pressure directs her attention toward internal processes such as body movements and anxious thoughts, and this attentional shift undermines performance in a number of ways.

First, self-consciousness distracts athletes from the task of the moment such that, as Beilock puts it in *Choke*, they "are not devoting enough attention to what they are doing and rely on simple or incorrect routines." This is precisely what happened to Siri in her final chance to qualify for the Olympics in Dallas, where she forgot to execute the rudimentary measure of drinking to stay hydrated on a very hot day—a beginner's error that even most beginners don't commit.

Pressure-induced self-consciousness also harms performance by reducing movement efficiency. Athletes move more efficiently when their attention is focused on key features of their environment rather than on their own body. A 2005 study conducted at the University of Nevada–Las Vegas and published in the *Brain Research Bulletin* found that college students shot basketball free throws more accurately when they were asked to concentrate on the back of the rim than they did when they were told to focus on snapping the wrist when the ball left their hand (an element of "good technique"). Psychological pressure has a similar effect, inducing a state of self-consciousness that effectively shifts the athlete's attention from the "rim" to the "wrist."

Endurance sports do not require the same kind of coordination that games like basketball do, but self-consciousness is known to reduce movement efficiency in running, swimming, and other forward-motion activities. In a 2011 experiment, scientists at the University of Münster in Germany observed that runners consumed more energy at a fixed pace when they thought about their body movements or their breathing than they did when they concentrated on the external environment.

Yet another way in which pressure-induced self-consciousness sabotages performance is unique to endurance sports, and it is explicable only in terms of the psychobiological model of endurance performance. Simply put, self-consciousness increases perceived effort.

Racing in a state of pressure-induced self-consciousness is like fire walking while giving your full attention to the painful heat in your feet rather than focusing on where you're going. As an athlete, you're much better off directing your attention externally, to the task at hand, which distracts you to some degree from your suffering, allowing you to push a little harder.

The negative effect of an internal attentional focus on perceived effort and endurance performance was demonstrated in a clever study conducted by Lars McNaughton at England's Edge Hill University and published in the *Journal of Science and Medicine in Sport*. Trained cyclists completed 16.1-km indoor cycling time trials under three different conditions. During one time trial, each cyclist watched a video screen displaying an avatar representing him and showing his progress toward the finish line. In a second time trial, the subjects watched a screen on which their avatar raced against a virtual competitor. In the remaining time trial, the screen was blank. McNaughton found that the cyclists performed best when they were engaged in a virtual race and did worst in the blank-screen condition.

These differences in performance corresponded to differences in the athletes' attentional focus. They reported being most *internally* focused when the screen was blank, offering no visual stimulation. Their attentional focus was most *external* in the battle of avatars, which drew the athletes into forgetting themselves and becoming absorbed in their task. Ratings of perceived effort were no higher in the avatar-versus-avatar trial than they were in the blank-screen trial despite a 3 percent difference in power output, indicating that an internal attentional focus reduced performance by making the same intensity of pedaling feel harder, while an external focus had the opposite effect.

Choking was not a factor in this study because the participants felt little pressure. But it proved that self-consciousness reduces endurance performance, and we know from other research that perceived pressure promotes self-consciousness, especially in certain vulnerable individuals. This vulnerability is not necessarily inborn, but may result from traumatic experience. For example, people who suffer from post-traumatic stress disorder exhibit heightened activity in the dorsolateral prefrontal cortex, known as the brain's internal critic, when performing under pressure.

Siri Lindley did not have PTSD, but she had an overactive internal critic that was probably related to the trauma of her parents' divorce and was almost certainly the source of her tendency to choke under pressure. The irony is hard to ignore. The reason Siri latched onto the goal of becoming an Olympic triathlete was that she believed it would free her from the self-doubts that had dogged her for so long. But it was this very weakness that had caused her to miss out on the Olympics. In order to rebound from her failure and achieve some future feat of greatness in triathlon that would silence her internal critic, Siri would need to . . . silence her internal critic. In order to get what she needed, she needed to have it—or at least some semblance of it—already. Quite a pickle.

AFTER THE HEARTBREAK OF missing out on the Olympics, Siri Lindley decided to make a coaching change. Her friend Loretta Harrop, who had qualified for the Australian Olympic team, encouraged Siri to work with her own coach, Brett Sutton, who trained a select group of athletes at a mountaintop camp in Leysin, Switzerland. All Siri knew about Sutton was that he was a notorious taskmaster who had exiled himself from his native Australia in the wake of a sexual scandal involving an underage swimmer, but who also had a remarkable record of producing world-beating athletes. She decided to take a chance on him.

Siri gave a richly detailed account of her unforgettable first few days at Sutton's camp on the *Competitor Radio Show* in 2013. She flew into Geneva in July 2000. At baggage claim she waited and waited, but her belongings never arrived. Only her bike showed up. After filling out the necessary paperwork, she drove 2 hours to Leysin. As soon as she got there, Sutton ordered her to set up her bike on a turbo trainer and do a 3-hour ride.

"I don't have any cycling clothes!" she protested.

"That's okay. You can wear what you have on," Sutton said.

Siri looked down at her jeans and sweater with disbelief. Sutton nodded. Without further protest, Siri set up her bike, climbed on, and started to pedal. Next to her on another bike was Loretta Harrop, who rode with her head down and said nothing to the friend she had talked into coming all this way.

The next morning, Siri (whose luggage had been delivered during the night) met up with Harrop and the other campers and rode her bike 20 km to the base of the mountain, where the nearest swimming pool was located and where Sutton awaited them. He handed Siri a sheet of paper that described her swim set for the day. She added up the parts and discovered that it came to 6,000 meters in total distance. Siri had never swum farther than 4,000 meters in a single workout. An hour and a half later she crawled out of the pool, shoulders rubbery with fatigue. As she toweled off, Siri looked around for Sutton but couldn't find him. He had disappeared.

"Where's coach?" she asked Harrop.

"Back at camp."

"What! Isn't he supposed to drive us home?"

Harrop looked at Siri pityingly.

"No. We ride."

Siri hadn't even eaten yet. Not so much as a sip of coffee had passed her lips since the previous day. Harrop suggested that Siri ride up the mountain with Jane Fardell, who was supposedly the weakest cyclist in the group. Jane dropped Siri halfway to the summit, leaving the newcomer to straggle into camp alone, 20 minutes after everyone else. Siri staggered into her apartment, fell into bed, and passed out. She woke up seemingly minutes later to the sound of knocking at her door. It was Sutton.

"Time to run," he said. "Get your stuff together."

Siri got her stuff together and met the others outside. Realizing she had forgotten something, she placed her full water bottle on top of Sutton's car and dashed back into the apartment. When she came out, she saw that only one sip of water remained in her bottle. She opened her mouth to remonstrate but Sutton cut her off.

"That's plenty," he said. "You'll be fine."

They drove down the mountain. At the bottom, Sutton told the athletes to get out and run home. Siri's jaw fell open. Had she heard him correctly? Was she now expected to run up the same 20-km hill she had just cycled up after completing the hardest swim of her life? Outrage powered Siri to the top, but barely.

In the evening, Siri called her mother. She hadn't gotten three words out before she broke down.

"I'm so scared, mom!" she wailed.

The next day, Sutton asked Siri to describe her goals. Siri counted them off. She wanted to win a World Cup race, and another U.S. championship, and a world championships medal. As she spoke, Siri's body tensed, her voice tightened, and her breath became shallow. These things did not go unnoticed.

"You know what, Siri?" Sutton said. "Forget about all of that. Starting today, you're retired. The way you look at this sport and the pressure you put on yourself are just all wrong. You started doing triathlon because you loved it. Let's go back to that. Let's just see how fit, how fast, and how strong Siri Lindley can be—and have fun doing it."

An invisible weight was suddenly lifted off Siri's shoulders, leaving behind a lightness of being she hadn't felt in a long time. Sutton's invitation to let go and just enjoy being a triathlete again felt so natural and right. Strangely, the prospect of continuing to train the way she had been forced to do the day before seemed far less intimidating the moment Siri stopped thinking beyond it.

The training didn't get any easier, though. In fact, it got even tougher. The fact of the matter was that, despite the intensity of her yearning to achieve greatness as a triathlete, Siri had previously not trained very hard—not compared to some of the women, including

Sutton's athletes, who stood in the way of her goals. Siri did not know it, but a large body of psychological research has demonstrated that the more time people spend fantasizing about desired outcomes—everything from passing school exams to losing weight—the less effort they put into pursuing them and the less likely they are to achieve them. Distinct from mental rehearsal, or practicing a sport in the mind at rest, which is proven to enhance performance, fantasizing about desired outcomes is a maladaptive coping skill that may be associated with lack of confidence in one's ability to make these outcomes happen through one's own efforts. Siri's nightly visualization of the Sydney Olympics had been intended as mental rehearsal but functioned as fantasy because of the unrealistic perfection of her imagined performance.

Under Brett Sutton, Siri was compelled to redirect her energy from dreaming into doing. Every day the coach presented her with a challenge she did not believe she could meet. But each time she surprised herself and found a way. As the days turned into weeks, Siri could feel her confidence rising. Her former yearning to achieve great things slowly transformed into a quiet, evidence-based belief.

In August, Siri and Harrop flew to Hungary for a World Cup race. It was to be Siri's first test of Sutton's methods. She expected little. Sutton had not reduced her training workload one iota in anticipation of the race. Her legs felt like wood. She lived in a fog and craved sleep constantly. Two days before the competition, Siri called her mother for another venting session.

"This is stupid," she told Astrid. "I shouldn't even be here. I can barely move."

Less than 48 hours later, Siri finished second in the race, 34 seconds behind Harrop. After just six weeks on Sutton's program, she had come within a whisker of achieving one of her major goals—a goal that, like her other ambitions, had been crowded out of her thoughts by the demands of the moment ever since her arrival in Switzerland.

The lesson was not lost on Siri. Sutton had sent her to Hungary on tired legs intentionally, to ensure that she raced without expectations—just in case she had not yet entirely let go of her self-sabotaging goal obsession. Set free to focus on racing rather than winning, Siri proved to be faster on tired legs than she had been previously with fresh legs and a self-conscious mindset.

The following weekend, Siri raced another World Cup, this one in Lausanne, Switzerland. She won. Behind her in second place was Switzerland's own Brigitte McMahon, who five weeks later claimed the first Olympic gold medal ever awarded in the sport of triathlon.

Siri closed out her season with a World Cup race in Cancun. She won again. By now she was completely sold on Sutton's mind-over-muscle approach. After taking a break for the holidays, Siri returned to the Swiss Alps to prepare for the 2001 season. She got off to a relatively slow start with a sixth-place finish in Gamagori, Japan. She followed that up with a third-place result in Ishigaki and then hit her stride, winning her next two World Cup starts. Siri was now the second-ranked female triathlete in the world.

Her purple patch hit a snag, however, in Rennes, France. While running barefoot on the beach between laps of a double-loop swim leg, Siri stepped on a sharp rock, tearing the fascia in her right foot. She gutted it out to the finish but was unable to run for two weeks afterward. The timing couldn't have been worse. Three weeks after the Rennes World Cup came the U.S. pro championship in Shreveport, a qualifier for the 2001 world championships. To claim a spot on the American team Siri had to place among the top six—a small order when she was healthy, but on her bum foot she managed only to limp through 1 km of the 10-km run before the pain became unbearable and she pulled out. Another crushing disappointment.

Siri took five weeks off to heal and rebuild her fitness and then returned to World Cup racing in Toronto on July 7. She had the swim of her life, emerging from Lake Ontario within spitting distance of Barb Lindquist and Sheila Taormina. The three Americans worked together with Teresa Macel on the bike to build a huge lead over 22 chasers. Siri dropped her coconspirators immediately after the bike-run transition and went on to complete the 10K run in 34:37, a time that would have made her competitive in the men's race held later in the day. She won by more than 2 minutes and had all but showered and lunched before Lindquist finally crossed the finish line in second place.

Siri's astonishing performance in Toronto created a conundrum for the International Triathlon Union (ITU), organizers of the world championships. Siri Lindley was now unquestionably the best female short-course triathlete on the planet, but she had failed to qualify for the sport's premier non-Olympic showcase. The 2001 world championships were to be held in Edmonton just 21 days after the Toronto World Cup. Some ITU officials favored granting Siri a wild-card slot, while others cited the venerable maxim, "Rules are rules." With only days left before the race there was still no decision, so Siri made the trip, just in case.

The festivities surrounding the world championships included an "aquathon"—a short swim-run-swim race that many athletes used as a tune-up for the main event. Siri was allowed to participate and she won, putting even more pressure on the ITU brass to let her compete in the world championship. But on the eve of the competition, the officials were still vacillating. In an effort to distract herself, Siri went out for a nice dinner with her mom. Siri was on her second glass of wine when she got the call. She was in.

If there had been any risk that the importance of the world championships would cause Siri to forget everything she had learned about the art of letting go and revert to her former anxious mindset, the manner in which she got to the start line did away with it. Although she still hoped to win, the hope of winning did not occupy her thoughts in the final hours before the big event. That space was taken up instead by gratitude for the mere chance to try.

Race morning dawned wet and cool. Siri ate a banana and a slice of whole wheat toast with peanut butter, suited up, and made her way to the race venue at Hawrelak Park, where she was directed to join a wetsuit-wearing lineup of 60 women. Strangely desultory music played over the public address system as the competitors were paraded one by one onto the starting platform and introduced to the sodden crowd of spectators. Wearing number 60, Siri was presented last, finding her place on the start line mere moments before the gun sounded.

Siri dived into the lake and sprinted. Her position at the far right end of the field made it impossible for her to find the feet of the highest-seeded racers at the opposite end. When she looked up to sight the turn buoy, she was horrified to see that she was behind not only the lead pack but the first chase pack as well. This time, though, Siri did not panic. Instead she stayed in the moment, put her head down and redoubled her efforts. On the second lap, she hitched herself to the rear of the chase pack, which dragged her to shore 40 seconds behind the lead group.

Siri blasted out onto the bike course astride her black-and-white Litespeed Vortex. Giving no thought to saving her legs for the run, she pedaled with utter abandon over the drizzle-soaked pavement in pursuit of the six-woman lead group, which included all three of the American women who had beaten out Siri for the U.S. Olympic team and her friend Loretta Harrop. Midway through the first of six laps, Siri found herself cooperating with three athletes willing to work as hard as she was: Kathleen Smet of Belgium and Germans Joelle Franzmann and Christiane Pilz. Together they began to inch their way toward the leaders.

The skies opened up, dumping a hard, cold rain on the racers and forming treacherous puddles on the course's many sharp turns. Another echo of Sydney. Siri carved those turns with as much speed and lateral lean as she would have done in the driest conditions.

On the second lap, her foursome passed the aftermath of a crash. Nicole Hackett and Sheila Taormina and their bikes lay sprawled on the glistening street. The accident had disrupted the cooperative efforts of the lead pack's surviving four members, giving Siri's group an opportunity. Siri shifted into a higher gear and took aim at the familiar names printed on the backsides of the women ahead of her:

Lindquist, Gutierrez, Harrop, Reback, Zeiger. Before the next circuit was complete, Siri's group had caught and merged with Harrop's. Over the remaining three laps, the leading contingent, having lost its incentive to push, swelled to 19 athletes as other chase groups closed their respective deficits.

Approaching transition, Siri forced her way from the rear of the bunch to the front, aware that her inflated race number gave her the disadvantage of having to run with her bike all the way across the transition area to get to the spot where her running shoes awaited, whereas top-seeded racers such as Michellie Jones would be able to rack their bikes near the entrance and run unencumbered. Siri dismounted first and charged across the carpet with her bike at her side while Jones, Harrop, and the other strong runners stuffed their feet into running shoes. When at last Siri came to transition slot number 60, she yanked on a pair of racing flats and a white cap bearing the Polo RLX logo. She grabbed her number belt and fastened it on the go, exiting the transition area a half-step ahead of a stupefied Michellie Jones, and still in first place.

Siri set off at a murderous pace that only Jones could equal. In the space of a few yards, the race was reduced from a 19-strong battle to a two-woman duel. Just outside the transition area, the lead pair came upon an aid station. Siri grabbed a bottle off the table, drank, and tossed the empty container in the direction of a garbage barrel. It landed dead center. Siri thought, *This might be my day!*

The sense of destiny gained traction as she continued. Siri felt surprisingly good, strength flowing out of her from some previously untapped source. Jones, meanwhile, was on the rivet. Siri continued to press a tempo that was unsustainable for either woman, confident that Jones was the closer of the two to the breaking point. Sure enough, after half a lap of clinging to Siri's back shoulder, the Olympic silver medalist snapped.

At the completion of the first of three laps, the American's lead was more than 10 seconds. Siri might have relaxed a bit at this point, but she kept on running as though Jones, or someone else, were right there with her. After two laps, she had 30 seconds in hand. Still she did not relent. Siri's unyielding pace of 5:35 per mile, coupled with her balled fists, furrowed brow, and raised upper lip, informed onlookers that she intended to leave everything she had to give on the racecourse. What might have been a de facto victory lap was instead a fearsome display of unbridled going-for-it. Yet as hard as Siri was pushing, she still felt fantastic. It wasn't quite pleasure or even comfort she experienced but a sense of being one with her immense effort.

Siri kept on spurring her flanks until she was within reach of the finish line. Then she stopped abruptly, two feet short of her destiny, and grabbed the plastic banner in both hands. Raising it overhead, she stepped over the threshold wearing a smile of total, ecstatic fulfillment.

"This is the greatest moment of my life!" Siri announced minutes later, echoing the words she had spoken after becoming the U.S. champion three years earlier. But this time Siri knew that no greater moment was possible, or needed.

She was right. More than a decade later, Siri still regards her triumph in Edmonton as an unsurpassable zenith of personal happiness. In that moment, she filled the void she had carried inside her since childhood. With one final step in a long, hard journey, she claimed the peace and self-acceptance she had sought in her pursuit of greatness in triathlon.

It's not that Siri needed to bear the title of world champion to love herself; she had already transformed into the person she wanted to be through her total commitment to a dream. Paradoxically, it may seem, Siri had to let go of that dream and find contentment in the moment-to-moment process of chasing it in order to complete the personal transformation that was her deeper ambition, and yet it was this very act of letting go that enabled her to fulfill the outward dream. Crossing the finish line first was merely symbolic of the journey's end.

IF CHOKING IS A condition of heightened self-consciousness that intensifies perceived effort and hampers endurance performance, then its opposite would be a mental state in which self-consciousness disappears, reducing perceived effort and boosting performance. Does such a thing exist? It does.

The psychologist Mihály Csikszentmihalyi called it "flow" and defined it as a state of complete immersion in a purposeful activity. Endurance athletes describe the flow state as one in which they seem to become the thing they are doing. The part of the mind that normally watches the part that is focused on the task at hand vanishes, leaving the athlete's consciousness directed externally in a way that feels right and yields exceptional performance. Siri Lindley's choking problem was essentially an anxious tendency that kept her from racing in a flow state in the most pressure-packed races.

Neuroscientists have observed that several changes in brain function tend to accompany the flow state. The brain's electrical activity always unfolds in wave patterns. Normal consciousness is associated with a high-frequency beta wave pattern. In the flow state, brain rhythms drop down to the borderline between low-frequency beta and theta waves. Flow is tied also to sharply reduced activity in the prefrontal cortex, the part of the brain that gives rise to a sense of self and that includes the aforementioned dorsolateral prefrontal cortex—the brain's internal critic. And at the molecular level, several neurotransmitters, or brain messenger chemicals, are released during flow. Among these are norepinephrine, which enhances mental focus, and endorphins, which are the source of the famous "runner's high."

It is not necessary to measure brain waves or neurotransmitter levels to figure out if an athlete is operating in the flow state. You can just ask. Athletes know when they are in flow because the feeling is unmistakable—it's that sense of absolute unity with one's effort that Siri Lindley experienced in the 2001 ITU Triathlon World Championship. Perception of effort does not disappear during flow. Hard work still feels hard in this state, but the feeling becomes enjoyable in a way that is difficult to put into words.

A handful of studies have supplied evidence that the more flow an athlete experiences during an endurance test, the better she performs. One such study was conducted in 2012 by Alan St. Clair Gibson and his colleagues and published in the *International Journal of Sports Physiology and Performance*. Eight trained cyclists were asked to complete a pair of 20-km time trials on stationary bikes on separate occasions. It is exceedingly unlikely that any athlete will ever complete consecutive time trials of the same distance in exactly the same time, and sure enough, none of these athletes did. Some of the cyclists performed slightly better in the first time trial, others in the second. Gibson and his colleagues collected physiological and psychological data during both time trials in an effort to ascertain *why* the cyclists performed better in whichever one they completed faster. They found no major differences in any of the physiological variables. But what they did find was that the cyclists consistently reported higher levels of positive affect—a sign of flow—in their better ride.

As this study hints, flow is not entirely controllable and hence cannot be regarded as a coping skill in itself. It appears that a number of factors have to line up just right for flow to occur. Insofar as flow is controllable, anything that helps an athlete race less self-consciously promotes the flow state. And flow, in turn, is the ultimate prophylactic against the self-sabotage of choking. Learning how to exploit these flow facilitators, therefore, is a vital coping skill for all endurance athletes.

Physical preparedness is one such factor. Research has demonstrated that people are more likely to experience flow when performing tasks in which they have a high level of mastery. Other investigations have revealed that well-trained athletes exhibit reduced activity in parts of the brain that are related to physical self-consciousness. These things are linked. Well-trained athletes have an easier time achieving flow *because* they are less physically self-conscious.

Any factor that tends to increase self-consciousness during a race makes flow more difficult to attain. One of these factors is negative thoughts. In a 2014 study that appeared in *Medicine and Science in Sports and Exercise*, a team of scientists led by Samuele Marcora invited volunteers to pedal stationary bikes to exhaustion at high intensity on two occasions separated by two weeks. Between the tests, half of the subjects were trained in the use of positive self-talk, a coping skill that many athletes use instinctively to neutralize negative thoughts and preserve flow during competition. The remaining subjects received no training in positive self-talk. When the endurance test was repeated, the subjects trained in positive self-talk improved their time to exhaustion by 17 percent. Even though both tests were performed at the same intensity, these subjects reported significantly lower ratings of perceived effort in the second test. The subjects in the other group did not improve between tests and their perceived effort ratings did not change.

Some athletes are especially prone to negative thinking in competition. Athletes who lack self-belief, as Siri Lindley once did, have a harder time tamping down their internal critic in races. Many of the negative thoughts that such athletes experience issue from excessive focus on the desired outcome. All athletes begin their races wanting to achieve their goals, but those lacking self-belief are so anxious about their goal that it pulls their attention away from the task of the moment. They feel that if only they can achieve their goal, *then* they will have self-belief to carry into the next race. But it doesn't work like that. The self-belief has to come first.

So where does it come from? It comes from letting go, as illustrated by Siri's surrender to Brett Sutton's methodology. Counterintuitive though it may be, caring a little less about the result of a race produces better results. An athlete who believes in herself whether she succeeds or fails is able to put her goal out of mind and race in the moment, and to race in the moment—in flow—is to race better. The athlete who lacks self-belief can gain it by consciously pushing her goals and the worries that surround them out of her mind and teaching herself to stay focused on the task of the moment throughout the training process that leads up to the next big race. The progress that issues from this head-down, "just do it" approach cultivates self-belief in a way that no amount of visualizing the perfect race can.

Siri learned this lesson through her work with Brett Sutton. Self-belief cannot be manufactured through obsessive yearning toward one's goals or through the elimination of all "distractions." In fact, it requires the opposite: an empty mind and total immersion in the process that builds the proof of potential that is the only solid foundation for true self-belief.

"Real confidence comes from real results and real training," Siri told writer Timothy Carlson in 2014. "It must be truthful."

ALMOST ANY OTHER ATHLETE who stood in Siri Lindley's position in July 2001 as the newly crowned triathlon world champion would have stayed in the sport at least through the next Olympics. But Siri did not. Although she did race one more year, just to see if, having made it to the top, she could stay there, she knew she had already gotten everything she needed from the sport.

When Siri announced her retirement in November 2002, she was still the highest-ranked triathlete in the world. A few months later, she reemerged as a coach. Borrowing Brett Sutton's model, Siri set up an elite training camp in Boulder. Her first athlete, Canadian Jill Savege, won the 2003 Pan Am Games Triathlon. Another early protégé, American Susan Williams, won the bronze medal at the 2004 Olympics in Athens. Many more successes followed, among them a pair of victories by Mirinda Carfrae at the Ironman World Championship®. Today Siri is widely regarded as an even better coach than she was an athlete.

Perhaps not surprisingly, what sets Siri apart from other coaches is her heavy emphasis on the mental side of the sport. Having worked through the psychological issues that held her back as an athlete, Siri believes she has a formula to help other athletes do the same. A single word is tattooed on each of her wrists: "GRATITUDE" on the left wrist and "BELIEVE" on the right. These two words encapsulate

Siri's coaching philosophy. "Gratitude" is about letting go of desired outcomes and fully embracing the privilege and process of pursuing goals and dreams. "Believe" refers to the confidence that arises naturally through this process, a self-trust that is the antithesis of the doubt-fueled fixation on goals and dreams expressed in Siri's nightly fantasy of having the perfect race at the 2000 Olympics.

Siri's reputation as a "triathlete whisperer" draws many struggling athletes to her. A salient example is Leanda Cave, a British triathlete who had great success as a short-course specialist before moving up to the Ironman distance, where she struggled. Her big dream was to win the Ironman World Championship, but the race intimidated her. After a promising debut in 2007, when she finished eighth, Leanda dropped out of the 2008 race, in the aftermath of which she asked fellow pro Dede Griesbauer, "Does it ever get any easier?" Leanda was informed that it did not, and indeed it didn't. She finished 20th and 10th in the next two Ironmans. Then she went to Siri.

Leanda Cave is a shy person. As a girl she had a hard time even making eye contact. Her self-esteem was low and she had few friends. Shyness is, of course, a form of self-consciousness, an overactive internal critic that is projected onto others. Leanda's internal critic did not hold her back as a short-course racer, but at the more painful and mentally challenging Ironman distance it did. "There are times you have a conversation with yourself while fighting hard to stay focused and stay within the race," she told slowtwitch.com. "There is something in my head that says, 'Stop! You're in so much pain!'"

The first time they spoke, Siri told Leanda, "I believe you can win Ironman." Siri repeated these words again and again over the following months. In the meantime, she consistently challenged Leanda in her training much as Brett Sutton had once challenged Siri.

At first, Leanda was flummoxed by Siri's continual insistence on her belief in Leanda's ability to win Ironman and by the punishing training Siri prescribed. Gradually, though, Leanda came to realize that Siri was carrying the burden of belief for her so that Leanda could let go of it and focus on the process. And the hard training served to nurture true belief within Leanda. After one year of working with Siri, Leanda placed third at the 2011 Ironman World Championship. A short time later a reporter asked Leanda what her new coach had done for her.

"Siri encouraged confidence to come out of me," she said.

The process continued in 2012. A couple of days before that year's Ironman, Leanda's seventh attempt at the event, Siri sat down with her for a final strategy session, an encounter Siri recalled for me in 2014. At the end of the meeting, Leanda told her coach, "I believe, now, Siri."

Siri felt a lump rise in her throat, and her vision swam. Two days later, Leanda won the 2012 Ironman, a surprise to many. But not to everyone.

CHAPTER FIVE

THE WORKAROUND EFFECT

THE CLASS OF 1980 at Langley High School in McLean, Virginia, was chock-full of gifted athletes. Both the boys' cross country team and the girls' tennis team won state titles in the 1979–1980 school year. But the top jock on campus was Willie Stewart, whose primary sport was rugby. To understand how good Willie was at rugby, you need only know that in his secondary sport, wrestling, he went undefeated in his senior season and won the Virginia state championship at 145 pounds.

After graduating in June, Willie took summer employment with a roofing company where his older brother Steve worked as a foreman. It was a short-term gig to keep Willie occupied while he continued to play rugby and worked on getting into college and resuming his wrestling career. He neither expected nor wanted the job to be a life-changing experience.

Fate had other plans.

The crew had just started on a project of replacing the roof of the Watergate building in Washington, D.C. One morning Willie found himself laboring underneath the building's massive rooftop cooling tower. Willie and a coworker were using a rope to remove debris from the old roof. The coworker tossed a rope head to Willie from a plat-form several feet above him. Willie reached out to grab it and the frayed end lassoed itself around his left arm, just above the elbow.

In the same instant, the other end of the rope got caught in the blades of a giant fan located at the edge of the cooling tower. This caused the end attached to Willie's arm to pull toward the fan with incredible force, lifting him bodily. When he hit the ceiling, his body stopped and his arm kept going, the noose of rope squeezing the flesh off Willie's arm like clenched teeth scraping kabob meat from a skewer. The violent snapping of bones and tearing of sinew produced a sickeningly loud cacophony that Willie would never forget. The hand was taken clean off and all of the forearm muscle was ripped away, leaving behind a wand of naked white bone.

Willie dropped to the ground, landing on his side. He saw a glove on the ground near him. His hand was still in it. Blood gushed from the ragged tissue of Willie's upper arm. His biceps muscle, detached at the bottom end, dangled loosely. He scrambled out of the tower, fall-ing when he attempted to use his phantom left arm to support him-self against the roof surface. He got up, scrambled a few more steps, and fell again. This time he stayed down. Another coworker removed his belt and tied it tightly around Willie's mangled upper arm. The jury-rigged tourniquet failed to stanch the torrential blood flow and succeeded only in intensifying the victim's pain. Instinctively, Willie took two fingers and pressed the dangling end of his biceps up under the sheath of skin. Moments later, the bleeding slowed to a trickle.

Through it all, Willie remained clearheaded—lucid enough to realize that he ought to seek help instead of waiting for help to find him. He stood up and handed his severed hand to his brother, then hobbled over to the edge of the roof, where he signaled to a crane operator on the ground below. A basket was lifted to roof level. Wil-lie climbed in and was lowered to the street. He ran several blocks down New Hampshire Avenue to George Washington Medical Cen-ter, wearing a borrowed shirt that hid his grisly wound from public view—and from his own eyes.

At the hospital, Willie was rushed into an operating room, but was forced to wait there for his breakfast to digest before he could be knocked out and operated on. (There wasn't much the surgeon could do except cut the humerus bone flush with the surviving flesh and close up the wound.) In the meantime, a sheet was drawn over Willie's head so he wouldn't have to see the mutilated appendage. When at last the Cocoa Puffs had cleared Willie's stomach, a general anesthetic was administered.

Thirty-four years later, when he recounted this story to me, Willie was able to recall what happened next with perfect clarity. As he waited for oblivion to overtake him, he overheard a doctor and a nurse talking about him.

"I think he's finally out," the doctor said.

"Took long enough," the nurse said.

"I can hear you," Willie said from under the sheet.

Seconds later, he could no longer hear them. He remained unconscious for two days and then woke up to a new life.

The new Willie Stewart was revolted by meat. But far worse than this new aversion was the bitter depression that settled over him. Willie felt he had nothing to live for. He was convinced that he would never have another girlfriend and that his days as an athlete were over. Willie's family and friends assured him that there were plenty of girls who couldn't help but swoon for a strapping young man with a prom king's smile and a class president's charm who just happened to be missing one arm. But on the subject of his sporting future they were mum, silently agreeing that a one-armed man could not be an athlete.

Who could blame them? In 1980 there was little support for, or even acknowledgment of, impaired athletes. What few opportunities did exist gained little exposure. Nor did rehabilitative specialists encourage disabled persons to exercise and to pursue athletics as aggressively as they do today.

Willie received worker's compensation and lived with his parents, so he felt no pressure to find another job. Partying became his new occupation. He took up with the sorts of troublemakers and escapists he had always avoided in high school. Getting blitzed with these new associates allowed him to briefly forget his grief. But more often than not, Willie's nights out ended in brawls with guys who had looked at him the wrong way.

After several months of this routine, Willie's parents talked him into seeing a psychologist. Although Willie did not resist the counseling, it produced no change in his behavior. Eventually, his folks decided they'd had enough of their son's sloth and dissolution and asked him to find somewhere else to live. He found a cheap house to rent and continued to loaf about, party, and scuffle.

Two years after his accident, a friend of his mother invited the now 20-year-old Willie to run a 5K race with him. Beginning a second life as an athlete was the furthest thing from his mind, but he surprised himself by accepting the offer. Early on the next Saturday morning, the family friend swung by to pick Willie up. He couldn't tell if the young man was hung over or still drunk. Nevertheless, when the starting horn blared, the competitor in Willie awoke, and he ran as hard as he could. Although his performance was unspectacular, when he crossed the finish line he experienced a feeling he had not known for a long time: the thrill of achievement. It was the first healthy emotion he had enjoyed in as long as he could remember.

As bracing as it was, this episode might not have led anywhere if not for something that happened a short time later, on the afternoon of Sunday, February 21, 1982. Willie was back in his usual spot—on a recliner in the living room of the house he rented—when ABC's coverage of the recently completed Ironman triathlon came on TV. He watched in wonder as Julie Moss crawled across the finish line in soiled shorts to take second place in the women's competition. Somewhere deep inside Willie, a flame was ignited. Feeling inspired (and impulsive), he immediately went out and bought a white-and-red–striped one-piece Scott Tinley triathlon racing suit. He put it on and drove to Lake Elsa (now called Lake Audubon), and dived in.

Swimming with one arm is not impossible. In fact, competitive swimmers do it all the time as a technique drill. Although Willie had never been a competitive swimmer, he had spent many a summer day splashing around in open water, and he had no fear. He just put his head down and executed a clumsy yet serviceable modified front crawl. But if swimming with one arm is not impossible, it is exceedingly inefficient and energy-sapping for the inexperienced. After 100 yards of thrashing, Willie was exhausted—and 100 yards from shore. He took his time floating back to the safety of land, where he hopped onto a bike and pedaled for a couple of miles. He then ditched the bike and ran a half-mile to the nearest McDonald's, bought two Big Macs, and wolfed them down. He liked the way he felt.

Willie's attitude began to change. He decided to rejoin his old rugby club, Northern Virginia RC, but not right away—he spent a full year preparing. During that time Willie conditioned his body with unprecedented zeal, mostly through running. To test himself, he participated in road races, starting with 10Ks and working his way up to full marathons. By the time he showed up at his first rugby practice, he was fitter than he'd ever been.

If Willie's new teammates and opponents were inclined to treat him with kid gloves, they never got the chance. He hit them first, and he hit them hard, exhibiting greater ability and ferocity than he'd ever shown in high school. Certain adaptations were necessary, but Willie prided himself on his adaptability. A couple of his signature wrestling moves were self-discovered, and he had always fought each opponent differently, molding his wrestling style to what he learned of his foe's weaknesses. Willie used the same approach to evolve a new style of rugby. No longer able to break tackles with a conventional stiff arm, for example, he did it instead by using his residual limb as a bludgeoning instrument.

His secret weapon, though, was his newly acquired endurance. The exceptional stamina Willie developed through his extracurricular pursuits left his rugby opponents gasping behind him. In his very first tournament he won the MVP trophy. After that he quickly advanced from Northern Virginia's D squad to the C squad to the B squad.

The coach of the A squad was a crusty Englishman named Chris Brook. Through the team grapevine Willie learned that Coach Brook had vowed Willie would never play for him. Willie could guess the reason, and it stung. Scoring four or five tries a game, he was unquestionably the best player in the entire organization. Willie was still smarting from the slight when Billy Smith, who coached the rival Washington Rugby Club, pulled the frustrated athlete aside after a match and invited him to join *his* A squad. Willie accepted the invitation and crossed the Potomac. The next time Washington and Northern Virginia clashed on the rugby pitch, Willie played the game of his life and led his new team to a one-sided victory. As he left the playing field, Willie got in the face of his former coach.

"Miss me?" he asked.

The move across the river paid off in another way. One of Willie's fellow Washington players offered him a job as a bike messenger in D.C. Five hundred bucks a week under the table. *What the hell*, he thought. Willie bought a cheap Ross mountain bike and a few days later he was riding along busy downtown streets with a sack of letters slung over his shoulder. The hardest part of riding with one arm was braking. The most reliable way of stopping was crashing, which Willie did often. One day, he slammed into the back of a bus. An elderly woman shouted from the curb, "You shouldn't be out here!"

Willie felt anger rise up in him, but the feeling was arrested by a sudden thought. *She might be right.* Perhaps he really shouldn't be out there. Willie didn't mind hurting himself, but he could not bear hurting someone else. And he never wanted his disability to be blamed for a screwup or failure. Perhaps it was best to avoid putting himself in situations that only reminded him of his incompleteness. But at the same time, he didn't want his missing arm to be the reason he couldn't do something (such as ride a bike safely), and he needed the job. So Willie decided to give it 30 days. If after a month of practice he remained a public menace, he would quit.

Thirty days later, Willie was popping wheelies and riding down the steps of the Lincoln Memorial like any other bike messenger. He owed his progress entirely to blind trial and error—to falling down and getting back up and falling down again (but not as soon), and so on, just as he had learned to ride a bike the first time. In this manner Willie slowly developed a repertoire of techniques for one-armed cycling, such as shifting his center of balance when applying the rear brake with his right hand so that he didn't sail over the handlebar. In the process, his trepidation gave way to exhilaration. Willie became so smitten with cycling that he sometimes hopped in the saddle after an evening rugby practice and rode through the night to the beach at Ocean City, Maryland, to watch the sun rise. After a giant breakfast, he'd turn around and pedal 10 hours back home.

Willie's athletic rebirth got him thinking about the future. At the time of his accident he'd had no idea what sort of career he ought to pursue. He now felt a strong desire to help others with disabilities. In 1986, Willie moved to Breckenridge, Colorado, to take a job with Disabled Sports USA. His main duty there was hoisting kids onto chairlifts. It wasn't glamorous work, but it was a start in the direction he wanted to go in his professional life. Being surrounded by snow all day inspired Willie to take up cross-country skiing as a way to keep in shape for rugby during the winter. But it soon became something he did for its own sake. He skied before work and again after work, and he even jumped into the occasional race.

At one race, Willie was approached by Kendall Butts, head coach of the U.S. Disabled Ski Team, who invited him to Park City, Utah, to take a VO_2max test. Willie agreed. The result—a score of 60 milliliters of oxygen consumption per kilogram of body weight per minute—was stratospheric for a 185-pound rugby player. Unable to conceal his excitement, Butts drew up a training plan for Willie and told him that if he followed it, he might make the Paralympics one day—perhaps even medal. Within a year, Willie had raised his VO_2max 10 points and lowered his marathon time from 3:40 to 2:42 (and lost 40 pounds, ending up at his old high school wrestling weight). In 1998, he qualified for the Winter Paralympics in Nagano, Japan. Four years later, in Salt Lake City, he won a silver medal in the Nordic relay event.

As much as he relished this achievement, Willie preferred to compete against able-bodied athletes. He got little satisfaction from doing well "for a guy with one arm." He wanted to do well by the same standards that applied to athletes with four working limbs.

Willie's mind often wandered back to that fateful day when he watched Julie Moss crawl to the Ironman finish line. Although he had never had much interest in endurance sports before his accident, that galvanizing moment had planted a seed of desire inside him. It not only pushed him into an ever-ascending post-accident athletic career but also pulled him ceaselessly toward an ultimate destination: the Ironman World Championship in Hawaii, where 1,600 of the world's best pro and amateur triathletes—only half a dozen of them disabled—gathered each year to compete in a forbidding environment. Willie looked ahead to the crossing of that particular finish line as a symbolic completion of his journey back to full living.

Willie moved a step closer to this destiny when he attended a Challenged Athletes Foundation event in San Diego, where he met Jim MacLaren, who had done Ironman as a single-leg amputee. MacLaren urged Willie to stop dreaming about Ironman and give it a shot. By this time Willie was married. His wife, Lynnsey, had raced the 1985 Ironman and was itching to return to the Big Island. What's more, the couple now lived in Southern California, home to a vibrant triathlon community. Everything was lining up. It was time for Willie to complete the journey.

First, though, Willie had to find out if he could swim—not just keep his chin above water for 100 yards, but really swim. His first test was discouraging. Within a single lap at the Loma Linda Medical Center swimming pool, he was hyperventilating and had a bellyful of chlorinated water. But the rude awakening only intensified Willie's determination to master the challenge.

Applying the same 30-day rule that had delivered him to mastery of one-armed cycling, he swam every day for a month. Again Willie relied on unguided trial and error to feel his way toward competence, eventually coming up with a personal technique that was heavy on kicking and body rotation. When the month was up, he felt confident that he could cover 2.4 miles—the Ironman swim distance—within the official 2-hour cutoff time. In 2002, he applied for one of the half-dozen Ironman slots awarded each year to disabled athletes by lottery. Only four others applied.

Six months before the race, a local television news crew tracked Willie down at the pool, where he had just completed a workout, and gave him the good news, Publishers Clearing House–style. But instead of a check for $10 million, he was given race number 306.

His first thought was this: *What have I gotten myself into?*

WILLIE STEWART'S STORY is remarkable but not exceptional. Today it is quite common for amputees to participate in endurance sports. Physicians and physical therapists actively encourage patients with lost limbs to get involved in competitive swimming, cycling, and other activities. But the docs and PTs can't take credit for discovering sports as a vehicle for recovery. Long before health professionals added athletics to their treatment repertoire, victims of dismemberment were drawn to endurance sports on their own.

The psychology behind this attraction isn't difficult to understand. What bothers many amputees most about their condition is the inability to do things that "normal" people can do. The category of normal activities is not limited to everyday tasks such as opening jars and driving a car. Participating in marathons, triathlons, and bike races is also normal for a certain segment of the population. There is no better way for an amputee to feel normal than to successfully perform the most physically challenging tasks that able-bodied people do. This is why some men and women who have no interest in endurance sports before losing a limb choose to chase finish lines afterward. Before the accident it was enough for them to open jars and drive a car and know that they *could* run a marathon if they ever felt like it. After the accident, many feel a compelling need to get out there and prove it.

Willie Stewart summed up this mindset succinctly in a conversation with Challenged Athletes Foundation founder Bob Babbitt. "Sport makes me whole," he said.

In 1985, psychologists at Canada's Laurentian University studied the psychological impact of sports on disabled individuals by subjecting a large number of disabled athletes and nonathletes to a battery of questionnaires and then comparing the results. In a paper published in *Psychological Reports*, the researchers concluded that disabled athletes have "higher self-esteem, exhibit greater life satisfaction and happiness, are more externalized, and attain more education than disabled nonathletes. Psychosocial functioning of disabled individuals may be enhanced through active participation in athletic events."

Other research has shown that sports participation enhances body self-image and functional capacity in amputees. On the basis of such findings, the medical community made it standard practice to encourage amputees to participate in athletics. Amputee soldiers in particular are now being pushed into sports, and they are willing takers. In the United States there is today a veritable pipeline from the battlefield to the racecourse. Organizations such as Ride 2 Recovery and the Wounded Warrior Project have transformed thousands of wounded American veterans into endurance athletes.

Not surprisingly, a number of these men and women participated in sports before they got hurt. A 1993 survey of competitors in the Fifth National Triathlon for the Physically Challenged found that a majority had been athletes longer than they had been disabled. So there's a chicken-and-egg dynamic at work. Not only do disabled individuals become psychologically healthier through sports, but sports also cultivate the psychological wherewithal to make the best of life—partly through the pursuit of athletics—after the loss of a limb.

Many athletes discover that dismemberment actually makes them *better* athletes—at least mentally. Willie Stewart was inarguably a better rugby player with one arm than he had been with two. Every competitor wants to prove himself, but when Willie returned to the rugby pitch after his accident he was single-minded in this desire. "Losing my arm gave me incredible focus," he says. He means this quite literally. During games, One-Arm Willie (as he became known) was blind to every detail of his environment except those specifics— such as a narrow seam between defenders—that he could exploit to put the ball past the goal line.

It would be wrong to say that losing an arm made Willie a better endurance athlete, as he had never tried endurance sports before the accident. But there's no doubt that he brought to endurance sports the same focused mindset that made him a better rugby player, and this mindset was as great an asset on the racecourse as it was on the rugby pitch. In races, Willie's superior focus manifested as inhibitory control, a coping skill I mentioned in the Introduction, which enables endurance athletes to attend to helpful stimuli and tune out negative stimuli and thereby achieve greater speed with equal perceived effort.

Many athletes who suffer injuries or other physical setbacks find in them opportunities to gain mental fitness. If a race is like a fire walk, then a physical setback is like a backward slide on the bed of hot coals. The loss of physical capacity effectively increases the distance an athlete must cover to reach the furthest point he had reached prior to the setback. It is natural for an athlete to want to get back to that point despite the greater distance. The obvious way to chase this goal is to simply try harder than ever before. If successful, the athlete may discover along the way that the greater physical capacity he enjoyed before his setback was a kind of crutch that prevented him from exercising his full mental capacity.

The truth of the matter is that the stronger or more capable the body is, the weaker or lazier the mind can afford to be. In a 2014 interview with Flotrack, Chris Solinsky, a former American record holder at 10000 meters, confessed, "I've discovered over the last couple of years that I don't know if I've been as tough as I thought I was." This discovery was prompted by a fitness-robbing injury that left Solinsky struggling to keep up with teammates in workouts for the first time in his life and made him realize that his prior physical dominance had deprived him of the chance to develop the mental skills to cope with such adversity.

Some athletes gain not only mental fitness but also physical fitness—after first losing it—through an injury or some other setback. It happens by way of a process I call the "workaround effect." When the body loses the ability to achieve a desired level of performance in the accustomed way, the brain responds by seeking out new ways to get the same level of performance out of the body, ways the athlete might never have discovered otherwise. That's the workaround effect.

This phenomenon is not confined to sports. An example of the workaround effect in the arts involves Django Reinhardt, the legendary jazz guitar player. At age 12, Reinhardt received his first guitar. By the time he was 18, he was a virtuoso on the instrument. But then the middle and ring fingers of his fret hand were badly burned and left paralyzed by a house fire. Instead of giving up music, Reinhardt learned to play the guitar all over again. The fruit of his efforts was a unique soloing style that became known as hot jazz. Music critics judged the new style better than the old, and it would very likely never have been born if a loss of physical capacity hadn't challenged Reinhardt to do more with less.

The workaround effect comes in several flavors. Some I will discuss in later chapters. The flavor we're discussing here is known to scientists as neuroplasticity. The brain is highly *plastic*: It has almost unlimited ability to reorganize itself in response to roadblocks affecting its normal operations. For example, the brain of someone who loses her sight rewires itself in ways that sharpen the other senses. Something similar happens when an athlete returns to training after suffering an injury with lasting physical effects. Unable to stimulate bodily movement in the way it did previously, the brain explores alternatives, eventually settling on the most effective of these.

In a 2014 experiment, Anita Haudum of the University of Salzburg studied the workaround effect in running. To simulate an injury affecting the legs, she stretched a length of elastic tubing between the hip and the ankle of each member of a group of volunteers and instructed them to run. As you would expect, they found it rather awkward in the beginning to run with this constraint. Electromyography (EMG) showed that running with the elastic tubing required far more muscle activation compared to unconstrained running. But in *Perceptual and Motor Skills* Haudum reported that after seven weeks of training with the elastic tubing, the volunteers exhibited much improved efficiency. Through the magic of neuroplasticity, their brains had found a new way to run that required scarcely more muscle activation than did their unfettered stride. This unconsciously learned new stride was not, in fact, visibly different from the subjects' natural stride, yet it was achieved through different patterns of brain and muscle activation. In effect, the subjects had found a new way to run the old way.

As Willie Stewart discovered in learning how to ride a bike and to swim with one arm, persistent trial and error (or what he calls "guided discovery") is the only way to master a familiar activity that has been made new again by an imposed constraint such as injury. It is impossible for an athlete faced with such a situation to consciously deduce how best to modify his technique and then programmatically acquire the new movement pattern. He must instead simply create and allow for opportunities to let it happen on its own.

Another example of the workaround effect in endurance sports concerns the runner Serena Burla. Raised in Wisconsin, Serena started running in the third grade. From the very beginning she hated to lose, crying inconsolably whenever another girl reached the finish line ahead of her. She didn't lose often until she got to high school, at which point she failed to make the leap from statewide dominance to national prominence, placing no better than 12th in the Midwest regional qualifier for the Foot Locker National High School Cross Country Championships.

From 2003 to 2006, Serena ran on scholarship at the University of Missouri, where she was again an excellent but not quite outstanding performer, finishing sixth in the NCAA Championship 10000 meters in her senior season. Having no prospects for a professional running career, she quit the sport after graduating. A short time later, though, she met Isaya Okwiya, the Kenyan American coach of a new post-collegiate running team, who persuaded her to get back in shape.

Serena's comeback was progressing well when she developed a painful spot in her right hamstring. The usual treatments brought no relief, so she had it checked out and learned that a cancerous tumor the size of a golf ball had formed on her biceps femoris, one of three muscles that make up the hamstrings. In early 2010, Serena went under the knife. The surgeon, Dr. Patrick Boland of New York's Memorial Sloan Kettering Cancer Center, ended up removing not only the tumor but nearly the entire muscle.

When Boland explained to Serena the necessity of what he'd done, she asked him if her running career was over. He refused to give an opinion. "We'll just have to see," he said. But privately he wasn't hopeful.

"I thought she'd be able to walk," Boland later told *Runner's World*, "but I felt pretty sure she wouldn't be able to run again competitively."

If it *was* possible for Serena to return to elite status as a runner, her brain would have to somehow find a workaround to compensate for the missing muscle. Through intensive rehabilitation and a cautious but persistent return to running, neuroplasticity worked its magic. When she graduated from rehab, Serena was able to lift more weight with the "bad" hamstring than she could with the other. The two muscles remaining on the back of her right thigh were literally doing the work of three.

The first time Serena's coach saw her run after the surgery, he noticed that a trademark outward flaring of her lower right leg had vanished. Without conscious interference, her brain had taught her leg a new way to run. And as her training progressed, Serena began to notice that she tended to become sore in certain spots where she never had before—another sign of a workaround.

Serena experienced psychological changes that complemented the physical. While her passion for running was greater than ever, its expression altered. Her burning need to win was replaced with profound gratitude and appreciation for simply being able to run, feelings that are common among athletes who have overcome career-threatening injuries. She no longer sweated the small stuff, like subpar workouts, and she became more accepting of the challenging aspects of her sport, such as the discomfort of running hard in a state of extreme fatigue. Cancer had left her with a desire to live without regret, and this desire motivated her to get more out of important workouts than she had been content with in the past. All in all, her mind had become a greater asset to her as a runner.

Eight months after the operation, Serena ran the New York City Marathon, her debut at that distance, stunning everyone by finishing as the fourth American in a time of 2:37:06. During the race, she ran by the hospital where her surgery had been performed. She pointed at her right thigh and shouted, "Thank you!" Over the next three years, Serena lowered her marathon time three times, eventually running 2:28:05 in Amsterdam in 2013. The following year, she became the U.S. national champion at the half-marathon distance.

Numbers don't lie. Serena was a better runner with two hamstrings muscles in her right leg than she had been with three. It wasn't *really* magic. Many athletes have found ways to do more with less. Collectively, these examples prove that setbacks resulting in the loss of physical capacity, be it temporary or permanent, present an opportunity to make compensatory physical gains through the workaround effect and to become mentally fitter. Major injuries, minor injuries, sickness, starting over after time away from training, getting older—these hated setbacks and others are all potential blessings in disguise.

Neuroplasticity is a hardwired coping skill, operating automatically whenever an athlete practices an old skill under a new constraint. But in order to benefit from the workaround effect, an athlete must first exercise another, psychological coping skill, one that requires a conscious choice and that Willie Stewart relied on intuitively: adaptability.

For the athlete who has suffered a physical setback, adaptability begins with the belief that practicing an old skill is worthwhile despite the existence of a new constraint. Adaptability is losing a limb and thinking, *I believe I can still ride a bike and swim—maybe faster than most people.* Adaptability is having a hamstring muscle removed and thinking, *I believe I can still run—perhaps better than ever.* Adaptability is responding with a similar mindset whenever a physical setback occurs. If you do, your body and mind will follow suit, the body adapting by finding new efficiencies and the mind by elevating mental fitness through heightened focus or inhibitory control (as in the case of Willie Stewart), greater appreciation for the gift of movement (Serena Burla), or some other positive change.

Disabled sports are also known as adaptive sports. Willie Stewart would tell you that all sports are adaptive sports—or should be.

THE IRONMAN WORLD CHAMPIONSHIP makes no special accommodations for disabled competitors aside from reserving a handful of entry slots for them. Challenged athletes start at the same time as everyone else, cover the same course, and are required to meet the same time cutoffs, all unassisted (with the exception of a lift from the swim exit to the transition area for nonambulatory racers).

Willie Stewart wouldn't have had it any other way. Indeed, he took full advantage of his status as just another competitor by placing himself at the center of the front row of athletes treading water behind the start banner that hung over Kailua Bay just after sunrise on October 19, 2002. An hour earlier, monsoonal rain had been falling. The downpour had since ceased, but the four-foot waves that had accompanied the shower continued to roll in, lifting and dropping the racers in a languid rhythm.

All triathletes have strengths and weaknesses. Running was Willie's strongest discipline because it was the one in which his missing arm affected him least. (A study found that runners are only 3 percent less economical with both of their hands clasped behind their back than they are normally.) Cycling was affected somewhat more than running for Willie because, although cycling is a legs-dominant sport, he could not ride in the aerodynamic position used by athletes with two arms. Swimming was Willie's weak link due to the obvious challenge of swimming with one arm. For him the Ironman's full-contact, 2.4-mile open-water swim was going to be all about survival.

At seven o'clock, the traditional starting cannon blasted and some 1,600 athletes began to whip the Pacific, creating a seaward-moving field of whitewater. Willie's plan was to ride in the wake of the faster swimmers in front of him as long as he could and then settle into his own tempo. No sooner had he relaxed than he was overtaken by a steady flow of swimmers, many of whom inadvertently slapped, kicked, and dunked him as they passed by. A veteran of contact sports, Willie wasn't bothered. Nor did he lose his focus when he got beyond the protection of the cove and encountered the largest swells seen in the 24-year history of Ironman. Every few strokes he swallowed a mouthful of throat-burning brine, gagged, and kept going.

Willie's fingers touched the asphalt surface of the boat launch ramp at the end of Kona Pier at 1:16:54 on the race clock. There were 1,124 athletes ahead of him at the swim exit, 479 behind him. Willie passed at least a dozen competitors in his mad dash up the ramp and into the transition tent. This, too, was part of his plan to exploit every opportunity to gain a second or a position.

Willie strapped on his bike helmet with deft movements of the right hand, mounted his bike, and pedaled out of the transition area and onto the 112-mile bike course. The route had been changed since the year before. Previously, it had taken riders straight out of Kailua-Kona and into the lava fields hugging the West Coast of the Big Island on the Queen Kaahumanu Highway. It now started with a loop that took riders to the Old Kona Airport State Recreation Area on the extreme northern outskirts of Kailua and then back into Kailua village before dumping them onto the Queen K. The changes introduced several new tight turns and short, steep climbs and descents—the kind of technical riding that is most difficult to do with one arm.

In future races, Willie would have the aid of a prosthesis, but today he had none.

If there's anything more difficult for a one-armed cyclist to do than make sharp turns and negotiate short, steep climbs and descents, it's ride in a crosswind. Ironman is famous for its crosswinds, and when Willie penetrated the lava fields, he was summarily introduced to them. Merely staying upright was as challenging as maintaining a 20-mph rate of forward progress. Willie feared crashing into another rider and taking him out even more than he feared being blown over. He knew his disability would be blamed, and that was unthinkable.

To minimize the risk of sideswiping a fellow competitor, Willie stopped to drink from his squeeze bottle instead of riding no-handed and drinking on the fly. Hating the time lost to these hydration breaks, he kept them infrequent, pausing every 30 minutes or so, or about half as often as he would have done on a solo ride. As the day warmed, Willie became increasingly parched.

Despite inadequate hydration and a dozen stops, Willie passed many more riders than passed him. He completed the bike leg in 5:48:55, having moved up almost 100 places, and was now just outside the top 1,000. Willie again blazed through transition, taking less than 2 minutes to trade his cycling shoes for running shoes and exit onto the 26.2-mile run course.

Before the race, Willie had boldly vowed to run the marathon in less than 3 hours, something only a handful of athletes—nearly all of them professionals—do at Ironman each year. Willie started the run on pace to achieve his goal. He felt strong and passed competitors one after another. His mood became euphoric. *I can't believe I'm really here*, he thought as he ran along coastal Ali'i Drive, seeing firsthand the fabled vistas he had seen in scores of photographs and video images in his years of dreaming about doing this race.

Eight miles into the marathon, Willie began to feel very hot. That's because it *was* hot—86 degrees. At 10 miles, he was completely spent. The thought of having to cover another 16 miles to reach the finish line made him want to weep. His pace slowed from 7 minutes per mile to 8, from 8 to 9. Some of the runners Willie had passed now returned the favor. His prized mental focus was powerless to halt the inexorable slowing. Yet he refused to walk. No matter what, he promised himself, he would not walk. Then an older gentleman who was walking passed Willie. Moments later, Willie broke his vow and walked also, but only because it appeared he could go faster that way.

Approaching 18 miles, Willie saw a cluster of approaching vehicles in the distance ahead on the shimmering Queen K Highway. They surrounded the women's race leader, Natascha Badmann, who was about to tie a bow on a third consecutive Ironman victory. As Badmann came face-to-face with Willie, she smiled and chirped, "Hi!"

Willie was not one to be overawed by a brush with celebrity. But in that moment, he recalls, a kind of energy transfer took place. Although Badmann was on her way toward glory and a big payday, she seemed happy just to be out there, able to do what she was doing. The feeling was infectious. Willie caught a second wind. Having flipped back and forth between long bouts of walking and short stretches of running over the preceding miles, he was able now to run steadily. He started passing other runners again. The closer he came to Kailua Village, the faster he ran. As he sprinted down the iconic final stretch on Ali'i Drive, he felt he could run another 5 miles. Willie stopped the clock at 10:48:15, having covered the marathon in 3:36:49. He had passed nearly 500 competitors during the marathon to finish 532nd—within the top third of the field. And, although it wasn't his main concern, he had won the disabled division.

Willie returned to Ironman three times before moving on to new challenges. These have included 100-mile mountain bike races, 100-km trail runs, 24-hour adventure races, and kayaking the Grand Canyon. In 2006, Willie won the Catalina Marathon—not the disabled division or his age group but the whole race.

Once in a while a fan or friend will say to Willie, "Boy, imagine what you could have done with both of your arms!"

His answer is always the same:

"I wouldn't have done any of it."

CHAPTER SIX

THE GIFT
OF FAILURE

MAURO "SANTO" SANTAMBROGIO WAS facing the wrong way as he
approached the finish line of stage 9 of the 2010 Tour de France in
the Alpine village of Saint-Jean-de-Maurienne. Instead of looking
ahead at the race clock to see how many riders had finished ahead
of him (40) or how much time he'd lost to the stage winner (8:09), the
red-and-black-uniformed Italian member of the BMC Racing Team
rode with his head swiveled rearward, eyes guarding his grimacing
team leader, Cadel Evans, whom Santo had virtually dragged through
the final 30 kilometers of the 204.5-km stage after the Aussie cracked
on the last big climb of the day.

Upon completing the stage, Cadel pulled even with Santo, threw
a bony arm over his shoulder, and coasted alongside him, helmet to
helmet, toward a gradual stop, whispering weary words of thanks
into his ear. He then apologized for letting the team down—or tried
to, but he choked up. Suddenly Cadel dropped his head to Santo's
chest and erupted into unrestrained sobbing. Santo clenched his
teammate in claw-like hands, eyes gleaming with compassionate
anguish. Seconds passed like minutes, Cadel's torso quivering to the
staccato rhythm of his emotional spasms.

A throng of photographers quickly gathered around the dramatic tableau. The veteran shooters among them were stunned to witness the notoriously stoic Aussie displaying such raw feeling. Indeed, none of them could recall seeing *any* cyclist weep so wretchedly at a Tour de France stage finish. But they understood. Cadel had lost much more than a single stage of the world's biggest bike race. A dream had perished on the road to Saint-Jean-de-Maurienne.

Dreams die every day in this hard world, and it's always painful, but Cadel's did so in especially cruel fashion. For most of his life, Cadel had possessed the aura of a Chosen One, a man born to win the world's greatest bike race. Since the day he snatched a wrench from his father's toolbox and used it to pry the training wheels off his first bike, Cadel had been locked into a steady ascension toward the pinnacle of the sport of cycling, moving a step closer to his apparent destiny with each passing year. The trajectory had continued until Cadel stood just one small step from the mountaintop. Then he stalled. And that was frustrating. Then he took a step backward. And that was maddening. Now he was in freefall. And that was almost unbearable.

To have any hope of becoming a champion of the Tour de France, a person requires certain advantages. Cadel had had all of them. An early start on the bike? Check. The first thing the four-year-old Cadel did after removing the training wheels from his bike was to take it on epic rides over the primitive dirt roads surrounding his family's modest home in the tiny village of Barunga, an isolated aboriginal community in Australia's Northern Territory. He routinely pedaled away from the house after lunch and failed to return before nightfall, forcing his parents to go looking for him. Years later, as a professional cyclist, Cadel would credit these early adventures as an important factor in his development as an athlete. What he had thought was play turned out to have been preparation.

Opportunities? Check. Cadel came of age just when the young sport of mountain biking, to which he was particularly suited, was taking off in Australia. His precocity on fat tires quickly earned him an invitation to enroll at the Australian Institute of Sport, located in

Canberra. At AIS, Cadel was able to work with top coaches and train with other gifted young athletes on the finest equipment. Just one year after Cadel arrived at AIS, mountain biking became an Olympic sport. Cadel qualified and finished ninth in Atlanta. He was still a teenager.

Talent? Check. At AIS, Cadel underwent a comprehensive fitness examination that included tests of aerobic capacity, power-to-weight ratio, and lung volume. He cranked out the best numbers in the 14-year history of the Institute. Cadel's maximum rate of oxygen consumption (or VO_2max) was more than twice that of the average healthy young adult male, and his power-to-weight ratio was already superior to that of most Tour de France winners.

Cadel made his Tour debut 10 years later, in 2005, his transition to road cycling having been initiated when he competed in the World Junior Time Trial Championship on a borrowed bike and won the bronze medal. As fate would have it, Cadel's first Tour de France was Lance Armstrong's last (until he came out of retirement four years later). Everyone knew the American would win for the seventh time in a row. The more interesting question was who would stamp himself as the heir apparent. Three weeks later, that question had a clear answer. Cadel finished eighth, ahead of all other Tour rookies. What's more, he was younger than any rider ahead of him. If he improved in future Tours, as was only to be expected, his chances of winning the Big One at least once looked very good indeed.

He did improve. In the 2006 Tour, Cadel kept himself in the mix in all of the big mountain stages and rode two solid time trials to finish fifth overall. When the winner, Floyd Landis, was disqualified for a doping violation, Cadel slid into fourth position.

Few cycling pundits predicted that Cadel would leap all the way from fourth place to first in the 2007 Tour, but the preternaturally talented Aussie was included on everyone's short list of contenders. He kept the pressure off himself by setting an incremental goal of making the podium. It was a wise move. Having allowed himself to race one last time as the man of tomorrow, Cadel climbed better than ever and demonstrated much improved time trial ability. In the third week of the race, he jumped abruptly from fourth place overall to second when yellow-jersey wearer Michael Rasmussen and second-place rider Alexander Vinokourov were booted for doping.

On the morning before the decisive stage 19 time trial, Cadel stood 1 minute and 50 seconds behind new race leader Alberto Contador. He was already on the podium. Cadel could afford to ride the time trial defensively, to protect his position, or he could attack it, taking a long shot at the win. He took the shot. Rising to the moment, Cadel turned in the best race of his career, finishing second to Levi Leipheimer and later being declared the stage winner when the American's results were voided because of (you guessed it) a doping admission. The victory was bittersweet, though. Cadel came up just 23 seconds short of overtaking Contador and arrived in Paris as the runner-up.

Cadel's near miss caused a sensation back home. He became an instant national hero and was voted Australia's most popular sportsman in a major media poll. A classic introvert, whose reticence was often misperceived as sullenness or prickliness, Cadel shrank from the attention. The whole country now expected him to win the next Tour. Cadel had been on an upward trajectory his entire career. Every single year he got a step closer to the mountaintop. Now there was but one step left to take. The only way Cadel could make further progress was to claim the sport's biggest prize. That was pressure enough even without all the scrutiny.

And it wasn't just his own expectations and his nation's hopes that Cadel was burdened with. Pretty much the entire cycling world expected him to win the 2008 Tour de France. Like every major sporting event, the Tour is wagered on, and when betting closed on the eve of the 2008 race, Cadel stood as the favorite, with three-to-one odds. The money placed on his name was looking smart after stage 10, when Cadel donned the yellow jersey of the race leader for the first time in his career. He managed to keep it on his back until five days later, when he cracked on the final climb of stage 15 and lost the *maillot jaune* to Luxembourg's Frank Schleck.

Cadel slid as far back as fourth place in the succeeding days. His frustration boiled over after stage 16, when an overzealous cameraman impeded his progress from the finish line to the team bus. Cadel put his head down and rammed the camera with his helmet. The video went straight to YouTube, where it earned Cadel a few new fans and a great many more detractors.

Cadel regained enough poise to ride another heroic time trial for stage 20 that lifted him to second place in Paris, 58 seconds behind Carlos Sastre of Spain. For the second year in a row, Cadel had lost the Tour de France by less than a minute.

What a difference a year makes. Cadel had been thrilled to take second place in 2007. Earning the same result in 2008 left him nauseated. At 31, he was now a veteran of four Tours de France. He couldn't help but wonder if he'd missed his chance.

Another year passed. Cadel came to the 2009 Tour with an uncompromising attitude. "To me," he said afterward, "the goal was to win it and nothing else. A bad 2009 Tour would have been to finish second or third."

He finished 30th. The 2009 Tour was over for Cadel Evans almost before it started. In stage 4, a team time trial, Cadel's Silence-Lotto crew lost an almost insurmountable 2 minutes and 35 seconds to the victorious Astana team, whose roster included Cadel's chief rival, Alberto Contador. It was a completely unexpected disaster for which the entire team bore blame.

Cadel had no one but himself to blame, however, in stage 15, the toughest mountain stage of that year's Tour, in which he surrendered another 86 seconds to Contador. But that was nothing compared to the nearly 4 minutes he forfeited in stage 16.

Critics were ruthless. More than a few commentators chose to interpret Cadel's calamitous 2009 performance as a revelation, not an aberration. Cadel was no man of destiny after all, they said. Instead, he represented an altogether different archetype: the tragic athlete of limitless promise who lacks the final ingredient, that *je ne c'est quoi*, needed to reach the mountaintop.

"Evans is a great rider," wrote one blogger, "but to me there's always been something missing, a lack of strength or a weakness displayed when he's pushed in climbing." The general knock on Cadel was that he was careful to a fault; he lacked panache. True champions, people said, know when to go for it.

Cadel redeemed his 2009 season by finishing third in September's Vuelta a España and then winning the world championships road race. But by then, he had already decided that he needed to make a change. An American-owned racing team sponsored by Swiss bike manufacturer BMC had shown interest in hiring Cadel away from Silence-Lotto, and he was tempted to accept, knowing he probably would never win the Tour without a stronger team. Two weeks before the world championships, Cadel met with BMC team member George Hincapie, one of the most respected riders on the pro circuit, at a Zurich hotel. Hincapie later recounted the meeting in a 2011 book about Cadel.

"I really think you're going to like this team," Hincapie said. "I really believe I can help you podium at the Tour de France."

Cadel stared daggers at Hincapie.

"I've already done that," he growled. "I've podiumed two times at the Tour. I want to *win* it!"

When Cadel lined up for the opening prologue of his sixth Tour de France the following July, he wore the red-and-black kit of the BMC Racing Team. His results up to that point in the 2010 season had been solid—they included a stage win in the Giro d'Italia and a victory at the Flèche Wallonne one-day classic—and his Tour started well. In stage 3, he found himself on the right side of an unexpected split in the peloton and he finished the day third in the overall rankings. Five days later, he claimed the yellow jersey despite crashing and landing hard on his left side.

It was a pyrrhic victory, however, for the crash left him with a fractured elbow. Cadel rode the next day's mountain stage in terrible pain. Unable to deliver full power to the pedals, he was towed up the final climb by his teammate Mauro Santambrogio, finishing more than 8 minutes behind the leaders and completely out of contention. After crossing the line, Cadel buried his face in Santambrogio's shoulder and wept as a man does when his greatest aspiration has been ripped from his hands and tossed into the fire. He would finish the Tour in 25th place.

A dream died. Or did it?

IN 2013, MARK SEERY, a psychologist at the State University of New York at Buffalo, tested the pain tolerance of college students by asking them to immerse one of their hands in frigid water and hold it there as long as they could bear to. Afterward, the students filled out a questionnaire that elicited information about their childhood exposure to adversity. The results, published in *Psychological Science*, revealed that the students who had the fewest adverse experiences while growing up had a low pain tolerance. But so did the students who had suffered through a whole slew of childhood traumas. The students who kept their hand in the icy water the longest were the ones who'd experienced neither heaven nor hell while growing up, but something in between.

These findings were greeted with little surprise by Seery's fellow psychologists. Similar results had come out of research on the phenomenon of resilience. The mother of all coping skills, resilience is defined as a general ability to respond to adversity. Resilience is the quality that keeps a person engaged in challenging situations long enough to develop specific coping skills with which to overcome them, and, like pain tolerance, resilience is greatest in men and women who as children experienced some but not too much adversity. In the aggregate, studies on the phenomenon indicate that a person with a high tolerance for pain is likely to also have above-average capacity to cope with the stress of a job layoff or a cancer diagnosis, and this same person is more likely as well to have experienced a moderate amount of psychological trauma in his or her past. It would appear that a certain amount of misfortune is needed to toughen the mind against suffering and hardship, but excessive trauma leaves scar tissue.

Elite sports competition features inherent challenges that demand great resilience from athletes, and resilience, again, requires past adversity. It's not surprising, then, that men and women with psychological trauma in their personal history seem to be overrepresented at the highest levels of many sports. In a 2012 paper titled "The Rocky Road to the Top: Why Talent Needs Trauma" and published in *Sports Medicine,* sports psychologists Dave Collins and Aine MacNamara argued that "the knowledge and skills [that] athletes accrue from 'life' traumas and their ability to carry over what they learn in that context to novel situations certainly appear to affect their subsequent development and performance in sport." If this is true, then having things too easy in life can actually put developing athletes at a significant disadvantage.

Some experts have proposed that resilience may be especially beneficial to endurance athletes. Adversity exists in every sport, but a bike race is much more similar to immersing a hand in frigid water than is, say, a basketball game. All athletes experience failure, and resilience is needed to bounce back from it. But an endurance athlete's resilience is tested in every single race, in those moments of great suffering when something inside the athlete seems to ask, *How bad do you want it?*

Examples of champion endurance athletes who experienced significant psychological trauma in childhood are strikingly abundant. Frank Shorter, who won the 1972 Olympic Marathon for the United States, was subjected as a boy to appalling abuse at the hands of his father. Later in life, Shorter acknowledged that the experience may have made him a better runner. In a 2011 interview he said, "I found out as long as you know the pain is coming . . . and you have an idea of how bad it's going to be and how long it's going to [last], you develop an ability to ride it out. And I think in a way it may have transferred a little bit over into my running."

Scientists have much more to learn about how this sort of transfer occurs, but they have picked up interesting clues from brain-imaging studies. Research involving survivors of the devastating 2011 tsunami and earthquake in Japan, for example, revealed that symptoms of post-traumatic stress disorder were less likely to occur in individuals who exhibited greater volume (suggesting greater functional capacity) in a part of the brain called the anterior cingulate cortex. The ACC plays a crucial role in situations of internal conflict, such as the tug-of-war that is fought between the desire to slow down and the desire to keep pushing in a race. Endurance exercise itself is known to strengthen the ACC. It is possible that the coping skills a person acquires in overcoming certain traumatic experiences also strengthen the anterior cingulate cortex, producing more resilient endurance athletes.

Whether champion athletes have more adversity in their past than others do or not, many of them see themselves as having been tempered by suffering. At the 2012 Olympics, psychologist Mustafa Sarkar and colleagues at the University of Gloucestershire conducted interviews with eight gold medalists and then looked for themes in their remarks. In a summary of their findings published in the journal *Reflective Practice*, the researchers reported that "the participants encountered a range of sport and nonsport adversities that they considered were essential for winning their gold medals, including repeated nonselection, significant sporting failure, serious injury, political unrest, and the death of a family member. The participants described the role that these experiences played in their psychological and performance development, specifically focusing on their resultant trauma, motivation, and learning."

Notably, a number of the adversities the athletes cited were setbacks that occurred *within* the sporting context. This finding suggests that athletes need not experience appreciable trauma in everyday life to become resilient. Sport itself has a way of cultivating mental toughness. But it also means that athletes who passed through relatively trauma-free childhoods may really *depend* on facing adversity within their sport to develop elite-level resilience. Athletes who have been gifted with exceptional talent and other blessings that enable them to sail to the top of their sport—athletes like Cadel Evans—may therefore be doubly disadvantaged where resilience is concerned. It's not that they are necessarily mentally weak—no one who knew him ever said that Cadel lacked toughness—but they might not be as resilient as they need to be in order to finish, say, *first* in the Tour de France rather than *second*.

Are such athletes then doomed to stall out one step shy of the mountaintop? History says no. There are noteworthy examples of "over-fortunate" athletes who nevertheless were resilient enough to find the additional resilience they needed to take that last step. In particular, the maddening frustration of repeated failure to achieve a coveted goal has sparked many a mid-career breakthrough in athletes "spoiled" by having been given every advantage.

The American middle-distance runner Nick Symmonds presents an interesting case study of this phenomenon. The son of a surgeon and a teacher, Nick enjoyed an all-American upbringing in Boise, Idaho, where he became an Eagle Scout and won multiple state championships in track and field. Despite his athletic success, Nick turned down scholarship offers from big-name schools to attend Willamette University. As a Division III institution, Willamette offered no financial support to athletes, but the Symmonds family's ample means permitted Nick to choose the college he liked most without weighing other considerations. After he graduated in 2006, Nick signed a contract with Nike and subsequently amassed five consecutive national championship titles at 800 meters. Along the way he perfected a signature come-from-behind racing strategy, lurking at the back of the field through the first lap and then running down everyone in the second.

But while he had no peer within the United States, Nick could not break through to the podium level in major international championships. He failed to qualify for the 800-meter final at the 2007 world championships and again at the 2008 Olympics, and he finished sixth and fifth respectively at the 2009 and 2011 world championships. Each time he stalled out one step shy of the mountaintop.

In their paper on resilience in athletes, Dave Collins and Aine MacNamara observed that "low points" often become "turning points" in the development of resilience. Nick's low point came in the final of the 800 meters at the 2012 Olympics, which is widely regarded as the greatest half-mile race in history. The winner, David Rudisha of Kenya, broke the world record. Nick ran the fastest time of his career and one of the fastest times ever run by an American. But he finished fifth, and he wasn't even the top American in the race—Duane Solomon took fourth.

A photograph of Nick captured immediately after the race shows him with his hands on his head, his face wearing an expression of stunned disbelief. Behind the rueful countenance, a powerful psychological transformation was taking place. In that precise moment, Nick decided he'd had enough of falling short. He was *fed up* with missing out on the medals.

At the start of the next season, Nick vowed to abandon his familiar come-from-behind strategy and just go for it. Following through on this promise would be as simple—but also as terrifying—as leaping out of an airplane with faith in a never-before-used parachute; a matter of letting go. At the 2013 USA Track and Field Outdoor Championships, fear won out. Nick was slow off the line, got boxed in at the rail, and was beaten again by Duane Solomon.

Nick faced Solomon again just one week later in London. This time Nick swore to himself that he would not allow his younger rival to get away from him. In principle, nothing could have been easier than for Nick to key off Solomon, who invariably set a vicious early pace, and shadow him through the race's early stages. But to actually do it Nick would have to overcome every half-miler's greatest fear: hitting the wall.

"I knew that if I blew up and died I would have to write it off as a learning experience," he said after the London showdown.

When the race started, Solomon sprinted into the lead and Nick chased right after him, a look of almost theatrical determination stamped on his face.

"This is early aggressive running from Nick Symmonds," observed television commentator Tim Hutchings. "We're not used to that."

Nick stayed on Solomon's heels until the two men came off the final bend. Far from blowing up, Nick discovered that he had enough strength left to lift his pace and ease away from Solomon to take the win in 1:43:67—the second-best time of his career.

At the 2013 world championships, Nick was even more aggressive, moving into the lead of the 800-meter final with a full lap left to run, a new mantra echoing in his mind: *Don't waste this opportunity*. He remained in the lead until just before he hit the tape, when Ethiopia's Mohammed Aman squeezed past him. Nevertheless, Nick walked away with his first international medal—silver—and he had failure to thank for it. Repeated failure to attain the highest level in his event gave him the very ingredient whose lack had resulted in those failures.

Failing repeatedly is like walking on a bed of hot coals toward a wall that keeps receding as you approach it—a Sisyphean nightmare. Eventually, the cycle of frustration causes an athlete to feel either defeated or angry. The latter response is much more likely than the former to disrupt the cycle and enable the athlete to reach the flag. Robert Wicks, a psychologist and author of the book *Bounce: Living the Resilient Life*, has referred to this type of angry resolve as "sweet disgust." The phrase aptly conveys the idea that there is an element of healthy wrath in the fed-up mind state that fuels positive change. Sweet disgust is really the opposite of defeat. It is a determination to fight back, something that is hard to do effectively without anger. All else being equal, the angrier party in a fight wins. In psychobiological terms, sweet disgust enhances performance by increasing potential motivation, or the maximum intensity of perceived effort an athlete is willing to endure.

In 2001, Sabine Janssen and colleagues at the Dutch University of Leiden induced anger in volunteers and then subjected them to a test of pain tolerance. On a separate occasion, the volunteers took the same test in a neutral emotional state. Janssen's team reported in the *Journal of Psychosomatic Research* that the subjects' pain tolerance was significantly greater when they were angry. Nine years later, Henk Aarts and colleagues at Utrecht University reported in *Psychological Science* that inducing anger markedly improved performance in a hand-grip strength test. Pain is not quite the same thing as perceived effort and strength is different from endurance, but they are similar enough that we should expect anger to affect perceived effort and endurance performance in much the same way.

Does this mean that an endurance athlete should go out of his or her way to become an angry person? Certainly not. But it does indicate that one can use failure as a motivator, albeit a "dark" motivator tinged with anger. This constructive form of anger is a useful coping skill that is available to all endurance athletes who experience repeated failure.

When Cadel Evans failed to win the Tour de France for the sixth straight year, he became fed up. His 25th-place finish in 2010 left him devastated, haunting him afterward like nothing else he had experienced either within or outside of sport. But Cadel had a feeling that this failure—and indeed all of the disappointments that preceded and fed into it—might have been the best thing that could have happened to him. He told Rupert Guinness, in reference to winning the 2009 World Road Championship, "Missing out all those times kept me hungry. The more I look back on it as my career has progressed, the happier I was that I didn't win earlier. This is the scenario that has helped keep me hungry longer."

Would he ever be able to say the same thing about the Tour de France?

AS HE PREPARED FOR the 2011 Tour de France, Cadel not only made use of the sweet disgust his cumulative disappointments had provoked in him, but he also applied several concrete lessons he'd learned the hard way in his first six Tours. This type of behavior is also common in athletes who have become fed up with failure. The resilience that grows out of failure manifests itself in both creativity and heightened effort. Getting fed up can push athletes to try new things, such as Nick Symmonds's shift in race strategy. In other words, failure stimulates a kind of workaround effect, albeit a different flavor of workaround effect than neuroplasticity, the hardwired coping skill exploited by athletes who show adaptability in the face of the loss of physical capacity, which we discussed in Chapter 5.

Cadel appreciated this silver lining of failure as much as he did its motivating effect. "In these periods, you get stronger and learn so much," he said in the book *Close to Flying*. "You have to revisit the basics of what you do. Even just riding the bike with a broken elbow, you have to change your position and that change might turn out to be a good change for your efficiency that you didn't expect."

One of the lessons Cadel had learned was the importance of starting the race with fresh legs. He felt he had over-raced before the 2010 Tour, and he shared this opinion with the coaches and managers of the BMC team when he met with them in Legano, Italy, to plan out the 2011 season. They agreed on a schedule that would set him up to arrive in France with 30 to 33 days of racing in his legs, or about 10 days fewer than the year before.

The plan worked beautifully. In June, Cadel competed in the Critérium du Dauphiné, a one-week stage race that is used as a final Tour de France tune-up by many of the top G.C. contenders. He finished second to Englishman Bradley Wiggins, feeling stronger at the end than he had at the beginning.

Despite this performance, when pre-Tour wagering closed, Cadel's odds of winning stood at 25 to 1. The editors of roadcycling .com picked him to finish fifth. In a few short years, he had gone from Mr. Inevitable to Cadel *Who*? He was 34 years old, after all. Only one rider older than he was now had ever won the Tour de France, and no one had won the Tour after losing it six times.

Stage 1 of the 2011 event was a 191-km, mostly flat race that started on the Atlantic coast and worked its way inland to a short, uphill finish. With 8 km left in the stage, a crash split the peloton in half. Cadel was positioned ahead of the carnage. When the BMC team learned that Alberto Contador, heavily favored at four-to-six odds, had been caught behind, they whipped up the pace to gain as much time on him as possible. There was no better target for Cadel's bottled-up frustration than the Spaniard who, more than any other rider, had obstructed his path to the mountaintop. On the short climb to the finish line, Cadel launched a savage surprise attack and was able to gain 3 precious seconds on several other rivals, including Frank Schleck and Alexander Vinokourov. Cadel had not often displayed such aggressive opportunism in previous Tours. Having lost the 2007 edition by less than half a minute, he planned to scrap for every second this time.

Stage 2 was a team time trial. To forestall a recurrence of the catastrophic performance of Cadel's former Silence-Lotto team in this discipline at the 2009 Tour, Cadel and his BMC teammates had practiced the team time trial on a Formula One racetrack one month before the 2011 Tour began. Despite the rehearsal, just 2 km into the 23-km stage, two riders, Manuel Quinziato and Marcus Burghardt, were dropped, leaving only seven riders to share the load. The survivors rallied, though, and completed the stage in a tie for second place, 28 seconds ahead of Contador's Astana team. Cadel moved into third place in the G.C., just 1 second behind leader Thor Hushovd.

More crashes occurred in stage 3, a 198-km trek northward from Olonne-sur-Mer to Redon. Cadel, riding near the head of the peloton and encircled by teammates, escaped them. So insistent were Cadel's BMC lieutenants on keeping their leader at the front of the race and out of harm's way that they drew the ire of the top sprinters' teams, who had their own reason to stay at the vanguard in flat stages such as this one. George Hincapie, perhaps recalling his 2009 conversation with Cadel in Zurich, reminded the BMC boys that they weren't there to make friends—they were there to win the Tour de France.

In stage 4, misfortune struck. With only 15 kilometers left in the race, a rider clipped Cadel's rear derailleur, causing it to partially malfunction. Cadel was tempted to ride through the problem, but Hincapie, knowing from experience that it would only get worse, insisted that he stop and change bikes. After the switch, Cadel was off the back, well behind the 195 other riders in the race. Marcus Burghardt, eager to redeem himself after his lackluster performance in the team time trial, dropped back to shepherd his captain to the front. Within minutes, the German had led the Aussie into contact with his main rivals. Like stage 1, this stage featured an abrupt uphill finish. Contador, needing to shave seconds off his deficit, attacked on the run-up to the line. Teeth bared, Cadel chased down his adversary and took the stage win in a photo finish. In the space of less than 10 miles, Cadel had moved from last place to first to claim his first Tour de France stage win not awarded after the fact.

The next three stages were custom-made for the sprinters, but even so, Cadel's average finishing position on those days was 15th—extremely high for a rider who was neither contesting sprints nor supporting a teammate who was. The team's strategy of keeping Cadel near the head of the field and out of trouble was clearly succeeding.

Stage 8, featuring four rated climbs, including a Category III ascent to the finish, offered the top climbers their first opportunity to measure their form against one another. Cadel bested Contador and several others in a sprint to the line to claim third place on the day, 15 seconds behind the winner. The media were at last beginning to acknowledge Cadel as a threat. "Cadel Evans was perhaps the most impressive of the overall contenders on that climb," conceded reporter Barry Ryan in cyclingnews.com's live coverage of the event. The next day's route brought the field over eight rated climbs and again Cadel led the big boys to the finish, though without gaining time.

On Monday, July 11, the Tour took a break in the town of Saint-Flour, located in the Massif Central region. In a press conference held at the hotel where the BMC team was staying, a cheerful, relaxed

Cadel told reporters, "My coach and I worked very hard for this Tour and we have planned it very carefully, with months and months of work and years and years of experience. I am really happy with how it is." His situation was indeed ideal: Still in third place, Cadel was not yet burdened with the pressure of wearing yellow, and he knew himself to be well capable of tearing to shreds the two riders in front of him in the coming mountain stages.

The wellspring of Cadel's good spirits ran deeper than his favorable circumstances, however. Journalists noted a new air of calm surrounding the two-time Tour runner-up. His fellow competitors, too, observed that his demeanor was looser, even compared to high points in his previous Tours. What they did not know was that the source of this calm was anger—specifically, the sweet disgust that had germinated in Cadel after the 2010 Tour and that he had brought into this year's race. Anger is not often thought of as a calming emotion, but the fed-up feeling that transforms failure into resilience is just that. Athletes who have everything it takes to succeed but lack the highest level of resilience are psychologically dependent on things going their way—on not facing too much adversity—in competition. This dependency makes them nervous and emotionally reactive. The fed-up athlete, on the other hand, no longer hopes for the uncontrollables to work out in his favor. He has resolved to take total responsibility for his racing, to avenge adversities past and future. This simmering determination gives the athlete a sense of agency and control that is calming. Such was Cadel's mindset midway through the 2011 Tour de France. He now seemed like the last guy in the world who would ever head-butt a television camera. His temper was channeled and proactive now, no longer exposed and reflexive.

After the rest day, the Tour spent two days rolling through the Massif Central toward the Pyrenees, where fireworks were expected. Now more than 1.5 minutes behind Cadel in the General Classification, Contador had to attack. Frank and Andy Schleck were behind by only 3 and 11 seconds, respectively, but neither of the two brothers rode as strong a time trial as Cadel. So they, too, felt pressure to ride aggressively, lest they arrive at the start of the stage 20 time trial lacking the cushion they needed to hold off Cadel and win the Tour de France. But the expected pyrotechnics never materialized. The contenders did little more than feel each other out over eight major climbs in stages 12 through 14. Such timid racing drew criticism from fans, but it also intensified anticipation for stage 18, the "Queen Stage" of the 2011 Tour de France, a 200-km death march through the Alps from Pinerolo to Galibier Serre Chevalier that included three "beyond-category" climbs and now loomed as the last best chance for someone to wrest control of the race from Cadel Evans.

The BMC team's plan for the stage called for two of Cadel's domestiques, Marcus Burghardt and Brent Bookwalter, to place themselves in an early breakaway in hopes of being available to help Cadel on the final climb of the day, a 22.8-km scaling of the imposing Col du Galibier. But the plan unraveled when Bookwalter bonked on the penultimate mountain, the wickedly steep Col d'Izoard, and was forced to drop back early. Worse, three of the BMC men riding with Cadel—Hincapie, Quinziato, and Michael Schar—came unglued on the same climb, while Ivan Santaromita was feeling the effects of a knee injury he'd suffered in an earlier crash. Taking advantage of the BMC team's weakness, Andy Schleck, who had dropped from 3 seconds to 1 minute 18 seconds behind Cadel in stage 16, launched an attack. Cadel decided to let him go, not wanting to share the risk Schleck was taking by going for broke so far from the finish.

It all came down to arithmetic. Cadel could give away up to 77 seconds to Schleck on the stage and remain ahead of him in the overall standings. In the worst-case scenario, he could lose up to 3 minutes to Schleck and still have a chance of moving in front of him in the stage 20 individual time trial, judging by past discrepancies in their solo performances against the clock. But of course, he would prefer not to cut it that close.

At the summit of the Col d'Izoard, Schleck had a lead of more than 2 minutes on Cadel's group. The lanky captain of the Leopard-Trek team took tremendous risks on the subsequent descent in an effort to catch his teammate Maxime Monfort, who had been in the same breakaway as Burghardt and Bookwalter. Schleck succeeded in joining Monfort, and the two worked together to stretch their advantage to nearly 3.5 minutes over Cadel's group as they approached the base of the Col du Galibier. The lower slopes of the mountain were not particularly steep but they proved too much for Cadel's last surviving teammate, Amaël Moinard of France, who fell off the pace of the fast-dwindling chase group, leaving Cadel utterly friendless.

Cadel looked around the group for athletes who shared his plight—overall contenders whose hopes of winning the Tour would be dashed if Schleck's lead wasn't slashed before he reached the stage finish at the summit of the Galibier—and whom he therefore might enlist as coconspirators in a chase. He asked yellow jersey wearer Thomas Voeckler to help, but Voeckler shook his head. The Frenchman was redlining and had no intention of taking turns as a windbreaker at the front of a serious chase. Contador, too, appeared to be in the hurt box. Naturally, Frank Schleck wasn't about to chase down his brother and teammate.

The urgent voice of BMC sports director John Lelange crackled through Cadel's earpiece. Andy Schleck's lead had breached 4 minutes. Cadel had to go *now*, and he had to go alone.

No man is truly born to win the Tour de France. Cadel had figured that out. But he felt keenly that his entire life was a prelude to this moment. Cadel was 11 kilometers and 1,800 vertical feet from the most important finish line he had ever aimed at. If he covered this distance 2 minutes faster than Schleck, his great dream would indeed become a destiny. If he came up short, he would not win the Tour de France—not this year, not ever. Neither teamwork, nor cunning, nor attention to detail, nor any other ingredient of Tour success could help him now. Cadel's fate depended entirely on whether he had the sheer resilience to pull himself out of the hole he found himself in. If Cadel was still the same athlete he had been before the moment in 2010 when he wept on Mauro Santambrogio's shoulder, he would fail again, and more painfully than ever. If that last failure had transformed him, he had a chance.

Cadel stood up and lunged off the front of his group like a Doberman snapping his yard chain taut. Pierre Roland quickly countered the move and found Cadel's back wheel, dragging several others behind him. Cadel sat back down but continued to mash the pedals furiously. After all these years of racing on pavement, he still rode like a mountain biker, hunched way forward, his torso almost parallel to the ground. His face seldom showed much expression, but his effort was now plainly visible in the downturned corners of his open mouth.

None of the riders behind Cadel showed a hint of willingness to relieve him of the burden of full exposure to the buffeting mountain wind gusts that now met him head-on. So be it. Cadel stood again and took another dig, his bike rocking smoothly from side to side as he used virtually every muscle between his shoulders and his toes to wring power from the machine. His quadriceps bore the brunt of the effort in this posture. A burning sensation radiated from the muscles, becoming more intense with each pedal stroke until Cadel was forced to sit again.

As he passed under a banner marking 10 kilometers to the summit, Cadel learned that he had reduced his 4-minute deficit to Schleck by a paltry 10 seconds. At this rate, the Leopard-Trek rider would still finish the stage more than 2 minutes ahead of Cadel in the G.C. His only hope now was to push Schleck into faltering, but up ahead Schleck still looked strong. Indeed, he had just shaken the last remaining breakaway rider from his back wheel, Astana's Maxim Inglinskiy. Schleck was now the lone leader of the stage as well as the virtual leader of the Tour de France.

To encourage Cadel, John Lelange, who was riding behind him in a team car, reported the name of each cyclist to come unhitched behind him. First it was Sammy Sanchez, who had started the day fifth in the General Classification. Then Cadel's former mountain biking rival Ryder Hesjedal exploded. Moments later, American

Christian Vande Velde, a brilliant climber, lost contact. All of these men were using at least 10 percent less energy than Cadel by riding in his slipstream, yet his punishing pace was still too much for them.

Schleck passed under the 5-km banner and hit the steepest part of the climb, the road kicking up to a 9 percent gradient. For the first time since he launched his attack some 90 minutes before, he stood up from the saddle—something he tended to do only when he was beginning to struggle. At the same time, Schleck lifted his gaze toward the summit. Almost imperceptibly, he began to lose momentum.

Three minutes and eight seconds behind him, Cadel too had his eyes raised toward the summit. As he came around a switchback, he got a long view of the road ahead and spotted the scrum of vehicles surrounding Schleck. A shot of adrenaline catapulted him into another ferocious surge. At the back of the dwindling train of hangers-on, Alberto Contador, the man who had beaten Cadel by 23 seconds to win the 2007 Tour, shook his head in defeat and fell back. Lelange gave Cadel the news, provoking yet another merciless acceleration, years of dammed-up frustration being transferred from legs to pedals.

The pundits who had written him off had nothing to say now. Perhaps they had been right to argue that Cadel was missing something. But if so, he was missing it no longer. They wanted panache? Here it was.

Schleck was blind with fatigue, a ghost rider, his bike weaving crazily across the road. With only 1 kilometer to go, he nearly crashed into a temporary barrier on the other side of which lay a rocky precipice dropping hundreds of feet to certain death. At last the finish line came. As he crossed it, Andy Schleck pumped his right fist in a manner that looked more hostile than jubilant—a "take that" sort of celebration. He'd raced angry too, but he was nowhere near as fed up as the fuming Australian closing in from behind.

As Cadel powered toward the line, Frank Schleck, one of only three riders Cadel hadn't killed off, stole a march and sprinted across in second place, 2 minutes and 7 seconds behind his brother. Cadel finished 8 seconds later. Andy Schleck had leapfrogged Cadel in the overall standings, but his net advantage was only 57 seconds, significantly less time than he would need in order to stave off Cadel in the stage 20 time trial. Cadel's valiant chase had saved his Tour.

It wasn't over yet, though. Andy Schleck had one more chance to pad his lead over Cadel before the time trial. Stage 19 was another Alpine slog, marked by three beyond-category climbs and ending atop the famous Alpe d'Huez. Cadel suffered a scare between the first and second climbs when another mechanical issue forced him to stop and change bikes. But the mishap served only to put a fresh match to his fuse. Cadel's rivals took advantage of the contretemps and rode away from him on the next ascent. Cadel bombed down the backside of the mountain as though it were a videogame, where death is virtual and temporary, catching the group containing the Schleck brothers and Contador just before the start of the final climb. Cadel marked the Schlecks all the way up L'Alpe d'Huez, even tossing in a needless attack of his own, and finished the stage having lost no more time to anyone who could threaten him.

That night, the BMC team stayed at a Club Med near the stage finish. Cadel's teammates were on tenterhooks. They wanted him to win the Tour almost as badly as he did, but they had done all they could to help him. It was up to Cadel to close the deal. He stood third in the General Classification, 57 seconds behind Andy Schleck and 4 seconds behind Frank. Cadel had 42.5 kilometers to erase those deficits in the next day's time trial. The pressure was enormous, and yet at dinner he conversed with his teammates as though they were all getting ready for a regular training ride, not the most significant race of his life. He sipped from a glass of wine like a man who hadn't a worry in the world. The others were once again witnessing the calm of sweet disgust.

Some 16 hours later, Cadel rode an inspired time trial, flying up hills, charging down descents, and carving turns like a slalom skier until he stopped the clock at 55:40. It was the second-fastest time of the day, bettered only by Tony Martin of Germany, who would win the World Time Trial Championship two months later. Andy Schleck was

2 minutes and 34 seconds slower, his brother slower still. Cadel had taken the yellow jersey, and his lead of 1 minute and 34 seconds was big enough to render stage 21, the road to Paris, ceremonial.

When Cadel Evans completed that stage on the Champs-Élysées, he became the first Australian and the second-oldest person ever to win the Tour de France. But his fellow endurance athletes would do well to remember him as the guy who failed to win the Tour de France more times than anyone else before he won it.

CHAPTER SEVEN

TODAY'S WEAKNESS, TOMORROW'S STRENGTH

ONE OF THE MOST compelling images to come out of the 2012 Summer Olympics in London was a photograph taken outside competition, during the medal ceremony that followed the final of the men's double sculls rowing event. The photo shows the six medalists—representing three teams—standing side by side on a carpeted dock at the edge of Dorney Lake, site of the just-completed race.

What is striking about the image is the relative size of the athletes. The two in the middle look tiny—almost miniaturized—in relation to the pairs on either side of them. At the far left of the frame is Italy's Romano Battisti, dressed in a black warm-up suit. Like the others, he wears a ribbon-slung medal around his neck and holds a bouquet of multicolored flowers at his waist. Battisti is a big man: 6 feet, 3 inches tall and 203 pounds in weight. Beside him towers his boat mate Alessio Sartori, a veritable giant at 6 feet, 8 inches and 220 pounds. At the far right of the grouping looms Iztok Cop of Slovenia, wearing the blue-and-green unisuit and white undershirt he raced in. His dimensions are 6 feet, 3 inches and 198 pounds. To Iztok's left stands his teammate Luka Spik, another behemoth at 6 feet, 5 inches and 209 pounds. Sandwiched between these strapping duos and utterly dwarfed by them is the black-clad New Zealand team. Nathan Cohen is barely 6 feet tall and weighs 192 pounds. His partner Joseph Sullivan is a mere 5 feet, 11 inches and 178 pounds.

The central placement of the Kiwis amplifies the power of the image, and not only by exaggerating their comparative smallness. Olympic tradition dictates that gold medalists be placed in the middle of the lineup at medal ceremonies. In a sport that rewards size and punishes its lack, little Nathan Cohen and tiny Joseph Sullivan had beaten the Goliaths on either side of them.

JOE SULLIVAN WAS 9 years old when he watched the 1996 Summer Games in Atlanta from his family's home in North Canterbury, on the east coast of New Zealand's South Island. Before the Olympic flame was snuffed, Joe was consumed by the dream of becoming an Olympian, although he couldn't have said in which sport. His best talent at that time was general hyperactivity.

At age 13, Joe moved with his family to the small seaside town of Picton. He enrolled at the local high school, Queen Charlotte College, where he channeled his overabundant energy into cross country running and track and field. A slender kid of average height, Joe had the right physique for these sports and did fairly well.

When Joe was still a freshman, his athleticism caught the attention of a senior member of the rowing team, who encouraged the younger boy to try his hand at sculling. Within a week, Joe was building calluses with his new teammates in daily workouts on Picton Harbour, a busy fishing area where human-powered craft were frequently swamped by the wakes of passing trawlers. Joe was an unlikely rower. Successful oarsmen, in addition to being tall and heavy, tend to have a large wingspan relative to their height. Not only was Joe smallish, but he also had unusually short arms, an anatomical peculiarity that inspired his fellow rowers to call him "T-Rex."

Despite having the "wrong body" for rowing, Joe excelled. The biggest competition of the year for the Queen Charlotte College rowers was the Maadi Cup, the de facto New Zealand national secondary school rowing championship. It was held in late March, a couple of weeks before Joe's birthday. In 2003, when Joe was not quite 17, he won the boys under-19 double sculls event with Kieran Gaudin, plus two other races.

The winner of the 2003 Maadi Cup's premier event, the under-18 single sculls, was none other than Joe's future Olympic double sculls partner, Nathan Cohen, some 15 months older and representing James Hargest High School, located at the southern tip of the South Island. The victory was a watershed moment for Nathan, who like Joe was smaller than most of the rowers he raced with and against. "It showed me that if you wanted something enough and were willing to push yourself beyond all your perceived limits," he said years later, "anything was possible."

Nathan graduated a few months later and went off to Canterbury University. At the 2004 Maadi Cup, it was Joe's turn to step into the spotlight. Nasty weather conditions caused the race schedule to be compressed, and Joe was forced to race three finals—the under-17 and under-19 double sculls and the under-17 single sculls—in less than an hour. He won all three, flopping onto his back in ecstatic exhaustion after the last of them. That hour is still remembered as the greatest performance in the history of the Maadi Cup.

In 2005, Joe returned to the big show one last time and won three more races. He had established himself as the best rower his age in all of New Zealand. But when it came time for officials from Rowing New Zealand (RNZ) to select the double sculls team for the 2005 World Junior Rowing Championships, Joe was snubbed. National team selection in rowing is notoriously arbitrary—tainted by politics, prejudice, and personal allegiances. Joe's problem was his size. He just didn't *look* like a champion rower, so the selectors passed him over for an inferior athlete who did. This would not be the last time the sport's gatekeepers judged Joe by his stature rather than by his performance on the water. But if they thought they were discouraging him, they were mistaken.

"People have always told me I'm too small," Joe told *World Rowing* in a 2012 interview. "I like to prove them wrong."

The Marlborough Rowing Association, the local club to which Joe belonged, appealed his exclusion from the junior national team. RNZ's ombudsman (it is telling that the organization needs one) overturned the decision and Joe was permitted to represent his country in Brandenburg, Germany—provided he could come up with $10,000 to cover the cost of the trip. He supplied half of that amount from his own funds and got the balance from a booster. At the Junior World Championships, Joe proved them wrong indeed, earning a bronze medal in the double sculls with his partner (and former Queen Charlotte College teammate) Daniel Karena.

There are four levels of competition in international rowing: the junior category, for rowers 18 and under; the under-23 category; the lightweight category, for male rowers under 160 pounds and female rowers under 130 pounds; and the senior category, for the best rowers of any age. After making a statement in Brandenburg, Joe set his sights on breaking into the senior ranks, perhaps in time to qualify for the 2008 Olympics in Beijing. He never considered settling for the lightweight category, and he quickly silenced anyone who dared to suggest it.

Joe's first opportunity came in the summer of 2007. At that time, Nathan Cohen already had a seat in New Zealand's top double sculls boat with Matthew Trott. But just days before a World Cup event in Amsterdam, Trott fell ill and Joe was called up to replace him. He caught the next flight out of Auckland and reached his destination just hours before the first heat. The thrown-together Cohen-Sullivan pairing won the race easily, qualifying for the semifinals. In their semifinal round, Joe and Nathan moved from second-to-last in the early part of the 2,000-meter race to the runner-up slot at the end to earn a berth in the final, where they finished fifth.

It was a promising result for a pair that had scarcely even trained in the same boat before, let alone competed together. But Matthew Trott soon returned to health and reclaimed his seat in Nathan's boat, relegating Joseph to the under-23 bullpen to await his next chance to race with the big boys. That chance was a long time coming.

One week after Amsterdam, Joe took the gold medal in the single sculls event at the World Rowing U23 Championships, establishing himself as the best rower his age on the planet. This achievement had little effect, however, on RNZ's national team coaches and selectors, who were less impressed by Joe's victories on the water than they were concerned about his inability to lift as much weight or churn out as many watts on an indoor rowing machine as his rivals.

The following year, Joe successfully defended his world title, but the gatekeepers remained wary. Meanwhile, Nathan qualified to represent New Zealand at the Olympic Games in Beijing, where he finished fourth in the double sculls in a pairing with 2000 gold medalist Rob Waddell. Joe was not even among the six finalists considered for selection to that boat.

In 2009, now age 22, Joe won yet another World Rowing U23 Championships gold medal, this time in the double sculls. Even now he was not given a single opportunity to race at the senior level. His coaches justified the rebuff by explaining to him that his size made him "incompatible with other rowers," who struggled to match his rhythm.

This explanation was not entirely baseless. In 2007, a team of Greek and Serbian sports scientists explored the relationship between anthropometric characteristics (such as height and arm length) and stroke characteristics (namely stroke rate and stroke length) in elite junior rowers. They observed that certain body measurements were highly predictive of a rower's natural stroke pattern. In particular, rowers with longer limbs tended to take longer strokes, whereas rowers with shorter limbs chose higher stroke rates. In a summary of their findings published in the *Serbian Journal of Sports Sciences*, the researchers pronounced, "Our data indicated rowers with the same arm length, thigh length and sitting height will probably row with the same stroke rates and lengths. Therefore, rowers with the same arm length, thigh length and sitting height characteristics should constitute a successful rowing crew."

The only New Zealand rower Joseph Sullivan could be paired with whose body measurements were close to his own was Nathan Cohen. In April 2010, at long last, Joe was given a seat in Nathan's boat. This time, however, the two men did not leap straight into competition but instead completed a long stretch of uninterrupted training on Lake Karapiro in search of the synergy that is never perfect when two rowers are first brought together. They discovered immediately that their top-end sprint speed was terrific, and likely to be their ace in the hole in competition. But they struggled to find an efficient rhythm that would carry them through the middle half of a 2,000-meter race and set them up for a winning surge.

"We have had to make quite a few changes individually to get us rowing more together as an efficient combination," Nathan said in an interview with Auckland's 3 News. "It does take time to gel and pick up on each other's rhythm to get the speed back and make the boat go faster."

In rowing, the only thing harder than reaching the top is staying there. One's position is never secure. Joe and Nathan's goal in 2010 was to compete in the world championships, an opportunity they would get if—and only if—they excelled at World Cup events in Munich and Lucerne. They finished seventh out of 12 boats at Munich, but improved to third place in Lucerne. That was good enough to get the nod to represent New Zealand at the world championships, which were held that year on their home "turf" at Lake Karapiro.

Joe and Nathan achieved as much as anyone expected of them merely by qualifying for the final, where they were matched up against the reigning world champions from Germany, the defending silver medalists from France, and a British team that had dominated the 2010 World Cup series. The Kiwis beat them all, stunning the rowing world with an emphatic victory. Languishing in third place at the 500-meter mark, Joe and Nathan sprinted the last 500 meters 2 seconds faster than any other boat, perfecting the rope-a-dope racing style that was becoming their signature.

"I'm still shaking," Nathan told a reporter afterward. "I can't quite believe it. It is a dream come true. You train your whole life for it. I can't quite put it into words."

In their rapture, both men were forgetting something. They had not, in fact, trained their whole lives to win a world championship; they had trained their whole lives to win an Olympic medal, and their victory on Lake Karapiro offered no guarantee that they would.

The next stepping stone on the path toward that greater dream was the 2011 world championships in Bled, Slovenia. Joe and Nathan arrived there having won two of the season's three World Cups. Their latest victory at Lucerne had been yet another come-from-behind masterpiece. Mired in fifth place at 500 meters, they rebounded to win by a length and a half. In Bled, Joe and Nathan burnished their reputation as rowing's heart attack kids, beating out Germany by just six one-hundredths of a second to claim their second world title after having fallen more than 2.5 seconds behind the leaders early in the race.

The New Zealand pair continued to perform well through the Olympic trials in February 2012, which, true to the sport's Orwellian traditions, were maddeningly unstraightforward. "We don't know what trials will involve until the day [they take place]," Joe told a journalist before the process started. "We never know what the selectors are going to do."

The 2012 New Zealand Olympic Rowing Team was announced at a waterside press conference at Lake Ruataniwha on March 4. Joseph Sullivan and Nathan Cohen had done enough, and were named as their country's representatives in the men's double sculls.

"Obviously, we're not the most physically gifted athletes in our field," Nathan told an interviewer at the press conference. "We know we have to sort of out-race our competitors because we're not as strong, probably, not as big. So we try to get the most out of each other. That's what we're going to be building toward: getting ourselves in physical condition where we can go beyond our perceived limits."

A TOTAL OF 26 ROWERS, representing 13 countries, qualified to compete in the men's double sculls at the 2012 Summer Games in London. The smallest of these athletes was Joseph Sullivan. The second-smallest was Nathan Cohen. Collectively, the Kiwis gave up 1 foot in height and 15.4 pounds in weight to their next smallest rivals, the Germans. And together they were 3 feet shorter and more than 72 pounds lighter than the largest pair in the competition, the Lithuanians.

Elite rowers are tall and heavy for a reason. As suggested above, rowers with longer limbs take longer strokes and therefore their boats cover more distance per stroke. Being heavy is not a virtue in itself for rowers, but strength is. Strength comes from muscle, and muscle is heavy.

Not only are bigger people more likely to become elite rowers, but even among elite rowers, greater size tends to predict greater success. In a 2004 study, Australian researchers quantified the relationship between body mass and 2,000-meter race times in a group of 15 world-class male single scullers. The "correlation coefficient" for this relationship was very high: 0.87. A perfect correlation coefficient of 1.00 would have meant that race times improved in exact proportion to increases in weight. Height and performance were closely coupled as well, with a correlation coefficient of 0.86.

In all endurance sports, not just rowing, anthropometry is destiny. A 200-pound man has never won the Tour de France and a 5-foot, 2-inch woman probably will never take the gold medal in the Olympic 200-meter butterfly. Body measurements such as height, weight, and limb length have significant effects on performance in endurance sports, so these variables are highly constrained within the elite population. This is truer now than ever because of how competitive endurance sports have become at the elite level.

The greatest runner in the world in the early 1950s was a Czecho-slovakian man named Emil Zátopek. He had thick quads and beefy shanks. This leg shape is extremely rare among today's elite run-ners—and it's no mystery why. Science has shown that mass below the knee is very costly in terms of its effect on running economy. It's no accident, then, that the best runners in the world today, the Ken-yans and Ethiopians of the Rift Valley area, tend to have exception-ally slender calves.

Yet there are outliers—endurance athletes who reach the highest level of their sport despite having anatomical proportions that are at the margins of the physically allowable for greatness in the mod-ern competitive environment. Consider swimming, a sport that is ruled by rangy athletes with flipper-like feet. (The current women's world record holder in the 400-meter freestyle, Katie Ledecky, stands 5-feet, 11 inches tall and wears size 11 shoes.) Then there's Janet Evans. Standing 5 feet, 5 inches tall and wearing size 6 shoes, Janet is not exactly the prototypical world-class swimmer. Yet during her career Janet won a combined eight Olympic and world championship gold medals (and broke seven world records to boot).

These achievements are particularly astonishing given how free-style races are usually won. Like tall rowers, tall swimmers are able to cover more distance with each stroke. In international competi-tion, the winner of any given freestyle race is usually the athlete who takes the fewest strokes. Janet routinely took the *most* strokes, and won nevertheless. How?

Janet overcame her size disadvantage—or rather, she turned this weakness into a strength—by developing an unorthodox stroke char-acterized by a very high turnover rate and a straight-arm recovery, which became known as the "windmill technique."

This is another example of the workaround effect described in Chapter 5. When athletes reach the highest level of a sport despite having the "wrong body," they do so by means of this effect. Recall that the workaround effect (or this particular version of it) is mediated by neuroplasticity. An athlete who loses physical capacity through injury or some other kind of setback may recover her performance capacity by rewiring her brain in a way that allows her body to do more with less. There is evidence that having the "wrong body" for a sport may stimulate the brain in a similar way. More specifically, an athlete's efforts to keep up with competitors who are better equipped physically for her sport may inspire the athlete to get creative with her movement patterns and make up for physical inferiority with a more efficient technique that generates more speed from equal effort. (The windmilling Janet Evans was indeed one of the most efficient swimmers ever tested.)

In the language of fire walking, becoming more efficient through the workaround effect is like figuring out how to walk lighter on your feet, so that less heat is felt and you can get farther along the bed of hot coals before reaching your maximum tolerance for the pain of intense heat.

Some of the most intriguing evidence for this particular form of the workaround effect comes from running. As in all endurance sports, a strong aerobic capacity is critical to success in running. Yet some runners manage to win at the highest level despite having a low aerobic capacity relative to other elites, and they do so by developing superior running economy. In other words, they make up for the inability to consume as much oxygen as their competitors by finding ways to run faster at any given level of oxygen consumption.

Interestingly, the most economical elite runners never have the highest aerobic capacity, and the runners with the highest aerobic capacity are never the most economical. One of the most economical runners ever tested was a Kenyan male middle-distance specialist who had a personal best time of 3:35 for 1500 meters despite having a pedestrian VO_2max of 63 ml/kg/min (a number that is more typical of a 4:20 1500-meter runner).

A very high aerobic capacity is a kind of physiological crutch that allows runners who are blessed with it to get away with being somewhat inefficient, whereas a lower VO_2max may serve as a constraint that leads to efficiency-boosting workarounds, much like being too big or too small.

Not all athletes whose bodies are imperfectly suited to their sport are able to exploit neuroplasticity to become more creative and efficient with their bodies, however. Real-world evidence indicates that a certain coping skill operates behind successful efforts by athletes to compete with physically superior rivals via the workaround effect. I call this coping skill *bulletin boarding*.

Athletes in team sports often talk of "bulletin board material"—insults, taunts, challenges, and disrespectful words uttered by members of one team about another team and posted in the offended team's locker room for use as motivational fodder—often with good results. Bulletin board material exists in endurance sports too, though it more often takes the form of skepticism concerning the ability of an athlete to achieve his goals. Bulletin boarding as a coping skill emerges when an athlete who is the object of such skepticism uses it as motivation to prove doubters wrong.

This coping skill is essentially a protective reaction against threats to the ego. Neuropsychologists have identified the ventral anterior cingulate cortex and the medial orbitofrontal cortex as two areas of the brain that "light up" when a person's ego has been attacked and he responds not by cowering or playing deaf but instead by rallying in his own defense. This pattern of brain activity is the neurological substrate of bulletin boarding, and bulleting boarding is the salient coping skill of every endurance athlete who achieves greatness despite having the "wrong body" for his or her sport.

As a young swimmer, Janet Evans confronted repeated judgment and discrimination on the basis of her size. It all went onto her internal bulletin board. When Janet was 12 years old, an official at one competition tried to force her to race with the 10-year-olds. She was 4 feet, 10 inches tall and 68 pounds, after all. But her spirit was large. Janet insisted on racing against her peers. The official relented and she won the race.

This same mindset led Janet to develop her windmill technique, the workaround that elevated her to greatness. The superior size of the girls she raced against was an unspoken challenge to Janet's desire to "measure up," a challenge she responded to by finding a different way to get from point A to point B. "I developed [the windmill technique] when I was a kid, and I wanted to get down the pool the fastest," she said in one interview. "I figured the fastest way to get to the other end was to turn my arms over as fast as I could."

Like Janet Evans, Joseph Sullivan and Nathan Cohen loved to prove people wrong. They were aided in their efforts to overcome their size disadvantage by the chip that each carried on his shoulder as a victim of size bias. Each worked around the problem of being smaller by developing a high-cadence sculling style.

Their strokes were far from identical, however. Having found a style that worked for them individually, Joe and Nathan were then required to call upon neuroplasticity to blend those styles and create a team style that was different from every other team's, yet somehow better. In their three years of training and racing together, the undersize teammates discovered how to cancel out each other's weaknesses and combine their strengths. Joe was a better starter and finisher, while Nathan did his best work in the middle section of the race, so they apportioned responsibilities accordingly.

In competition, they quickly learned that no matter how well they meshed, they were unlikely to ever reach the 1,500-meter mark of a 2,000-meter race in the lead. Everything would depend on their strength over the last 500 meters, where their high stroke rate would serve them especially well. For while the ability to take long strokes is generally more important than the ability to stroke rapidly, and while the biggest rowers naturally take the longest strokes, the authors of the Greek-Serbian study described earlier noted that rowers of all sizes tend to shorten and accelerate their strokes when sprinting. "Probably the reason," they explained, "is that a high stroke rate in on-water rowing gives the boat better propulsive efficiency and better velocity because of the more frequent oar blade work in the water." As smaller men with a higher stroke rate, Joe and Nathan were thus at a disadvantage relative to their bigger rivals in the first three-quarters of a race but moved into the catbird's seat during the final push, when everyone was sprinting.

Joe and Nathan were well aware of this advantage. "We are more efficient, which allows us to pick up speed at the end of a race," Nathan said in a pre-Olympic interview. Their rivals understood this too, and in London they would surely try to neutralize the Kiwis' strength by exploiting their weakness, aiming to get so far ahead of them in the first part of the race that nothing short of a miracle would allow them to close the gap before the finish line.

THE NEW ZEALAND OLYMPIC rowing team arrived in England on Monday, July 23, and took up accommodations at Royal Holloway University on the western outskirts of London, close to the Olympic rowing venue at Dorney Lake. Joe and Nathan were in a state of renewed confidence. Their last phase of training before leaving New Zealand in late May for the year's first World Cup in Lucerne, Switzerland, had not gone well. Despite working harder than ever, rowing up to 125 miles per week, they were unaccountably sluggish on the water. The national team selectors openly voiced regret for having named Joe and Nathan to the Olympic squad. Feeling the heat, their coach forced them to change their setup and seat positions in search of a solution.

In Lucerne, things got worse. Joe and Nathan placed dead last, losing even to a lowly Egyptian pair that hadn't qualified for the Olympics. The partners began to snipe at each other, the bond they had forged through countless hours of shared struggle weakened by failure and immense pressure. The New Zealand team moved on from Lucerne to Belgium for one last block of hard pre-Olympic training. Joe and Nathan's struggles continued.

In mid-June, the team travelled to Munich for the next World Cup and their final chance to compete before London. Joe and Nathan were now in a condition approaching panic. Then a discovery was made. Two days before the heats, by pure chance, the rowers noticed a subtle warp in their right oars. It explained everything. Almost invisible to the naked eye, this small misalignment had demoted the world's top-ranked double sculls team to the basement of elite rowing. The problem was quickly fixed and Joe and Nathan easily qualified for the Munich World Cup final, where they finished second to Norway. Their swagger was back.

In England, their first order of business was to get out onto Dorney Lake and familiarize themselves with the course and conditions. Joe and Nathan got their first opportunity on the morning after their arrival, four days before the heats of the men's double sculls. The lake was crowded with crews churning out short, fast sets to sharpen up for racing. The New Zealanders felt fit and ready. Later that day, Joe was even able to laugh about the warped-oar fiasco with a reporter for the *New Zealand Herald*. In another interview, with John Alexander of *The Marlborough Express,* Joe reiterated once more that "getting a good start and not letting the opposition get too far ahead is crucial as far as tactics are concerned."

Conditions on the lake were nearly perfect for Saturday morning's heats. Times would be fast. Joe and Nathan were scheduled to contest the third of three heats against Great Britain (a strong medal favorite), Argentina, and Estonia. Nathan studied the other heats meticulously, as was his habit, while Joe put on a pair of headphones and turned his attention inward. All they needed to do in order to pass on to the semifinals was avoid finishing last. Even so, Joe became so anxious during their warm-up that he threw up between his legs, right onto the boat.

They got a decent start, by their standards, reaching 500 meters in third place, less than a second behind the leading Brits. Nathan sat at the bow, making the calls. Joe sat in the stroke seat, ignoring the other boats and everything else outside of Nathan's calls and his own effort. At 1,000 meters, Argentina had a nominal lead over the Brits, while the Kiwis remained in the third spot, now slightly farther back. With 500 meters to go, Nathan called a surge and their boat accelerated. They passed the fading Argentines and then the Brits to win the heat with a time of 6:11.30, a new Olympic record.

The semifinals took place three days later, in the early afternoon of Tuesday, July 31. Conditions had deteriorated since the heats. The sky was half-clouded, the air cool, and the water surface rippled. Most competitors wore a base layer under their unisuits. Joe and Nathan did not. They drew the tougher of the two semifinals, facing Argentina, Germany, Italy, Australia, and Ukraine. The New Zealanders had to finish among the top three to reach the final.

The starting horn sounded and Argentina shot to the front. The field stayed tightly bunched for the first 250 meters, but then gaps emerged. Joe and Nathan fell back to fifth place with only an overmatched Ukrainian pair behind them. At 500 meters, the Kiwis were 1.7 seconds off the lead. From there, Argentina's Ariel Suarez and Cristian Rosso continued to broaden their advantage. Joe and Nathan overtook the Italians to move into fourth place, but at the halfway mark of the race they were still 3 seconds behind the leaders and a full second away from the last qualifying position for the final.

Nathan was calm. He barked two syllables that instructed Joe to maintain a steady effort as the race entered its second half. But the inspired Argentine team maintained their faster tempo and added another second to their gap on the rest of the field. Unless Suarez and Rosso suffered a major late-race collapse, Joe and Nathan now had almost no hope of winning the race regardless of how strongly they closed.

At last, the Kiwis began their trademark surge. Inch by painful inch they reeled in the Italians and then the Germans. Soon there was nothing but empty water between Joe and Nathan's boat and the Argentines. Rosso stole several looks over his right shoulder at the fast-gaining New Zealand boat. His inattention caused his right oar to nick the water during the recovery between strokes, breaking the boat's momentum. If it had been a 2,020-meter race, that mistake would have cost his team victory. As it was, Suarez and Rosso beat Joe and Nathan by 0.39 seconds.

The Southlanders had not rowed their best race, but they were in the final, and in a sport in which a tiny warp in the blade of an oar can ruin the dreams of a lifetime, this success was not to be taken for granted. Indeed, the defending Olympic champions from Australia and the medal-favored Germans finished behind Joe and Nathan and the Italian team in fourth and fifth places, earning early trips home. In the other semifinal, Slovenia, Lithuania, and Great Britain made it through.

Dorney Lake—rechristened Eton Dorney for the 2012 Summer Games—is a man-made body of water that was designed exclusively for rowing. It is shaped as a perfect rectangle of 2.2 kilometers' length. Permanent grandstands are located at the midpoint and near the finish area, but for the Olympics additional temporary seating was erected so that a total of 30,000 fans could be accommodated. At 11:50 in the morning on Thursday, August 2, 2012, every seat was occupied.

"Ladies and gentlemen, the Olympic final of the men's double sculls," boomed a sonorous male voice with a high-born English accent over the PA system.

A boisterous cheer went up from the 30,000. The Brits are proud of their rowing tradition and had high hopes for their representatives in this race.

The sky was almost entirely clouded over, but the air was calm. Six spear-shaped boats floated motionlessly with their sterns just touching the starting docks. A race official lay prostrate at each station, holding the vessel in place. The New Zealand scull occupied lane 5, with the Italians on one side and the Argentines on the other.

The announcer introduced the 12 athletes, drawing another round of cheers when he named the host country's entrants, Bill Lucas and Sam Townsend. Joe and Nathan's faces remained emotionless behind their dark sunglasses as their names were spoken.

As in their semifinal race, they were the only rowers without a base layer under their unisuits.

An electronic horn signaled "get set." One second later, the boats were released. All six crews went out extremely hard, five of them intent on leaving the Kiwis behind, the Kiwis equally determined not to let that happen. Joe and Nathan turned over their oars at a steady rate of 38 strokes per minute, visibly faster than the other competitors, but after 200 meters they began to slip behind.

A small cadre of VIPs on cruiser bikes pedaled alongside the boats on a narrow path tracing the edge of the lake. Keeping up with the action required that they maintain a steady speed of close to 12 mph, a challenge for some.

Drawing strength from the crowd support, Lucas and Townsend nosed their way into a slim lead. It was short-lived, however, as the Slovenians were better able to sustain the pace of the torrid start. They passed 500 meters at 1:33.87 on the race clock, eight-tenths of a second ahead of the Brits. Joe and Nathan were in last place, 2 seconds off the lead and 1 second outside of the bronze medal position, which was held by Lithuania. Focused solely on his own performance and on Nathan's voice, Joe was oblivious to their circumstances. Nathan knew they were behind but not by how much.

The Slovenians pulled hard to widen the gap. In the bow seat, Luka Spik grimaced with each dig, like a powerlifter maxing out on the bench press. Between strokes, he occasionally glanced to the left, toward the New Zealand boat, which sat a length and a half behind his own.

Not far enough.

The Slovenians pulled harder still and at 750 meters they had a full boat length on their next closest pursuers and nearly two lengths on Joe and Nathan.

"Work to do for Cohen and Sullivan in Lane 5," observed BBC television announcer Garry Herbert.

The six boats separated into three distinct echelons with Slovenia far in front, Great Britain and Argentina battling for second position, and New Zealand bringing up the rear with Italy and Lithuania. Luka Spik and Iztok Cop passed the halfway point of the race at 3:13.09, having enlarged their gap on the Kiwis by another four-tenths of a second over the last 500 meters.

Nathan's heart rate was pegged at 200 beats per minute, Joe's at 202. Both men were in a state of extreme oxygen debt, sucking up as much air as their bodies could absorb but not enough to meet the demands of their straining muscles. Their shoulders and thighs were on fire. A feeling akin to suffocation was concentrated in their lungs and windpipes.

Nathan could see the Lithuanian boat slipping back toward them in lane 2, and the stern of the Argentine boat was just visible in lane 4. But where were the others? Nathan reminded himself to stay calm. *We've been here before,* he thought.

The boats came upon the first major spectator area on the right-hand side of the lake and a riotous din enveloped them. Even Joe, usually too focused to notice, heard the ruckus and soaked up its energy. As hard as he and Nathan were working, and as much as their consciousness was dominated by their suffering, a small compartment in the minds of both men remained passive, waiting. Joe waited for Nathan to call the final surge. Nathan waited for his instincts to tell him when to make that call. Their closing sprint was always unleashed somewhere near the 1,500-meter mark, but numbers never determined exactly where. Nathan instead trusted a deep bodily wisdom cultivated through experience.

But the Italian team of Alessio Sartori and Romano Battisti had a surprise in store. Just past the midpoint of the race, their boat scudded ahead as if a sudden wind gust had punched an invisible sail. Sartori's cheeks flapped like a bellows as his lungs emptied at the end of each pull, while Battisti's face was frozen with his teeth bared. They rocketed into the lead, reaching the flags that marked 500 meters to go more than 2.5 seconds in front of the Kiwis.

Joe and Nathan entered the last quarter of the race in fourth place, having drawn even with a slowing British boat. Nathan finally

shouted the command to surge. The abrupt uptick in effort was signaled by a deeper swaying of their backs at the end of each pull.
Their perfectly synchronized movements were fusions of raw power
and graceful efficiency, evoking a thoroughbred's gallop. The seg-
ments of their bodies and the phases of their stroke blended into
something jointless and rolling, like spooling fabric.

Nathan could feel the redoubled power coming from the better
sprinter, Joe, seated behind him. He fought urgently to match his
partner's superior strength, which threatened to overwhelm him and
their perfect synchrony. Both men were in tremendous pain, but they
continued to stoke the source of that pain—their effort—as though it
were the most heavenly of pleasures.

The boats came upon the most populated area of the course. The
crowd noise rose in a deafening crescendo, taking on a hysterical
tone as the spectators noted the New Zealanders' last-gasp charge
toward the front. With 300 meters left in the race, the prow of their
boat was even with the stern of the Slovenians' second-place scull.

"Surprisingly, Cohen and Sullivan are finding it hard," remarked
the BBC's Herbert, a note of sympathy in the former Olympic rower's
voice.

Joe and Nathan lifted their tempo again. They began to slide up
on Slovenia and the leading Italians, but ever so slowly, and they
were running out of water.

Screams became shrieks as the Kiwis approached the Italians
and the Italians approached the finish line. At 1,780 meters, Joe and
Nathan pulled into the silver-medal slot. Seconds later, Sartori and
Battisti began to fail. Their surge at 1,000 meters had been a gamble.
If not for Joe and Nathan, it would have paid in gold.

Aware of the weakening of the pair to his left, Nathan called for
one final push. The New Zealanders were now taking 43 strokes per
minute, a crucial 3 strokes more than Sartori and Battisti could manage. Joe and Nathan yanked the oars with such ballistic force that
their rear ends threatened to leave their seats at the start of each
ferocious pull. Fifteen strokes propelled them from a half-length

behind the Italians into the slimmest of leads. Nathan swiveled his head left and right, like a fugitive preparing to dash across a busy freeway, confirming their position. His scowl became a toothy grin.

The New Zealand boat crossed the finish line at 6:31.67, just over 1 second ahead of the Italians. Joe and Nathan had rowed the last 500 meters in 1:33.90. Incredibly, this split matched the fastest time of any team in the *first* 500 meters of the race and was nearly 4 seconds faster than the next-best time for the closing quarter of the contest.

Joe did not know he was an Olympic gold medalist until the results were flashed on a giant video screen. Seeing them, he stood up to his full height of 71 inches and raised his T-Rex arms overhead. A dream of 16 years had come true. Nathan, still seated, spread his spent arms wide, chest heaving.

At the medal ceremony that followed, the medalists stood in a neat row, the winners at the center. Normally, athletes are arranged on a three-tiered platform with the Olympic champions at the highest level, so that they stand above the other honorees regardless of their relative size. But there was no platform available for this ceremony. It was just as well. Tiers would have disguised just how special the victory was, and the lesson it offered to any athlete who was ever told he had the "wrong body" for his sport.

CHAPTER EIGHT

THE ANSWER IS INSIDE YOU

A BUZZING CROWD OF sun-toasted spectators pressed against sagging blue safety fencing on either side of Ali'i Drive, challenging the boundary between grandstand and racecourse. The dense gauntlet of sweaty humanity terminated at a makeshift arch spanning the width of the simmering street. At the center of the arch hung a large digital clock, which briefly displayed a nice round figure—9:00:00—before moving on. Nine triathletes had passed under the clock so far, most recently a little-known Japanese pro named Hideya Miyazuka. The seething multitude now waited restlessly to see who would round out the top 10 finishers of the 1988 Ironman World Championship.

The serpentine shape of Ali'i Drive and the tight clustering of shops and restaurants in the village of Kailua-Kona kept approaching athletes out of sight until they were quite close, heightening the anticipatory drama. Presently a runner came around the final bend and into view. He wore a Speedo and matching singlet, his race number (10) identifying him as Pauli Kiuru, a rising star of the sport who hailed from Finland. The crowd erupted in a rapturous ovation, but it wasn't for Kiuru. It was for the runner right behind him, who wore an aqua-and-magenta one-piece racing suit, multiple earrings, and shoulder-length hair gathered in an elastic hair tie.

That runner was Paula Newby-Fraser, and she crossed the finish line at 9:01:01, only 12 seconds behind Kiuru. The 26-year-old Zimbabwean expat had broken the women's course record by a jaw-dropping 34 minutes and 24 seconds and had come within a hair of finishing 10th overall in the world's most competitive triathlon. Among the many elite male racers whom Paula had beaten was future Ironman champion Greg Welch, who finished 5 minutes behind her.

Paula was no upstart. She had placed third in her first Ironman World Championship in 1985. The following year, she won the race. By the start of the 1988 season, Paula was considered one of the top three female triathletes in the world. But nothing she had done previously had prepared the sport for her stunning performance at the 1988 Ironman, where she established herself as one of the best triathletes on earth, *period*. Her winning time would have made her the outright winner of every Ironman World Championship held through 1983, and the mark would not be surpassed by any other woman for 20 years.

Having reached the pinnacle, Paula built a throne there. She won her third Ironman title in 1989, finished second to arch-nemesis Erin Baker in 1990, and then went on a tear. In 1991, Paula beat Baker by 17 minutes. The following October, she lowered her course record to 8:55:28 and won the race by 26 minutes. In 1993, she put in another sub-nine-hour performance, and in 1994 she won her fourth consecutive Ironman title, her seventh overall.

The more Paula achieved, however, the less satisfied she became. The burning amazement that her dominating victories had once inspired in triathlon fans and journalists had given way to coolly admiring nods of reconfirmed expectations. They called her the Queen of Kona, a title that, although appreciative in spirit, made Paula feel somewhat taken for granted, as though her winning Ironman were not an achievement anymore but a birthright. Even the people close to her looked at Paula as some kind of invincible Cyborg.

"Friends said, 'I don't even need to wish you good luck,'" Paula recalled in a 2010 interview. "'It won't be any trouble for you to go and win.'"

They thought it was easy. But it wasn't. In 1993, an ankle injury severely restricted Paula's run training. It took everything she had to win that year's Ironman, but her grit attracted little praise; the credit went instead to her matchless talent—to the dumb luck of having won the genetic lottery at conception.

After the 1994 Ironman, Paula decided to make a change. She yearned to blow people's minds as she had six years earlier. She wanted to break her Ironman course record—demolish it, actually—and once again challenge the top men in the sport, who had gotten a lot faster since 1988. But to achieve these goals, Paula decided, she could not just train the way she always had. She would have to try something different.

Before she'd left Africa to start her career as a professional triathlete in the United States, Paula had come under the influence of Tim Noakes, a renowned exercise scientist at the University of Cape Town. Noakes had advised her to take a minimalist approach to training, doing the least amount of work necessary to win. Paula had heeded that advice throughout her career, and it had served her well.

Her less-is-more training regimen put her out of step with most professional triathletes of her era, who were locked in an arms race of ever-increasing training loads. In 1984, two-time Ironman champion Scott Tinley told *Triathlete*, "It seems every year the ante goes up. A few years ago, we did 300 miles [a week] on the bike and that was plenty. Last year it was 400. Now it seems like 500 is the magic mark. Each of us feels we have to do more than the next guy. I'm not so sure that's the right way to train, to improve. No one really knows."

When she started training for the 1995 season, Paula abandoned the methods that had worked for her in the past and joined the arms race. "I thought if I wanted to race like the men, I was going to train like the men," she told *Inside Triathlon*. She had also decided that her next Ironman World Championship would be her last, so why not pour everything she had left into it?

Paula's winning formula in previous years had consisted of 11,000 to 13,000 yards of swimming, 200 to 250 miles of cycling, and 50 to 55 miles of running per week. In 1995, she increased her cycling volume to 375 to 425 miles per week and bumped up her running volume by 20 percent. She completed individual rides as long as 150 miles, not alone or with athletes of equal ability but with Mark Allen, who had won Ironman five times himself and whose men's course record of 8:07:45 was a full 48 minutes faster than Paula's best time. Although she rode in Allen's slipstream, these rides were still far more challenging for her than they were for him.

The first real test of the effectiveness of Paula's new program came at the 1995 Wildflower Triathlon, a half-Ironman event, where she faced three-time and defending champion and course record-holder Donna Peters. Paula won the duel and then went on to record commanding victories at Ironman Lanzarote and Ironman Germany. Once again, the press predicted a cakewalk for Paula in Kona, but this time the premature coronation did not bother her. The pundits of the sport thought she could no longer surprise them. They had another think coming.

A couple of days before the race, Paula sat down for an on-camera interview with NBC Sports. "I've broken all the rules of training this year," she said with a sly smile. "So either I'm going to go out there and feel great or I've put myself so far down a hole I'm never coming out again."

On race morning, Paula arrived at the start area at Dig-Me Beach before dawn, dressed in an oversize white painter's cap and a loose, sleeveless linen top. An NBC Sports camera rolled film as a young female volunteer penned the number 33—Paula's race number, but coincidentally also her age—on her upper arms. Her smile showed no trace of nervousness.

Paula then made a short walk over to a VIP area on a cement pier adjoining the beach. Her training buddy, Mark Allen, was already there. The two legends went through their last-minute pre-race preparations together but mostly in silence, ignoring the brace of photographers snapping photos from the other side of the fence. Paula removed her street clothes, revealing a black two-piece racing suit underneath. She stretched a yellow swim cap emblazoned with the Gatorade brand name across her scalp and hitched a pair of goggles over the cap.

The sun rose. Paula left the pier and entered the 84-degree water of Kailua Bay to loosen up. At seven o'clock, a cannon boomed and the race started. Paula stroked her way into her usual spot among the second-tier male pros and the top male amateurs. The swimmer closest to her right flank, however, wore a yellow swim cap like hers, denoting another female pro. Its wearer was Karen Smyers, the runner-up to Paula in last year's Ironman and the reigning world champion at the shorter Olympic distance. Like Paula, Smyers owed her success to a minimalist approach to training. Unlike Paula, she had not abandoned the formula that had always worked for her.

Smyers's plan was to shadow Paula through the 2.4-mile swim leg of the race, follow Paula's rear wheel from the beginning to the end of the 112-mile bike leg, and stay glued to her hip through the early miles of the 26.2-mile run before attempting to drop her. At the halfway point of the swim, marked by a collection of party boats crammed with journalists, race officials, and special guests, Smyers remained within touching distance of her rival. As they approached shore, Paula lifted her pace and Smyers fell into her wake to gather herself for a final push. In the closing meters, Smyers pulled wide and sprinted past the seven-time Ironman champion to reach the exit ramp just ahead of her. Paula scrambled to her feet faster, though, and overtook Smyers on the ramp.

The rivals grabbed number-marked bags of cycling gear off crowded metal racks and hastened into the women's changing tent. Smyers exited first and received her bike from a race official. But she struggled to get her feet strapped into her cycling shoes, which she had pre-clipped onto the pedals, and Paula, who had put on her shoes before mounting the bike, passed her again at the transition area exit. The two women had exchanged the lead four times in the span of 3 minutes.

Standing on her pedals, Paula charged up a steep, three-quarter-mile hill leading away from the shore and then made a left turn onto the Queen Kaahumanu Highway, which would lead her into the searing lava fields of the Kona coast. She settled her forearms into the aerobars, put her head down, and began picking off the 51 athletes who had finished the swim in front of her. Less than 3 miles into the bike course, Paula passed Germany's Ute Mückel, one of only two female racers who had swum faster than her. A couple of miles later, she passed the other—fellow San Diego resident Wendy Ingraham—and became the women's race leader.

Karen Smyers was close behind, but not for long. As they left the protected topography of Kailua Village and entered the exposed lava fields, the riders were walloped from the right side by a vicious crosswind. The dreaded Mumuku winds are a factor in almost every Ironman World Championship, but on this day they were unusually fierce, gusting up to 60 miles per hour. Smyers suddenly felt as though her bike had gained 20 pounds, but Paula seemed impervious. The effort it took to stay on the defending champion's back wheel was too great; Smyers was forced to let her go.

Paula was not, in fact, impervious to the wind. She knew it would wreck her hopes of setting a new course record. But it would not stop her from winning the race by a record margin, so she focused on gaining as much time as possible on Smyers and her other pursuers. With each passing mile, Paula increased her lead by 10 to 12 seconds. By the time Smyers reached the Waikoloa Beach Resort at 24 miles, Paula had receded to a dot on the ribbon of asphalt ahead. When Paula turned left off the Queen K onto Route 270 some 10 miles farther down the highway, she had long since vanished from Smyers's sight.

Paula now embarked upon a lengthy, rolling climb toward the turnaround point in the tucked-away little town of Hawi. She fought gravity aggressively, her rear end out of the saddle once again, her unblinking gaze piercing through a light rain that had begun to fall in this lush nook of the island. At Hawi, a giant inflated Gatorade bottle marked the turnaround point. Paula was welcomed with warm cheers befitting Ironman royalty. She made a brisk loop around the oversized marketing prop and started the return trip to Kailua. Her lead over Smyers had grown to 5 minutes. Mückel and Ingraham were even farther back.

When Paula reached the outskirts of Kailua at 99 miles, her lead had doubled to 10 minutes. But she did not relent, leaving the saddle yet again to attack the last hill on the Queen K before swooping back down to the coast. The home stretch of the bike course was a south- ward push along Ali'i Drive to the Kona Surf Hotel, located 7 miles south of Dig-Me Beach. Paula padded her lead by another 90 seconds between these points to start the marathon 11:45 ahead of Smyers.

Paula's boyfriend, Paul Huddle, was covering the race for local television. When the magnitude of Paula's advantage was reported to him, he told viewers, "In the Ironman, it's never over till it's over. But with a lead like that, with Paula and her history, it's over."

The day had grown hot—90 degrees—and humid too. When she reached the first drink station on the run course, Paula, now wearing a cap stamped with the Mrs. T's Pierogies brand logo—grabbed every cup offered to her, as though intending to hoard them. But they were put to immediate use, the cool water going over her head and under the bib of her racing suit and the Gatorade down her throat.

Calm and calculating, Paula chose a conservative pace of 7:20 per mile, staying well within her perceived limit, out of respect for the heat. She had built a huge cushion—there was no reason not to rest on it in these conditions. More than a mile and a half behind her, at the Kona Surf Hotel, Karen Smyers did not enjoy the same freedom to adjust her effort to the weather. To have any chance of winning, she had to take some risks, and she did, tearing out of the bike-run transition at a 3-hour marathon pace.

A Princeton graduate, Smyers was good at math. She knew she would have to outrun Paula by almost 30 seconds per mile to overtake her before the finish line. When Smyers hit the 6-mile mark at the outskirts of Kailua Village on Ali'i Drive, she was 8 minutes behind Paula, having gained 37 seconds per mile. If she continued to close in at this rate, she would overtake the seven-time champion at 20 miles. But when she entered the lava fields, where the temperature at the surface of the Queen K Highway was now 112 degrees, Smyers was forced to slow down. Even so, she continued to gain ground. At 16 miles, Paula's lead had come down to 5:25. The way things were going, the homestretch on Ali'i Drive was going to be interesting.

Just when Smyers was beginning to fear that she would run out of road before she could catch her prey, she got word that Paula was walking. And indeed she was. Despite the precautions she'd taken, Paula had begun to overheat, her body begging her to quit. Never in 10 previous Ironmans had she felt so spent so far from the finish line. But within moments she had resumed running, her desire to win trumping her misery.

With 4 miles to go, Paula's lead was only 3 minutes. Her thoughts had become scrambled to the point where she could no longer figure out how fast she needed to go to have a realistic chance of keeping Smyers behind her until the finish. It was all she could do to keep from walking again. The next mile felt like a marathon in itself.

Not a moment too soon, Paula spied the oasis of an aid station on her left. She abruptly veered off the road and reached into a barrel containing sponges soaking in cold water. She grabbed as many as she could and squeezed them over her head as she darted back onto the Queen K. Head down, Paula ran smack into a burly male volunteer who was handing sponges to runners coming from the opposite direction. She caromed violently backward, landing hard on her bottom and rocking all the way back to her shoulders, curled into a fetal ball. The volunteer began to extend a helping hand toward her but then withdrew it, remembering he was not allowed to provide such assistance.

It wasn't needed. Paula had already sprung to her feet, the violence of the prior moment unremembered. Her addled mind had entered a kind of dream state in which even the most bizarre and terrible happenings failed to surprise.

With less than 1 mile to go and less than 2 minutes of her lead intact, Paula stopped short and doubled over, arms dangling limply toward the seething asphalt, either stretching her hamstrings or perhaps making a gesture of confused surrender (or both). Just as suddenly, however, she righted herself and wheeled around, looking for Smyers.

It was a bizarre image: the leader and seven-time winner of the Ironman World Championship standing at a dead stop at the 140-mile mark of the 140.6-mile race, facing the direction she'd come. The alarmed driver of a motorcycle bearing an NBC cameraman urged Paula to continue.

"You got it!" he said.

"I got it?" she asked, pronouncing the words with a boozy inexactness.

She began to shuffle.

Paula was within sight of the last turn of the race when she pulled up once more, staggering as though she'd taken a stiff jab to the chin. Smyers was now right behind her. Paula raised her arms skyward as though beseeching the wondering throng of spectators lining the course to tell her what the hell was happening to her. At this moment, Smyers made the pass, placing a steadying hand on Paula's back in the moment of eclipse.

As Smyers dashed away toward her first Ironman victory, Paula took a few wobbly steps, then bent over with her hands on her knees.

"Come on, Paula!" the spectators shouted. "You can do it!"

Again she tried to walk. The crowd struck up a thundering chant of "Paul-a! Paul-a! Paul-a!"

It fell on deaf ears. Paula sat down on the curb and robotically removed her shoes and socks. A bottle of Gatorade was handed to her and she guzzled it.

Paula was soon encircled by race officials, medical personnel, and fans. Many were still urging her to get up and finish.

"Just wait!" she said, irritably.

Paula then slumped off the curb onto the road and lay flat on her back, arms spread wide.

Paul Huddle came sprinting from the temporary television studio that had been constructed at the finish area, where, three hours earlier, he had declared the inevitability of his girlfriend's victory. When he saw her now, his eyes widened in shock.

"Let's get an ambulance right now!" he shouted, his voice cracking. "Nine-one-one! Who's got a cellular?"

A woman standing close by produced one and handed it to Paul.

"I think I'm going to die," Paula said as Paul struggled to make the zucchini-size device function.

By this time, the crowd around Paula was blocking almost the entire road. The race marshals at the scene made no effort to restore the integrity of the course boundaries. Their attention was completely absorbed in the spectacle of the greatest female triathlete of all time lying supine on the pavement almost within view of the Ironman finish line. Becoming more lucid, Paula kept up a steady dialogue with the medical personnel, and at one point she let them know that she had decided to finish the race after all—but she wouldn't be rushed.

"I have all day," she said.

Twenty minutes after she sat down, Paula stood up. The crowd applauded and Paula took a small, ironic bow.

She began to walk, still barefoot. The crowd walked with her down the middle of the street, blocking the progress of the few racers coming through. Paula was 15 feet away from the finish line when Fernanda Keller blasted by to claim third place. (Isabelle Mouthon had long since taken the runner-up spot.) Karen Smyers was among the first people to greet Paula behind the finish line. They embraced, Paula smiling wanly, Smyers close to tears.

IN THE IMMEDIATE AFTERMATH of her meltdown at the 1995 Ironman, Paula Newby-Fraser blamed the incident on a late-race nutritional blunder. With Smyers closing in on her, she told interviewers, she had panicked and rushed through aid stations without drinking enough. But later she would admit that she had lost the race before it even started.

"I got greedy," she told one reporter. "It's an old flaw in human nature: If you have success, you want more. So you think more is better instead of looking back at what has worked for you. I had a style. I knew what worked for me. But all around me, everyone was doing something else. That new philosophy for 1995 paid off on the bike. But then it bit me at the end when I collapsed."

Endurance athletes learn early on to equate hard work with improvement. It's a universal experience: The first bit of hard work a beginner does yields better performance, and a little more hard work produces even better results. But there is a limit to how much hard work an athlete can benefit from. Many lose perspective and exceed their limit. They come to see hard work as the only path to improvement. If they lose a race or fall short of a goal, they respond by working harder. If they begin to feel lousy in their training as a result of working too hard, they work even harder. Hard work becomes a kind of security blanket, a reflexive answer to every question, every doubt.

The problem with drawing an absolute equivalence between hard work and improvement is that it encourages athletes to ignore how they feel. According to the psychobiological model of endurance performance, remember, an athlete cannot improve except by changing her relationship with perceived effort. Training yields improvement by reducing the amount of effort an athlete experiences at any given speed. When an athlete's training is on track, therefore, she should find that she is able to go faster and faster at the same level of perceived effort. Inevitably, there will be days when the athlete feels lousy and even brief periods of challenging training when everything feels hard, but the overall trend should be toward less effort at the same pace. A trend in the opposite direction indicates that the athlete is training too hard and becoming chronically fatigued. If the athlete ignores this warning and refuses to reduce her training load, her competitive performance will suffer.

In a 2002 study published in the *Journal of Applied Physiology*, Asker Jeukendrup of England's Birmingham University put a group of cyclists through six weeks of varied training. During the first two weeks the athletes trained at their normal level. In week three, they were subjected to a massive increase in training load that continued through week four. At the end of that fourth week, the cyclists' perceived effort at a power output of 200 watts (a relatively low intensity for these individuals) was 8.9 percent higher than it had been three weeks earlier, indicating severe fatigue. Not surprisingly, their time trial performance was down 6.5 percent over the same span.

Any athlete who was silly enough to attempt such an abrupt increase in training load on her own could use the spike in perceived effort that ensued to catch her mistake and then give her body a chance to recover. This was shown in the third part of Jeukendrup's study, in which two weeks of reduced training caused perceived effort at 200 watts to drop to a level 9.5 percent lower than it had been after week one.

In the real world, athletes seldom double their training load from one week to the next, but they do routinely train a little too hard and ignore patterns of rising perceived effort even in low-intensity workouts. Each athlete has her own optimal training formula that is defined by individual physiological limits. Getting the most out of the training process requires that these personal limits be respected. An athlete gets herself into trouble when, instead of listening to her body and its intuitions, she begins to worry about what her competitors are doing and tries to "outwork" them. The answers to the most pressing questions that athletes face in their day-to-day quest for improvement ("Should I push? Should I back off?") lie within them.

A coach may either help or hinder this train-by-feel approach— hinder it by forcing a one-size-fits-all methodology on every athlete, or help it by encouraging athletes to share how they feel and by saving athletes from themselves when they are tempted to do too much.

But even the best coach cannot completely take the place of an athlete's gut instincts.

Bernard Lagat is a good example. He began his running career in his native Kenya, where nearly all promising young runners are subjected to severe, unindividuated training that causes large numbers of them to burn out quickly (a system that undermines to some degree the benefits of group training discussed in the next chapter). But instead of putting himself through this meat grinder Bernard chose to emigrate, attending the University of Washington, where he was coached by James Li, who shared Tim Noakes's philosophy of doing the least amount of training that sufficed for goal attainment. Li's measured program delivered three NCAA Championship titles to Bernard in his final year as a Husky.

After graduating, Bernard surprised many by staying with Li and continuing to train rather gently by elite standards. Unlike most of his peers, he ran just once a day, and every fall he took a five-week break from training. This balanced formula resulted in a remarkably extensive record of achievement that included 11 world championship medals between 2001 and 2014, and Olympic medals in 2000 and 2004. Bernard improved year after year without training harder, recording a career-best 12:53.60 for 5000 meters at age 36 and three years later becoming the oldest runner to win a world championship medal in a distance event, taking silver in the 3000-meter indoors.

In a 2011 interview for Flotrack, Bernard credited his prolonged greatness to moderation in training. "My coach always tells me, 'We do not need to do unnecessary mileage,'" he said. "'We do only the mileage that is going to benefit you.' My body reacts so well to that kind of training. I feel strong the entire way. At the end of the season, I feel, 'I can still do this, I can still run,' because I did not burn myself out."

How do athletes like Bernard Lagat manage to avoid the trap of the "hard work security blanket" while others, such as Paula Newby-Fraser, get suffocated by it? Research by Michael Mahoney of the University of California and other psychologists has shown that certain personality (or coping) traits are more common in athletes who allow themselves to become overtrained. One of these traits, perhaps not surprisingly, is compulsiveness; the other is perfectionism.

Psychologists distinguish two types of perfectionism: adaptive and maladaptive. Adaptive perfectionism is a never-satisfied mindset that can have a positive influence on performance. Maladaptive perfectionism, on the other hand, often leads athletes to engage in self-destructive behaviors such as overtraining. This variety of perfectionism is known to be associated with low self-esteem and insecurity. Athletes who harbor a general feeling that they are never good enough are prone to overtrain in their unending quest to prove their worth. Confident athletes tend to be much more able to shape their training on the basis of rational internal observation.

Bernard Lagat and Paula Newby-Fraser both conform to this pattern. Bernard, as anyone who has met him will attest, radiates self-assuredness. Paula, however, has battled insecurity throughout her life. A lack of self-confidence fed into her disastrous 1995 training experiment, and she knew it.

"Parents and schooling turned me into a total archetypal over-achiever," she said in a 2010 interview for slowtwitch.com. "I came from a totally different culture. Back home in South African schools, every flaw was exposed. You were held to such a high standard. My mother was a very accomplished person and I was always filled with insecurity. I didn't think I was good enough. I always felt like I could not live up to my parental influence. If I did well, I thought, 'Shoot, I have to do it again.' I do not think my success [in triathlon] was a fluke. I was not a one-off. But a little voice kept insisting that maybe I was."

The coping skill that is required to avoid overtraining is self-trust. An athlete must base her decisions on whether to push or back off on the messages that she receives from her own body rather than on what other athletes are doing or on a generalized fear of resting. This can be difficult for athletes who are lacking in the coping trait of self-assuredness, but understanding the psychobiological dynamics of overtraining—its true cause and cure—makes it easier. If Paula

Newby-Fraser was to walk away from the sport of triathlon on top, she would have to draw the right lesson from the lowest moment of her career and start trusting herself.

PAULA WANTED TO GET as far away from triathlon as she could after the 1995 Ironman. That meant getting far away from San Diego, her adopted home and the center of the triathlon universe. A decade earlier, Paula had spent a year in London, and she remembered it fondly. She decided to return. She rented an apartment in the city and spent a month riding the underground, attending the theater and the ballet, and neglecting her training.

The time alone—and away from her usual routine—gave Paula space to reflect, and reflection brought her heart and mind to a new place. London did not cure Paula of insecurity (she says she still struggles with the issue to this day), but it did grant her enough self-insight to know what her next step should be—*what felt right*. Paula realized how lucky she was to have a job as a professional triathlete, a rare and fleeting opportunity that she wasn't quite ready to give up. But no longer would she race to impress others or allow insecurity to influence her training.

At the beginning of 1996, Paula announced that she would go back to Kona, but with "no expectations." She dusted off her old, minimalist training methods and found a more appropriate daily training partner in her friend Heather Fuhr. The young Canadian pro was a weaker cyclist than Paula, but instead of forcing Fuhr to ride at her tempo, Paula slowed down. In return, Fuhr, the stronger runner, held back for Paula when they ran together.

These changes were complemented by a deepening of Paula's long-standing involvement in Buddhist practices. While she did not engage in daily meditation sessions, she read Zen literature and engaged in nonjudgmental self-observation during solitary activities such as gardening. She was beginning to see that her development as an athlete was tightly bound to her personal growth.

"Obviously, I am not ready to sit still and contemplate some of the big issues in my life," Paula told a writer for the Buddhist magazine *Tricycle*. "I sit for short periods and deal with the more external things, but there are other issues that require deeper work."

Through her spiritual explorations, she was becoming more centered in herself and less reactive to external judgments and expectations, an evolution that she was certain was helping her as a human being and that she hoped would help her as an athlete also.

While the steps Paula took at this point may have been small ones, her public statements demonstrated a growing self-awareness and self-acceptance. In Hawaii, she sat down in front of a video camera for a pre-race interview to be shown during NBC's coverage of the 1996 Ironman World Championship. Her tone was strikingly different from the year before. "I'd like to think I'm a little wiser and just a little softer towards my sport," she said. "I don't feel I come at it in such a hard way. You know, 'I have to go sub-9 hours. I'm here to set course records. I'm here to dominate.' It's okay not to win."

Sunrise on race morning revealed whitecaps on Kailua Bay. When the starting cannon thundered, more than 1,400 racers hurled themselves into choppier waters than Ironman had ever seen. Smyers was back to defend her title, and she handled the rough seas better than Paula, who reached the boats marking the turnaround point of the swim course more than 30 seconds behind her rival. By the end of the swim, the gap had swelled to 1 minute and 19 seconds.

In the transition area, Paula strapped on a helmet decorated with an American flag graphic, a tribute to her new status as a U.S. citizen. She moved without hurry despite having been apprised of her usurper's lead. Paula had gone less than 10 miles on her Felt B2 when a race official flagged her for following a male racer too closely and ordered her to dismount before continuing the race. Paula would have to sit for an additional 3 minutes inside a penalty box at the bike-run transition. She shrugged off the setback and kept going.

At 20 miles, Smyers took over the race lead. After turning around in Hawi, she met Paula head-on and was delighted—and more than a little surprised—to discover that her 79-second advantage at the start of the bike leg had grown slightly.

Paula had been holding back, however, and on the return trip to Kailua she began to push. As she approached the 70-mile mark, Smyers heard a helicopter moving ever closer from the rear and knew Paula was coming. The Queen of Kona sped up as she made the pass in a bid to demoralize Smyers, but Smyers knew the game and wasn't fazed.

When Paula wheeled into the Kona Surf Hotel parking lot, she handed her bike to a race official and calmly walked into the penalty box, where she drank Gatorade, stretched, and even answered a few questions for an NBC Sports reporter. While Paula was relaxing in the "sin bin," Smyers came into transition. She was still in the changing tent when Paula entered. They did not speak.

Smyers started the run 20 seconds ahead of Paula, but she was not the race leader. A rookie competitor, Natascha Badmann, had blasted through transition more than a minute earlier, having recorded the fastest women's bike split of the day. A 29-year-old former smoker with a teenage daughter and no prior athletic background, Badmann, who wore a girlish smile continuously as she ran and offered frequent thumbs-up and hang-ten gestures to spectators and fellow competitors, was a complete unknown to Paula.

In the previous year's Ironman, Smyers had felt almost magically strong on the run course. On this day, she did not. Paula passed her at 4 miles. Two miles later, Paula passed Badmann, noting the uncharacteristically strained grin the Swiss parvenu gave in response to her collegial nod. By the time she had passed through Kailua Village and reentered the lava fields, Paula was 45 seconds ahead of Badmann and 4 minutes ahead of a drain-circling Smyers.

Things seemed well in hand. But at the halfway point of the marathon, Badmann skated by Paula as effortlessly as Paula had earlier overtaken Smyers on the bike. Lead changes during the Ironman run leg are usually permanent. Indeed, in her 10 previous Ironmans, Paula had never taken the lead back from a woman who had passed her during the marathon. Knowing this, she now had to make the most important decision of her career. One voice, *that* voice, told her that she'd better go with Badmann—that if she let her get away, she would never see her again. But her instincts, her deepest intuition, told her to continue running her own race, guided by perception of effort—to stick to the highest speed she felt capable of sustaining to the finish. She let Badmann go.

Over the next several miles, Badmann stretched her lead out to a full minute, singing quietly under her breath at one point as her waifish body glided over the hot pavement. Badmann and Paula met face-to-face on an out-and-back spur of the race route. Badmann's smile was now easy and unforced. Seeing this, Paula reminded herself that she had come here not to win but to do her best. And yet, doing her best meant *trying* to win, if she felt capable, so she dug deep to chase down the rookie.

Badmann's advantage stopped growing and then began to shrink. Paula caught her 5 miles from the finish line. Badmann lifted her pace, refusing to go down without a fight. The veteran surged several times over the next 3 miles, but she couldn't shake her younger challenger. If Paula was worried, though, she didn't show it. The very last hill on the course lay at the edge of Kailua village, 1.5 miles from the end. Paula threw everything she had left into one more surge and at last broke Badmann.

Minutes later, Paula came upon the spot where she had sat down on the curb in humiliated defeat a year before. As she passed it, she lifted her hands in the same "What the hell is happening to me?" gesture she had made back then, but this time she wore a self-mocking grin. She crossed the finish line at 9:06:49 to claim her eighth Ironman title.

It would be her last. After 1996, Paula's athletic focus broadened to encompass other interests, including trail running and mountain biking. When she took her final bow at Ironman in 2001, it was just to see what she could do at age 40. She finished a respectable fourth, well behind Natascha Badmann, who won her third of an eventual six Ironman titles that day.

In 2009, Paula's venerable Ironman course record was finally broken—Englishwoman Chrissie Wellington lowered the mark to 8:54:02. Four years later, Aussie Mirinda Carfrae took it down to 8:52:14. Prior to this performance, Paula had offered Carfrae some advice in a recorded conversation.

"To me the greatest lesson as an athlete and in training is just don't get greedy," Paula said. "Know that you have to get up and go again the next day. Always save a little bit. I think that is what's precluding a lot of athletes from longevity and causing a lot of injuries right now. Everybody wants more. And the media is going to push you and hype you. And so is everyone else. You have to just have faith in yourself, and faith in [your coach], and just believe. Don't keep looking for more. When it's working, it's working. Don't mess with success, right?"

It was the deeply felt counsel of an athlete who had learned the hard way to look for answers inside herself.

CHAPTER NINE

THE GROUP EFFECT

CEMENT-GRAY CLOUDS HUNG LIKE a ceiling over Myslecinek Park, a sprawling outdoor recreation area located several miles outside the city of Bydgoszcz (pronounced *bid-gosh*) in northern Poland. The landscape was bleak and colorless, like a black-and-white photograph of an abandoned battleground. Undulant fields of crusty snow lay between thickets of denuded trees. Although it was officially spring—March 24, 2013—the air was gelid and given extra bite by gusty winds.

A 2,000-meter dirt track had been carved out of the snow and cordoned off with fencing and police tape. At one end of the loop stood a cluster of temporary structures—a few rows of long white tents, a grandstand packed with well-bundled spectators, and a pair of towers made of aluminum scaffolding. A bright yellow banner stretched between these towers read, "IAAF World Cross Country Championships BYDGOSZCZ 2013."

Beneath the banner stood 102 slender young men, underdressed in the colors of 15 nations. They hopped up and down and shook out their legs in an effort to discharge nervous energy, generate internal heat, and keep their muscles primed. The local time was 2:09 p.m. Their race—the last and most anticipated of the four contested on this day—would start in 1 minute.

Toward the left side of the lineup huddled a six-man American contingent, wearing navy blue and red. Chris Derrick, a recent graduate of Stanford University, had qualified for the world championships by winning the U.S. championships at St. Louis in February. Elliott Heath, another young Stanford alum, had punched his ticket to Bydgoszcz by finishing three spots behind Chris at nationals. James Strang had finished outside the top six but had been invited to make the trip to Poland after two runners who had come in ahead of him turned down their slots. Ryan Vail and Bobby Mack had been teammates at the 2010 World Cross Country Championships, also held in Bydgoszcz. Ryan had placed 44th in that race, Bobby 66th. Ben True was the team's wild card. A late bloomer whose primary high school sport had been cross-country skiing, he was improving every year.

Ten feet to the left of the Americans were the Kenyans, clad in black, green, and red. Although they stood near the far end of the start line, they were the center of attention. Spectators gawked openly at the bald-headed sextet. Video and still cameras lingered on them. Their competition tried to ignore them, but Ryan Vail's stomach did a somersault whenever he caught a sidelong glimpse.

Such notice and respect—and fear—were merited. Kenya's dominance of the World Cross Country Championships was like nothing else in sports. Since 1986, Kenya had won the senior men's competition 24 times and lost only twice. On a few occasions, the team had come close to achieving a perfect winning score of 10 points, the cross country equivalent of a shutout. (The top four finishers from each six-man team at cross country world championships earn points equal to their overall position. The lowest total wins.) The United States hadn't come within 50 points of Kenya in almost 30 years.

An amplified voice called the runners to their marks. They stepped through a human barrier of warmly dressed officials and bent over a chalk line drawn in the dirt. A gun fired and then fired again. False start. Bobby Mack heard the second report but kept running, just in case. The other runners had the same instinct, plowing heedlessly ahead until they came upon an official standing 30 meters from the start line and frantically waving a yellow flag in the international semaphore for "STOP!" The runners obeyed, but not before they had splashed through an icy mud puddle to reward their initial defiance.

They were herded back to the line. Two minutes later, the gun sounded again. The runners stampeded across a gloppy 150-meter straightaway toward the main loop and the first of many tight turns on the course. Those who failed to reach this chokepoint near the front of the cavalcade would have a hard time ever getting there. Few races throw runners into crisis from the very first step; in one way or another, the World Cross Country Championships always do.

Before leaving the States, Elliott Heath had asked his former Stanford teammate, Simon Bairu, a veteran of this event, for advice. "It's going to be the worst experience of your life," was all he said.

The colors of Team Kenya were conspicuous at the head of the charge. Japhet Korir had won the bronze medal in the junior race three years earlier on this very course. Jonathan Ndiku was a two-time junior world champion in the 3000-meter steeplechase. Geoffrey Kirui had a personal best time of 26:55 for 10000 meters. Hosea Macharinyang had won the Great Edinburgh Run, one of the world's most competitive 10K road races. Philemon Cherop had run under 61 minutes for the half marathon. And Timothy Kiptoo had run 15 kilometers on the road in 42:48, a time that only four Americans had ever bettered (none of them in this race).

Two minutes in, Kenya held the top three positions. Behind these men, runners were packed tightly all the way to the rear. The group flowed like a Chinese dragon through the narrow twists and turns of the muddy trail, an occasional wave passing from front to back as the runners hopped over one of several woodchip-covered earthen obstacles that course engineers had installed the day before.

Chris Derrick and Ben True had both started aggressively and held positions just inside the top 20. Chris felt good. His victory at the U.S. championships had given him a shot of confidence, and he believed he belonged where he now was. Before the race, his coach,

Jerry Schumacher, had said, "You're not the best runner in the race—but you shouldn't be scared of anybody." He wasn't.

The runners filed into a serpentine section of trail. Some of the turns were so tight and slick that racers were forced to come to a near stop to negotiate them, arms flung wide as they cornered, lest they skid out of bounds. The abrupt braking of the men at the front caused the bunch to compress in the manner of commuter cars behind a sudden rush-hour accident, and indeed there were more than a few collisions.

When the American team had reconnoitered the course the day before, they had scarcely believed what they saw. Elliott had slipped and fallen, aggravating a strained hip abductor muscle. Later in the day, a reporter asked Ben about the course. "It's definitely the hardest course I've ever seen in my life," he said. "I think it will be surprising if at least half the field doesn't fall at least one time during the race."

Just over a mile from the start, the runners hit "the Hill," as it was called, a quasi-precipice that had been a ski slope until the snow was removed from it 24 hours earlier. What the Hill lacked in length (about 200 meters) it made up for in pitch (about 15 percent). Had it been any steeper, the athletes might have been forced to use their hands to scrabble over the top. Spectators stood three-deep here, close enough to touch the passing competitors, many of whom wouldn't have minded a helpful shove.

No sooner had the runners topped the Hill than they found themselves in freefall down the backside. Fully exposed to the afternoon sun, this white-knuckle plunge was also the muddiest section of the loop. The options here were to let go and career downward like a runaway 18-wheeler or hit the brakes and get left behind by the daredevils. At the bottom of the slope, just where the runners reached terminal velocity, was a bunny-hop followed immediately by a hard right turn. At this point, the course mercifully flattened out and held straight for 100 meters or so. The leaders took advantage, lifting their pace and stringing out the field behind them.

At 5:34 on the race clock, Timothy Kiptoo completed the first of six loops. Sensors read a computer chip worn around his ankle, recording time and position, and then did the same for each runner behind him. The data were instantly compiled into individual and team competition rankings and displayed on a giant video screen visible from the spectators' grandstand. Kenya's fourth runner (and final scorer), Geoffrey Kirui, was currently in 14th place. The top American runner, Chris Derrick, was right behind him in 15th. Kenya led the team competition with 23 points. The United States was 99 points behind in sixth place.

IT HAS BEEN PROPOSED that Kenyans—particularly the Kalenjin tribe of the Rift Valley—have a "genetic advantage" as runners. It's a somewhat troubling notion whose origins are not entirely rational. After all, nobody has proposed that the Finnish dominance of running between 1912 and 1928 was the result of genetic superiority. Psychologist Adam Waytz of Northwestern University has explored this type of inconsistency, which he calls *superhumanization bias*. His studies have revealed that white people are far more likely to attribute superhuman qualities to blacks than they are to fellow whites who perform at a high level. So, when looking at white dominance of a particular sport, white people tend to look for a social or environmental explanation, such as a strong work ethic, but when looking at black dominance of a sport, they are more likely to look for an explanation in breeding. Even so, one cannot reject the idea that Kenyan runners have a genetic advantage merely because one doesn't like the race-based explanatory double standard that undergirds it. In principle, it is possible.

If a genetic advantage does exist, what might it consist of? One possibility is that some or all Kenyans possess a gene or group of genes favorable to running performance that are nonexistent in other peoples. For example, Kalenjins alone on earth might have a gene that strengthens a specific adaptive response to aerobic exercise, such as mitochondrial biogenesis. Biologists say that is extremely unlikely, however, as there are vanishingly few gene variants that exist exclusively within a single human population.

What's more, even if there were a running gene that the Kalenjin tribe had a monopoly on, it might not constitute an advantage in any absolute sense. There is no single genetic recipe for greatness in running, or in any sport. Scientists have identified a variety of genes that favor performance in particular types of sport, but they have not identified a single gene that is *essential* for greatness in any sport. As David Epstein remarked in *The Sports Gene*, "The gene variants that make one sprinter fast may be completely distinct from those that make her competitor in the next lane fast." The same principle applies to long-distance runners. Stephen Roth, director of the functional genomics laboratory at the University of Maryland, has said there are literally *trillions* of different possible genetic blueprints for bodies that are capable of reaching the highest level of running performance—and they're not all Kenyan bodies.

If Kenyans really do have a genetic advantage as runners, it may amount to nothing more than a greater *prevalence* of certain combinations of genes that are favorable to running performance. In this case, the most gifted Kenyan runners would be no more talented than the best runners in other populations. There would just be more of them.

The alternative to the genetic explanation of Kenyan dominance in running is the cultural and environmental explanation. Supporting evidence for this account is plentiful, and it begins with the fact that the phenomenon of national dominance of a sport is hardly peculiar to running. Indeed, there are rather few examples of sports that are *not* dominated to some degree by a single nation or by a small group of nations. The tiny island of Cuba has captured 67 Olympic medals in the sport of boxing since 1968, more than any other country. Half of the top 20 female golfers in the world are Korean and half of the top 20 female tennis players hail from Eastern European countries.

Germany has finished either first, second, or third in 13 of the last 16 soccer World Cups.

Nations that dominate a particular sport share one basic characteristic: Their people are *crazy* for that sport. To put it in a formula: National dominance of a sport is a function of the scope and intensity of its citizens' participation in it. If enormous numbers of a nation's people participate in a sport, and if many of them are willing to risk everything to achieve the highest level of success, that nation is certain to do quite well in global competition.

Kenya satisfies both of these conditions with respect to running. The process starts in childhood, with widespread exposure to long-distance running as a mode of transportation. Millions of Kenyan boys and girls run to school every day. What's more, when Kenyan children arrive at school, they discover that there are only two sports to choose from: running and soccer. Kenya has no tradition of success in soccer, but running is seen by young athletes as a realistic way out of the poverty that is so crushingly pervasive in the country. Kenyans are therefore willing to make huge sacrifices that runners of other nations might not in pursuit of success in the sport.

In his book, *Running with the Kenyans*, Adharanand Finn tells the story of Beatrice, a slightly plump Kenyan woman who never ran competitively in school and indeed hated running, yet who at age 20 chose to move alone to Iten—the epicenter of the Kenyan running scene—to try to make it as a professional runner, scraping by on handouts from her mother, who wholeheartedly supported her daughter's pipe dream. Nowhere else in the world is it commonplace for people with virtually no hope of succeeding as professional runners to give up everything to pursue the goal of making a living on the track or roads.

A national obsession with a particular sport does not occur in a vacuum. Something lights the match. In the early twentieth century, Finland was a poor, nonindustrialized country where many people worked outdoors and got around on foot and (during the winter) on cross-country skis. These fertile conditions produced Hannes

Kolehmainen, who won three gold medals in running events at the 1912 Olympics. Kolehmainen's triumphs ignited an intense running craze in his home country. Every Finnish boy wanted to be the next Olympic hero. The result was a quarter-century of Finnish dominance of distance running, a dynasty that produced a number of athletes whose performances far surpassed those of the man who'd started it all. Ultimately, the passionate and widespread participation in running that Hannes Kolehmainen inspired had a much stronger impact on the performance of Finland's top runners than did the conditions of poverty, lack of industrialization, and human-powered transportation that produced the first great Finnish runner.

Sociologist John Bruhn dubbed this phenomenon the *group effect*. The psychobiological model of endurance performance explains how it works in the context of sports like running. According to this model, you will recall, any factor that reduces the amount of effort an athlete perceives at a given level of exercise intensity will enhance performance. Among the less obvious factors that may exert this influence are certain social dynamics, including what psychologists call *behavioral synchrony*. When people work together, their brains release greater amounts of mood-lifting, discomfort-suppressing endorphins than they do when the same task is undertaken alone. This was shown in a 2009 study involving collegiate rowers that was conducted at Oxford University and published in *Biology Letters*. Twelve male athletes were subjected to a test of pain sensitivity on two occasions, once after rowing for 45 minutes alone and again after rowing for 45 minutes in synchronization with other rowers. The subjects proved to be significantly less sensitive to pain after rowing as a group, probably as a result of greater endorphin release in the brain.

Perceived effort is different from pain, but not so different. Most factors that increase pain tolerance or reduce pain sensitivity have a similar effect on perceived effort, and the group effect is no exception. Endurance athletes perceive less effort and perform better when training and racing cooperatively than they do alone. Fire walkers, if you will, get farther along the bed of hot coals when they clasp the hand of a fellow fire walker to the left and to the right. The group effect that is exerted through behavioral synchrony does not have to be acquired. It is a coping skill that exists latently in everyone, ready to be activated by the right situation.

What is the right situation? There are two—call them micro and macro—that are relevant to running and other endurance sports. One situation (micro) is any type of group workout or team competition in which a number of athletes work together. Whenever this happens, behavioral synchrony elevates performance. The other situation (macro) is a broader sport culture in which numerous groups of athletes train and race together often. When a sport culture is vibrant, comprising many groups of highly motivated athletes, behavioral synchrony achieves maximum intensity and effectiveness.

This two-tiered structure of the group effect ensures that success breeds success within sport cultures. In Kenya, success in the sport of running was made possible initially by widespread exposure to the activity, by the high altitude of the Rift Valley, and perhaps also by the prevalence of a body type featuring long legs and narrow calves (a proposed "genetic advantage" with some scientific support). These conditions created some great runners. These great runners then created a culture in which large numbers of men and women risk it all to join the Kenyan running pantheon. This culture does far more to elevate the performance of the country's runners than do the conditions that gave rise to it. Every day, hopeful athletes, talented or otherwise, arrive in Iten—runners willing to live in a closet-size room, survive on handouts, and run 100 miles per week for a slim shot at earning the opportunity to race internationally. With so many runners trying so hard together, the Kenyan running culture sustains a centripetal social force that pushes all to a higher level than they might attain in a less cooperative environment.

While it is still unclear whether Kenyans have a genetic advantage as runners, it is *certain* that they have a cultural advantage in the form of the group effect. When this advantage is taken into account, how much is left to be explained by genes?

Not much. The dominance of Kenya's runners is often framed in statistical terms that tend to exaggerate their superiority. For example, in 2014, 57 of the 100 fastest male marathon times were recorded by Kenyans. That's pretty amazing. But such numbers disguise the fact that the best Kenyans aren't really much better than the top runners from other places. The fastest mile time recorded by a male runner since 2001—3:46.91—was run by an American of British ancestry, Alan Webb. The long-standing women's world record in the marathon—2:15:25—is owned by an Englishwoman, Paula Radcliffe. Molly Huddle's American record for 5K on the road (14:50) is just 3 seconds, or 0.34 percent, slower than the fastest time ever recorded in that event by a Kenyan-born runner. If the group effect accounts for even half of this difference, then the vaunted Kenyan genetic advantage is not even two-tenths of 1 percent.

AT THE START OF lap 2, a subtle acceleration at the front of the race caused a gap to emerge suddenly between the first 20 runners and the rest. Chris Derrick was in the thick of the lead pack. Caught behind the split were Elliott Heath in 30th place, Bobby Mack in 52nd, James Strang in 61st, and Ryan Vail in 62nd. Ben True found himself alone between the two groups. Alarmed, he opened up his stride and flung himself into the lead pack like a desperado leaping aboard a passing boxcar. His goal coming into the race was to make the top 20. If he lost contact with the lead group this early, he could kiss that dream goodbye.

At 7:10 on the race clock, the leaders crossed another dirt obstacle. Japhet Korir got his feet tangled and sprawled onto his hands and knees, taking Uganda's Timothy Toroitich down with him. Seeing an opportunity, Ethiopia's Tesfaye Abera went to the front and surged, hoping to eliminate Korir from the lead group, but the Kenyan was up quickly and able to rejoin the leaders. Several runners at the rear of the group, however, were thrown off. Still feeling strong, Chris Derrick smoothly matched Abera's surge. Ben True was right on his heels.

For the second time, the field entered the twistiest, most treach-erous part of the course. Abera decided to take some chances on the tighter turns in hopes of separating himself from more cautious pur-suers. But as he rounded a hard left bend, he lost control and skittered toward the extreme right edge of the trail, his right thigh making contact with the flimsy police tape marking the course boundary. Several runners behind him suffered greater mishaps. One slammed into a metal stanchion holding up the police tape, another toppled face first into the mud, and a third lost a shoe and was forced to stop to replace it.

The runners were now basted in mud, a few spatters reaching as high as their cheeks. What skin was still visible on their legs was raw from contact with snow and ice. Under the hood, however, their engines were running hot. Ben got rid of his skullcap. James tossed his gloves to Neely Spence, who had finished 13th in the women's race earlier in the day.

They hit the Hill a second time. Australia's Collis Birmingham led the field up and over. Where the course widened out at the bottom, a group of men gained a sliver of separation from the rest. Chris was tucked immediately behind them, his jaunty stride continuing to exude confidence. He passed the 4-km timing point in 10th place, 1 second off the lead. There were two Kenyans ahead of him and one on his back. Ben held the 14th spot, with yet another Kenyan just behind him. Jonathan Ndiku, the Kenyan runner who had been in third place at the end of the first lap, had suffered an Achilles tendon injury and abandoned the race. Elliott Heath was still in 30th place, but Bobby Mack and Ryan Vail had advanced to 45th and 49th. As a team, the Americans had risen from sixth to fifth, and were now 69 points behind the first-place Kenyans, with four laps to go.

The lead runners again picked up the pace as they began a fresh circuit. They came upon the first obstacle of lap 3. Chris took two quick shuffle-steps to the top, leapt off, and came down awkwardly on his right foot. The ankle exploded in pain. Chris limped through the next several strides, putting as much weight on the hurt foot as he could bear, hoping the injured tissues would quickly numb up. They did—sort of—and he pressed on.

Three more runners popped off the back of the lead group, reducing its number to 17. Moments later, Ben, who had been hovering behind Chris, pulled even with him, and a wordless message passed between the teammates. *We're doing this!*

As the Americans pressed toward the front, a pair of Ethiopians slid toward the back, dangled briefly, and plunged away, like sailors falling off the angled deck of a sinking ship. The dwindling group approached the spot where U.S. team coach Robert Gary stood watching, and he took a quick head count.

"Group's down to 11!" he later recalled shouting. "Eleven in your group!"

He wanted Chris and Ben to understand what he hardly dared think: *You could both make the top 10.* Sixteen seconds later, Elliott ran past, followed closely by Ryan and Bobby, who were winning their own battle of attrition, passing runner after runner without speeding up. Gary informed them of Chris and Ben's position, knowing exactly what effect (the group effect) the information would have.

Back up the Hill they went. It seemed steeper and longer than it had the first two times around. The crowds were certainly thicker. The race was taking form, and partisans of the teams and individuals that were performing well were becoming increasingly animated in their expression of support. The narrowness of the loop allowed motivated spectators to sprint from one spot to another and catch the runners twice on each circuit. Many of the Americans present were now charging from place to place in a state of rising excitement.

Kenya's Japhet Korir and Eritrea's Teklemariam Medhin led the field over the course's high point. Only three runners remained in contact with them as they rumbled pell-mell down the hazardous backside, which was even more perilous on wobbly, fatiguing legs. Alarmed by the gap opening up in front of him, Chris shot down the descent like an avalanche. Ben ran more cautiously and found himself 20 meters off the lead at the base.

A select group of five Africans crossed the 6-km timing point at 16:32. Chris was 2 seconds behind in the 8th spot and Ben another second back in 11th. Kenya had lost ground, but the perennial champions still had four runners in the top 20 and led the team competition with 40 points. Elliott came through in 28th, having picked off two runners on the third lap. Bobby and Ryan were steps behind him in 33rd and 34th, having taken a combined 27 scalps on the last loop. With three laps complete and three to go, the U.S. team was still in fifth place but now just 4 points away from fourth-place Uganda.

Early in lap 4, Elliott rounded a muddy turn and felt his left leg whip out from under him as though the ankle had been lassoed. He just managed to avoid doing the splits, and a sharp pain zapped his already sore hip abductor. Like Chris before him, he ran through the pain until his body took the hint and went numb. No sooner had the throbbing calmed than Ryan and Bobby rolled by. Elliott, who at Stanford had earned a reputation for sacrificing himself for the good of the team (for example, by doing as many as three races in a single track meet), tried to go with them, but he just didn't have it. The Americans now had five runners in the top 30.

Up front, Chris and Ben were burying themselves in an effort to regain contact with the lead group of five Africans. Chris, however, was beginning to suffer. His whole body was tingling from a combination of cold and hypoxia. Meanwhile, his vision had become sepia-toned. He was less careful about where he placed his feet and he couldn't tell if Ben was still with him.

Just then, Ben drew ahead of his countryman and pressed toward the leaders. Feeling his pull, Chris fell in behind and the pair began to close the gap. At 18:06 on the race clock, as they hit another dirt obstacle, the Americans were back in the lead group, which had swelled to 10 runners. They rounded a sweeping right turn. Ben's right foot came down on a slick railroad tie hidden beneath a crust of snow and slid out from under him, but his skier's reflexes kept him upright.

Kenya's Korir and Ethiopia's Imane Merga were emerging as the strong men of the race. They pushed; the rest hung on. They hit the

Hill again, and again the lead group split. At the base of the following descent, Ben was 15 meters behind a gang of six, Chris another 5 meters adrift. He felt desperately weary. The prospect of catching up seemed infinitely more daunting than it had a lap ago. He passed the 8-km timing point in 10th place, 5 seconds after the leaders. Fewer than a dozen other runners came by before Bobby hustled through. He had overtaken 11 more competitors in lap 4. Ryan followed 3 seconds and four positions later, having passed eight. Elliott was hanging tough another second back in 30th place.

The team rankings soon appeared on the giant video screen. Kenya and Ethiopia were now tied for first place with 41 points. Eritrea was third with 57 points. The United States was fourth with 64 points.

When Robert Gary saw the numbers, he took off sprinting toward the nearest part of the course he could reach before Chris and Ben passed. "We've got five in the top 30!" he bellowed (or words to that effect). "We can medal!"

Robert himself had represented the United States at the 1998 World Cross Country Championships in Morocco. He and his teammates there had fully expected to take the drubbing the Americans took every year, and they weren't disappointed. Kenya won with a near-perfect 12 points; the Americans finished eighth out of 15 teams with 194 points. And so it was that when Robert—now Coach Robert—had met up with this year's world championship cross country team for the first time in Poland, he'd smiled inwardly at what he regarded as the naively optimistic goals the team tossed out. He was smiling outwardly now.

KENYA AND FINLAND ARE not the only places where the group effect has supported a running dynasty. In 1979, four of the top five finishers at the U.S. cross country championships were members of one team: the Greater Boston Track Club. Four years later, the GBTC took 4 of the top 10 places in the Boston Marathon (including first place, which went to Bill Rodgers).

As the home of the world's oldest marathon, Boston was ground zero of the running boom that swept across America in the 1970s. In 1974, Bill Squires, a coach steeped in Arthur Lydiard's revolutionary high-volume, low-intensity training method, became the first coach of the newly formed GBTC. Over the next several years, the Boston area produced a bumper crop of talented young runners. These were the conditions that brought initial success to the GBTC. But it was the group effect that eventually made it the most dominant team the sport had ever seen.

After Bill Rodgers won the Boston Marathon in 1975 (setting an American record in the process), the GBTC attracted young runners dreaming of greatness from all over the United States. Like Kenya's runners today, these men and women were willing to risk everything in pursuit of their dream.

A typical case was Andy Palmer, who played basketball in college and did not take up running until he was 24. At 6 feet, 4 inches, he was not designed for running and he demonstrated only modest aerobic talent, taking fourth place in his first two road races in the remote forests of northern Maine and southern Quebec. Nevertheless, Palmer decided to quit his teaching job and move to Boston to join the city's growing community of running bums. He trained with members of the GBTC, including Bill Rodgers, who hired Palmer at his running store so the young dreamer wouldn't starve.

Andy ran the Boston Marathon for the first time in 1979, the year the GBTC took four of the top 10 spots. He finished 266th with a time of 2:29:46. Four years later, Andy won a one-time event called the Boston Fest Marathon in 2:16:25. The local running community barely took notice. Such achievements were ordinary in the days when mailmen ran 120 miles per week. (Dick Mahoney, a full-time postal worker, was a member of the GBTC and a 2:14 marathoner.) The same year Palmer won his race, 84 runners, mostly Americans, finished in less than 2 hours and 20 minutes at the Boston Marathon. The winner, Greg Meyer, was yet another member of the GBTC.

That feat has never been duplicated. Money, of all things, spoiled the group effect within the GBTC and in American running as a whole. Before 1981, runners were forbidden to accept prize money or sign endorsement contracts. Then Bill Rodgers and a brave handful of his peers rebelled against their exploitation. The major running shoe brands began to pay the best runners to wear their gear. But they signed only the top names, like Rodgers, and passed over sub-elites like Andy Palmer. As a result, young runners with second-tier talent stopped quitting their jobs and moving to Boston to train with the greats.

The performance level of America's runners suffered. It wasn't because the best American runners had become less genetically gifted. It was because the most genetically gifted runners weren't being pushed by vast numbers of runners of equal and slightly lesser talent who were training like professionals. The nadir came at the 2000 Olympics in Athens, where no American runner finished higher than sixth place in a race longer than 400 meters. Without elite role models to inspire them, college and high school runners got slower as well. In the 1990s, only nine male high school runners broke 9 minutes for 2 miles, a decline from 51 runners in the 1980s and 84 in the 1970s.

After the disaster of the 2000 Olympics, leaders in the U.S. running community decided enough was enough. Postulating that the loss of the group effect was the cause of the decline of U.S. running, they sought to correct the problem by creating post-collegiate running clubs for athletes with elite-level talent. Their hope was that the runners who participated in these clubs would benefit from behavioral synchrony at the micro-level and achieve great performances that would in turn revitalize the broader running community.

It worked. Deena Kastor (née Drossin) joined the Mammoth Track Club after graduating from the University of Arkansas. She won two silver medals at the World Cross Country Championships (in 2002 and 2004) and a bronze medal in the 2004 Olympic Marathon. She was also victorious at the 2005 Chicago Marathon and the 2006 London Marathon. Dathan Ritzenhein joined the Nike Oregon Project after completing studies at the University of Colorado. He won bronze medals at the 2001 World Junior Cross Country Championships and the 2009 World Half Marathon Championships. Shalane Flanagan joined the Nike Oregon Project too and won a silver medal in the 2008 Olympic 10000 meters and bronze at the 2011 World Cross Country Championships. Americans were back on the podium.

The upward trend continues. At the 2013 World Outdoor Track and Field Championships, Americans won four medals to Kenya's three in the men's and women's 800 and 1500 meters. A year later, 20 American high school boys ran 2 miles in under 9 minutes *in one meet*.

By the time Ryan Vail graduated from Oklahoma State University in 2009, talented young American runners once again believed that pursuing the dream of running greatness was worthwhile. Ten years earlier, in a less encouraging climate, Ryan might have quit the sport after college, having never placed higher than fifth in an NCAA championship race (although he did lead his team to victory at the 2009 NCAA Cross Country Championships). But despite his lack of individual credentials, running shoe manufacturer Brooks saw enough potential in Ryan to offer him an endorsement contract. He moved to Portland, Oregon, to train with other young American pros, soaking up the group effect.

"I was always a team guy," Ryan told me. "I always ran my best when guys were counting on me."

Ryan's trip to Bydgoszcz in 2013 was his fourth time representing the United States at the World Cross Country Championships. He was still a team guy.

AT 22:41 ON THE race clock, Ben True pulled himself back into the lead group. Chris remained 10 strides back, gaining no ground. He couldn't understand it. Ben had never beaten him. Chris knew he could and should be up there with him right now. But the elastic bond between them had been stretched too far, and had lost its pull. Chris's pace seemed surreally slow, his body impossibly heavy. With sudden dread, he wondered if he was on the verge of hitting the wall, another experience he had not yet had in any race.

Korir led the top six in single file through the narrow, serpentine section of the course that had wrought such carnage on previous laps. It was the last place his pursuers expected an attack, so Korir attacked. Immediately his five chasers accordioned behind him, and two—Birmingham and Ben—came unhitched.

All too soon, the Hill was upon them. Ben's ears were filled with the screams of American spectators as he slogged toward the summit.

We can get team bronze, Ben!

We need every point, Ben! EVERY POINT!

At the start of the bell lap, it was a four-man race for the individual title. Ben started the final circuit in sixth place, 8 seconds off the front. Chris was now ninth, 7 seconds behind Ben. Bobby and Ryan came through side by side in the 21st and 22nd positions.

Ryan retains a vivid recollection of Robert Gary fixing his eyes on them and pointing ahead at a pair of runners, one wearing the red, green, and blue of Eritrea, the other the colors of South Africa.

"You have to catch those two!" he shouted. "If you get them, we've got bronze!"

Robert had no idea if this was actually true, but according to Ryan, the coach's words once again had the desired effect. Ryan and Bobby met their coach's stare with a look that communicated understanding, terror, and resolve. Then Ryan turned his head toward Bobby.

"Let's go!" he said.

"All right," said Bobby.

Ryan took off as though a new race had started. Bobby matched the acceleration, but almost immediately he was in trouble. He would later liken the feeling to pedaling a bicycle in a sand dune. He fell off the pace. Sensing the loss of his teammate, Ryan was overcome with a sickening anxiety, worse even than his deathly fatigue. *It's all on me now*, he thought.

Moments after he'd left his partner behind, Ryan overtook Canada's Mohammed Ahmed. He was now in 19th place. Looking ahead, he could see that Abrar Osman, the Eritrean runner Robert Gary had pointed out, had broken away from the South African, Elroy Gelant, whose personal record for 5000 meters was 17 seconds better than Ryan's. The American chased him relentlessly through the twisty part of the course. When the trail opened up, Ryan made his pass, surging as he did so to discourage any countermove. Eighteenth.

Approaching the Hill, Ryan could see Osman grinding his way upward. Osman's PR for 3000 meters was 13 seconds better than Ryan's. They were less than 600 meters from the finish line. If Ryan was going to catch him, he would have to push even harder. He hauled his unwilling body up the ski slope, contemptuous of his own suffering, as Osman disappeared over the top.

Charging down the other side, Ryan seemed to have lost ground, but when the trail leveled out the gap compressed and Ryan saw that he still had a chance. On previous laps, the course had bent sharply to the right here. This time race officials directed runners to veer left into the finishing chute. Mustering every last dreg of energy he had left, Ryan got up onto his toes and sprinted. He was on Osman's right shoulder before the Eritrean could react. The pair sped elbow to elbow down the home straight until Ryan pulled ahead to finish 17th.

Ryan's split time of 5:40 for the final lap was the fourth-fastest in the entire 102-man field. Only the three medalists—Korir, Merga, and Medhin—had run faster. Ryan had outrun four of the five Kenyans who remained in the race. He had closed faster than 2:04 marathoner Feyisa Lilesa and four other Ethiopians.

From the finish area, Ryan Vail and his mud-spattered compadres shuffled over to the press tent, trading high-fives. They had much to celebrate—more, in fact, than they yet knew. Ben True had taken 6th place and Chris Derrick 10th. Bobby Mack had finished 7 seconds behind Ryan in the 19th slot. Inside the press tent, Bobby and Ryan's interview with Flotrack was interrupted by the delivery of the official team score sheet. The Americans believed they'd done just enough to capture the bronze medal. But they were wrong. This is what they saw:

Ethiopia: 38 pts (gold)
USA: 52 pts (silver)
Kenya: 54 pts (bronze)

Back home, American running fans hailed Team USA's historic defeat of mighty Kenya as the "miracle in the dirt." But it wasn't a miracle. It was the group effect, a force that all athletes can exploit to attain far greater heights together than they ever could alone.

CHAPTER TEN

WHAT DO YOU EXPECT?

THOMAS VOECKLER COULD NOT believe his luck. Halfway through stage 5 of the 2004 Tour de France, the 25-year-old Frenchman found himself more than 16 minutes in front of the main field as part of a five-man breakaway and on track to finish the day in possession of the overall race leader's yellow jersey. Nobody had anticipated this turn of events, least of all Thomas himself. He was not exactly a superstar in the sport of cycling. In four years on the pro circuit, he had collected only a handful of wins, most of them in minor races. The previous year he'd finished 119th in his Tour de France debut, more than 3.5 hours behind the victor, Lance Armstrong. Yet here was Thomas now, poised to snatch the *maillot jaune* off the selfsame Armstrong's back, having benefitted from a perfect storm of events and circumstances conspiring in his favor.

The stage had begun under a hard rain in the northern French city of Amiens and from there rolled southward into taunting headwinds. The first breakaway attempt came almost immediately and others followed in quick succession. Thomas tried to insinuate himself into most of them, but each attack was neutralized by teams that did not want certain dangerous riders within them (Thomas himself did not count as dangerous) to get away.

As the race approached the town of Tilloy-lès-Conty, some 16 kilometers into the 200-km stage, Sandy Casar of the Française des Jeux team launched a well-timed assault on a small hill. Dutchman Jakob Piil promptly joined him and a few moments later the trio of Stuart O'Grady, Magnus Bäckstedt, and Thomas Voeckler came across the gap. All of these men were judged nonthreatening, so the peloton let them go. The five escapees set about working together to build what they hoped would become an insurmountable advantage.

They succeeded beyond their wildest hopes. Rarely is a breakaway given more than a quarter of an hour of leash in a "sprint" stage of the Tour de France (or in any stage, for that matter), but Thomas's group caught a break. Armstrong actually *wanted* to lose the yellow jersey so that some other team would have to do the work of defending it in the next few stages and his U.S. Postal Service team could relax a little before things turned serious in the mountains. To ensure this outcome, the Postal squad placed itself at the front of the peloton after the breakaway group had bolted and from this position enforced an unhurried tempo.

Still, they had no intention of giving up 16 minutes. But the weather had other ideas. The wind and rain caused the peloton to crash repeatedly throughout the stage. Each time the main group began to chip away at the breakaway's gap, a sudden pileup bogged it down and permitted the lead to stretch back out. Multi-rider crashes occurred at 116 km, 170 km, and 180 km.

Thomas was the highest-placed rider among the five members of the breakaway. All he had to do was finish with the group at least 3 minutes ahead of Armstrong and he would vault from 59th to 1st in the General Classification. Cat-and-mouse games among the five leaders in the last 2 kilometers of the race enabled the peloton to shrink the deficit, but Thomas's group still had 12:36 in hand at the end. Sprint specialist O'Grady won the stage. Thomas finished close behind in fourth place and leapfrogged to the top of the G.C., some 9 minutes and 35 seconds ahead of Armstrong, who wasn't the least bit worried to have fallen back to sixth place. And why should he have been? The defending champion had beaten Thomas by nearly 6 minutes in just the final time trial of the previous year's Tour. For his part, Thomas had no delusions of dethroning Armstrong. Yet although the new leader had already achieved more than he ever expected, and although he understood that he owed his ascension entirely to luck and opportunism, he did not plan to give up the yellow jersey without a fight.

"It's a little hard to believe it right now," Thomas said immediately after his coup. "I'm really happy to have the *maillot jaune*; it's something everybody dreams of. I hope to keep it as long as possible."

The next morning, Thomas Voeckler woke up to a new reality—the reality of life in the yellow jersey. The leader of the Tour de France, whoever he may be on a given day, is the ultimate athletic cynosure—a center of attention without parallel in other sports. The whole point of putting a bright yellow shirt on the leader of the Tour de France is to make him stand out. No other cyclist in the Tour is allowed to wear the same shade on his standard uniform. The man in yellow starts each stage at the middle of the front row of cyclists. He is often the only rider that the tens of thousands of spectators lining each stage can identify individually as the racers zip past in tight bunches at 30 mph. At least one television camera follows him from the start to the finish of each stage, beaming his image into hundreds of millions of homes and businesses around the world. His name appears in the first paragraph, if not the headline, of almost every stage summary published in newspapers and online. He is obligated to speak to the press before and after each stage and at all official Tour press conferences, and he receives more personal interview requests than any other racer. The leader of the Tour de France, whoever he may be on a given day, cannot help but be affected by all of this. On the morning that Thomas Voeckler donned the *maillot jaune* for the first time, the world was about to find out how he would be affected.

Frankly, the world expected little. The consensus among cycling pundits was that Thomas would remain in yellow no later than stage

10, the first mountain stage of the three-week Tour. It was hard to find fault with this prediction. Thomas had finished a whopping 25 minutes behind the winner of the first mountain stage the year before.

Stage 6 was a flat, southwesterly jaunt of 196 kilometers from Bonneval to Angers. A six-man breakaway escaped at 37 kilometers. Thomas's Brioches la Boulangère team moved to the front of the peloton to keep the deficit manageable. Later on, the Lotto and Quick Step teams helped with the pacemaking in order to set up their sprinters for a possible stage win. With just 1 kilometer left in the race, the breakaway was caught and Quick Step's Tom Boonen won in a field sprint. Thomas finished with the bunch and there were no changes to the General Classification.

Stages 7 through 9 followed the same script. Thomas got through them without losing a single second to Armstrong and the other big men. Then the roads turned upward.

Stage 10 featured nine categorized climbs. Climbing specialist Richard Virenque broke away at 33 kilometers in a bid to claim a victory for France on Bastille Day. Axel Merckx of the Lotto-Domo team went with him. Thomas's team again rode at the head of the main field to prevent the gap from getting out of hand. Virenque stood 12:35 behind Thomas in the G.C. The Brioches boys made sure his lead on the road did not reach beyond 11 minutes.

There was some uncertainty going into the stage as to whether the leading pretenders to Armstrong's throne—men such as Jan Ullrich and Ivan Basso—would attack the favorite or save their legs for the tougher days to come. In the end they held fire. But there was a measure of excitement on the seventh and most difficult climb of the day, a 5.5-km ascent of the Col du Pas de Peyrol at an average gradient of 8 percent. The contenders felt each other out with an aggressive but controlled tempo that was precisely calibrated to effect an initial culling. As they churned their way upward, riders fell off the back in an order that would prove to be a near-perfect inverse of their final placing in Paris.

In the previous year's Tour, Thomas had been among the first riders to crack in such a situation, but today he held on as the peloton shrank to 50 riders, then 40, then 30. While Armstrong and his main rivals remained stone-faced, Thomas's features and body language communicated tremendous suffering. Unable to generate enough power from the saddle, he stood up and stomped on the pedals with graceless, herky-jerky movements. The peloton shriveled to 20 riders, then 15, but still Thomas hung on.

Nothing in Thomas's career résumé indicated that what he was now doing was physically possible for him. So no one was surprised when at last he hit the wall, dropping his rear end back into the seat and drifting behind the 12 riders left in the top echelon. But when the summit banner suddenly appeared above the road ahead, Thomas became a new man. He leaped up, leaned precariously over the front end of his bike, and mashed the pedals. Merely catching Armstrong and the others would have been statement enough, but Thomas defiantly passed them all and was the first man over the top.

Two more climbs remained, neither of them as tough as the one just completed. Thomas made it through both without further crisis and finished the stage at the head of the peloton and only 6:24 behind Virenque. His perseverance on the Col du Pas de Peyrol bought him not just one more day in the yellow jersey but effectively two, as stage 11 included no major climbs.

Stage 12 was another story. It confronted the riders with a pair of Category I climbs in the last 40 kilometers of an otherwise flat 197-km ride. The first of these, the Col d'Aspin, brought the cyclists to an elevation of 4,914 feet over 12.3 kilometers at an average gradient of 6.5 percent. Armstrong's U.S. Postal team set a blistering tempo at the head of the race and riders began to drop off in twos and threes. Thomas again mashed and jerked as he struggled to hold his place among the smoothly pedaling alpha riders, misery plainly written across his face. But at the summit he was still there.

Next up was La Mongie: 12.8 kilometers at an average slope of 6.8 percent. The screws were turned again and a final culling took place. American climbing ace Floyd Landis exploded. Rising French star Sandy Casar popped. Future French time trial champion Sylvain Chavanel (a member of Thomas's Brioches la Boulangère team) slipped away like a fallen surfer in a riptide. Thomas looked more miserable than any of them, but still he refused to fold. Not until Jan Ullrich himself was under pressure did Thomas at last collapse and fade to the rear.

Moments later, the real fireworks began at the head of the race. Carlos Sastre attacked, Francisco Mancebo countered, and then Armstrong shot clear of everyone with Basso in tow. With the five-time champion now showing all of his cards, race officials put a clock on the growing gap between him and the yellow jersey wearer. The plucky Frenchman fought for every second, discovering a whole new universe of suffering over the remaining 6 kilometers of the stage.

When Thomas came around the last bend and into view of the summit, the large crowd gathered there erupted. He crossed the line 3:59 after Armstrong, who had moved up to second place in the General Classification, now only 5:24 behind Thomas.

The next morning, Thomas woke up to another new reality—this time the reality of being his country's latest hero. Overnight, the attention heaped upon him changed from interested to fanatical. French newspapers praised Thomas's *panache* (style) and *temperament* (character). When he got out on the road for the day's stage, he passed scores of spectators holding signs that read "Merci, Voeckler" and "Voeckler for President." French cyclists had given the Tour's host country little to celebrate since Bernard Hinault won his fifth and last title back in 1985. Thomas's campaign in yellow was bringing out some long-pent-up partisanship. And it wasn't only his countrymen who were embracing Thomas. His self-sacrificing efforts to honor the tradition of the *maillot jaune* won over cycling fans around the world, and his theatrical style of racing made him easy to root for.

It's not unusual for a motivated cyclist to "ride above himself" in a mountain stage of the Tour de France. But Thomas Voeckler's way of doing so was unique. Other riders tended to disguise their mounting distress with a poker face as well as a "poker body"—a feigned relaxedness on the bike. Only when they were moments away from the breaking point did their faces contort and their bodies thrash. And when they did break, they *broke*—disappeared, never to be seen again.

Thomas was different. His effort was on full display, often in the peculiar form of a distended tongue that wriggled and writhed against his chin. As he neared his limit, the tongue began to whip from one side of his mouth to the other and then vanished behind a plaintive frown or a biting of the lower lip with the upper teeth. At the same time the corners of his eyebrows sank cartoonishly, giving him a wounded look. As the eyebrows sank, Thomas's trademark paroxysmal pedaling style degenerated further and became a kind of seizure, as if the handlebar were sending blasts of electricity into his hands.

He kept up this pantomime of torture longer than seemed survivable before at last crumpling onto the saddle and drifting behind his tormentors. Minutes later, though, he was upright again and bounding back into the lead group wearing a sheepish grin. It was a spectacle that stirred the hearts of all but the most jaded watchers, and reminded them why they loved this sport.

Thomas was still deeply fatigued from stage 12 when he started the fiendishly difficult stage 13, which ended with the "beyond-category" climb of the Port de Lers. There were seven rated climbs in all, and each softened up the legs a little more. At the foot of the sixth climb, a Category I march up the sheer Col d'Agnes, the U.S. Postal Service team once again set a vicious rhythm at the front that left widespread destruction behind. Thomas hit the wall and dropped back. Seeing this, a journalist providing live online coverage of the race wrote, "Voeckler has cracked. I don't see his Brioches la Boulangère teammates. They are letting him get home on his own. They know he won't be in yellow tonight."

At the summit of the climb, Thomas was about a minute behind a lead group of 20 riders. Instead of marshaling his energy on the following descent, which led to the final climb of the day, Thomas went all-out, surprising Armstrong and company by rejoining them just in time to take one last beating on the Port de Lers.

The road bent skyward once more. Thomas clung to the rear of the group as long as he could, outlasting the likes of future Tour winner Sastre and former mountain biking world champion Michael Rasmussen before being ejected from the back about 14 kilometers from the summit.

With little more than half of his original advantage on Armstrong left, Thomas could not afford to lose ground to the American at the same rate of 40 seconds per kilometer as he had on the final climb of the previous stage, which had pushed him to the absolute limit. In fact, he would somehow have to find a way to stay within 20 seconds per kilometer of Armstrong's pace over the remaining distance if he was to keep the yellow jersey. In other words, he needed to find a new limit.

Too exhausted to pedal in his customary standing posture, Thomas put as much power as he could into each pedal stroke from a seated position, his head bobbing pigeon-like as he suffered his way up the 4,977-foot mountain. At 12 kilometers to the summit, Thomas had already lost 90 seconds. His team director, Jean-René Bernaudeau, bellowed into his earpiece, telling him he could still save the yellow jersey if he could only go a little faster. *A little faster?* He was already climbing harder than he ever had!

Just then, Thomas was passed by Christophe Moreau, a major G.C. contender who had suffered a flat tire at the base of the climb. Thomas hoisted himself up and latched onto his fellow Frenchman. His form was wilder than ever. The usual muscle combinations no longer working, Thomas turned the cranks with his knees bowing wide. But he was indeed going a little faster.

With 7.5 kilometers to go and less than 3 minutes of his overall lead still uneaten, Thomas was near the point of implosion. Moreau had dropped him, leaving the yellow jersey wearer alone in a personal hell of unimaginable weariness. Up ahead, Thomas saw the red-and-white uniform of his teammate Sylvain Chavanel, who had been part of an early breakaway. Thomas caught him. Chavanel had demolished Thomas in the 2003 Tour and had entered this year's race as the acknowledged leader of Brioches la Boulangère, the guy whom domestiques like Thomas were supposed to sacrifice themselves for. But their roles had reversed, and Chavanel now proceeded to bury himself for Thomas, towing the supposed lesser rider upward until he was in danger of tipping over.

With 5 kilometers to go, Thomas was 3:30 behind Armstrong on the road, 2:24 ahead on paper. Sweat-soaked hair plastered to his scalp, he stole several quick looks behind him, perhaps in search of rescue—some undefined *deus ex machina*. None came.

Just beyond the 3-km banner, the roadway narrowed and Thomas entered into a narrow gauntlet of spectators who leaned in with clenched fists and urged him on with livid faces, as though the future of the Republic depended upon the retention of Thomas's canary-colored blouse. That shirt was now fully unzipped and flapping in the wind, lending its wearer a ragged look that matched his internal state. With 1.5 km of climbing still to go, Thomas's deficit to Armstrong reached 4 minutes, leaving only 64 seconds to burn, less if Armstrong won the stage and captured the 18-second time bonus that came with victory on a summit finish. Sure enough, the American crossed the finish line one bike length ahead of Basso and the official countdown began.

The Brioches la Boulangère team car pulled alongside Thomas. Jean-René Bernaudeau stuck his head out the passenger window and vituperated at his failing athlete. Thomas was now able to pedal out of the saddle for only seconds at a time before sitting down to recover. A French television commentator screamed, "Allez! Allez! Allez!"—joining millions of his countrymen who were doing the same in their homes and at public gathering places. Sweeping around the final bend, Thomas lifted his head and squinted toward the finish banner, like an off-course ship's captain straining his eyes in search of land. Spotting the official time clock, he broke into a ravaged grin, his right fist clenched weakly. Thomas crossed the line 4:42 behind

Armstrong (and in 13th place overall in the stage). He had held onto the yellow jersey by 22 seconds.

"Not many people thought I would be able to keep the *maillot jaune* today, and not even me in some ways," Thomas told reporters outside his team bus. "Today I did it on guts alone."

The inevitable occurred at last in stage 15. An early attack by a desperate Jan Ullrich, who started the day in fifth place overall, proved Thomas's undoing. The other contenders had no choice but to respond and Thomas went off the back with the better part of four big climbs still ahead. He wound up ceding nearly 10 minutes to Armstrong and dropped all the way down to eighth place in the G.C. He had nothing left to give, not just that day but for the rest of the Tour. By the time he got to Paris, he had plummeted to 18th.

ANY CYCLIST WHO CAPTURES the yellow jersey in the Tour de France is riding well. But those who do often find that, once they have the yellow jersey, they ride even better. This phenomenon has given rise to an expression: "The yellow jersey gives you wings." In 2004, Thomas Voeckler became the latest in a long line of cyclists to ride above himself after taking possession of the ceremonial garment of the race leader (although never before had a rider who claimed it so unexpectedly kept it so long).

The yellow jersey does not have magical powers. It's just a piece of laundry, and the "wings" it confers are little more than extra effort. The yellow jersey doesn't increase the physical capacity of bike racers; rather, it inspires them to use more of the ability they already have. Specifically, it exploits the social nature of the human animal in a way that causes cyclists to genuinely expect more from themselves. The yellow jersey puts its wearer under a spotlight that intensifies both the sting of failure and the glory of success and thereby "raises the bar" that the Tour leader aims for on his bike.

Psychologists have a name for this phenomenon: *the audience effect*. The online *Psychology Dictionary* defines it as "the influence of the presence of other people on an individual's behavior." Psychologists believe that the audience effect is mediated by a so-called *sociometer*, a mechanism involving multiple regions of the brain, including the anterior insula and the inferior frontal gyrus. Through this mechanism people notice and interpret the attention of those around them and use this input to adjust their behavior in ways that are likely to earn more positive attention.

In essence, the audience effect coaxes people into holding themselves to higher standards. Consider a 2011 study conducted by psychologists at Newcastle University and published in *Evolution and Human Behavior*, which found that college students were more likely to clean up after themselves in a cafeteria when posters depicting human eyes were conspicuously displayed on the walls. The audience effect elevates people's standards not only for moral behavior but also for any kind of task performance that might be judged. We humans want to be seen as being "good at" whatever we do in the presence of others.

This includes exercise and sports. In 2003, researchers at Arizona State University asked student volunteers to bench press as much weight as they could in three different situations: in a noncompetitive group environment, in competition against other students, and individually in front of a passive audience. The results, published in the *Journal of Strength and Conditioning Research*, were startling. The subjects hoisted significantly more weight when working alone onstage than they did in competition, and moved the least poundage in the noncompetitive group environment. In fact, the numbers weren't even close. On average, the students hefted 13.2 percent more iron in front of an audience than they did unobserved.

Other research has shown that the audience effect becomes even more powerful when observers are not merely present but are actively encouraging the performer, as was the case for Thomas Voeckler when the cycling world rallied behind him at the 2004 Tour de France. In a 2002 study that appeared in the *Journal of Sports Science*, exercise physiologists at the University of Pennsylvania had subjects perform VO$_2$max tests on a treadmill under four different conditions: verbal encouragement every 3 minutes, every minute, and every 20 seconds, and silent observation. There were no differences in the effects of silence and encouragement every 3 minutes, but the subjects performed far better when they were encouraged once a minute and best of all when they were cheered on every 20 seconds. The reason was clear: The subjects exhibited higher blood lactate levels at the end of the test in which they received the most encouragement, indicating that elevated expectations for their performance had impelled them to try harder and get closer to their true physical limit in that test.

These findings help explain the home-court advantage that exists in all sports, including the various endurance disciplines. At the 2012 Olympics in London, for example, British runner Mo Farah won gold medals in the 5000 meters and the 10000 meters for the host nation in front of 80,000 roaring fans at Olympic Stadium. Both races were decided in the bell lap, and in each of them the crowd went utterly berserk during the climactic moments, its deafening sound palpably pushing Farah ahead of the other competitors. The 5000, which came second, was especially close, and afterward Farah credited his supporters for the win. "If it wasn't for them," he said, "I don't think I would have dug as deep."

A 2014 study led by Samuele Marcora and published in *Frontiers in Human Neuroscience* suggests that social encouragement boosts endurance performance not only by motivating athletes to "dig deeper" (or in Marcora's psychobiological terms, to tolerate a higher level of perceived effort), but also by reducing perception of effort relative to exercise intensity. In this study, 13 volunteers rode stationary bikes to exhaustion at high intensity on two separate occasions. In each test, the subjects looked at a computer screen that periodically flashed images of human faces. The images vanished so quickly, however, that the subjects registered them only unconsciously.

In one trial, the subjects were shown happy faces, while in the other they were presented with sad faces. Amazingly, the subjects lasted 12 percent longer in the happy-face trial. Heightened motivation was not the reason, though. Rather, exposure to happy faces lifted the mood state of the subjects and thereby reduced their effort perception. Returning to our fire-walking theme, encouragement in effect lifts the walker so that her feet do not press as deeply into the hot coals and less pain is experienced.

This secondary benefit of the audience effect demonstrates that the phenomenon is not merely a matter of increased motivation. Pure motivators make athletes try harder. The audience effect (assuming a supportive audience) not only makes athletes try harder but also makes them *feel capable of* trying harder. It is through this second influence that the audience effect genuinely raises an athlete's expectations for performance.

Studies like Marcora's suggest that racing for an Olympic gold medal in front of a massive crowd of supportive fans in one's motherland is not the only way to take advantage of the audience effect. Any athlete can do it simply by seeking out events with abundant and enthusiastic spectator support. An estimated 2 million spectators line the streets of the five boroughs at the New York City Marathon. All else being equal, a runner will probably perform better in this event than he would in a smaller marathon with sparser spectator support.

The specific makeup of a group of spectators influences the strength of the audience effect as well. In a 1988 study published in *Psychophysiology*, Stephen Boutcher of the University of New South Wales in Australia found that male subjects gave lower ratings of perceived effort when pedaling a stationary bike at high intensity if the experimenter was female. This finding is corroborated by the experience of many male participants in the Boston Marathon, who feel they get a special boost from passing through the famous "scream tunnel" of Wellesley College coeds at the midpoint of the race.

Spending time in the yellow jersey may be a once-in-a-lifetime experience for one in a million competitive cyclists, but resourceful endurance athletes at every level of competition can exploit the audience effect to raise their expectations for performance, for example by choosing races selectively, by seeding the crowd with family and friends, and perhaps even by cultivating a social media "fan" base.

FOR SEVEN LONG YEARS it appeared that wearing the yellow jersey would indeed be a once-in-a-lifetime experience for Thomas Voeckler. Then, in 2011, it happened again—Thomas snatched the overall lead of the Tour de France and held onto the *maillot jaune* far longer than most people expected. But if no one else expected it, Thomas himself did. For he was no longer the same cyclist he had been in 2004. In that year's Tour, he had relied on the audience effect to achieve a performance breakthrough. Being the center of attention had motivated him to try harder, and the support of his well-wishers had made him feel capable of riding faster than he ever had before. In subsequent races, however, Thomas relied on something else, which we might call the *success effect*. Thomas's heroics in the 2004 Tour changed him. Having discovered that he could ride with the very best when he set his mind to it, he did so repeatedly in subsequent years, winning a number of big races, including the 2008 Circuit de la Sarthe and the 2010 French National Road Race Championship.

Numerous studies have shown that experiencing success in the performance of a given task enhances subsequent performance in the same task by increasing self-efficacy, or perceived competence. Proof that believing one is good at something can elevate performance, independently of actually being good at it, comes from studies in which conditions are secretly manipulated in such a way that subjects' initial success is unmerited, duping them into believing they are better at the task than they actually are. For example, in a 2014 study published in *Proceedings of the National Academy of Sciences*, researchers at the State University of New York–Stony Brook created an online game and randomly distributed rewards for "successful performance" to some players. Although the rewarded players had not actually performed better than the other players initially, they went on to perform better as the game continued. That's the success effect, distinct from the audience effect.

At a deeper level, though, these two effects share a common mechanism. Both work by causing athletes and other task performers to expect more from themselves. In the audience effect, athletes aim for a higher standard of success when they are being observed than they do when their performance is unnoticed, all for the sake of being positively judged by their observers. In the success effect, athletes aim for a higher standard because a past success has heightened their sense of self-efficacy, engendering an expectation that they can perform better than in the past.

A variety of experiments have proven that, regardless of where they come from, expectations of success improve performance. In 2013, psychologists Ulrich Weger and Stephen Loughnan asked two groups of subjects to answer a series of questions presented sequentially on a screen. One group was told that the correct answer to each question would be flashed on the screen very quickly (like the happy faces in the Marcora study described above), so that only the subconscious mind would "see" it. In fact, nonsense phrases were shown. Nevertheless, these subjects did in fact answer more questions correctly. In a summary of their findings published in the *Quarterly Journal of Experimental Psychology*, Weger and Loughnan concluded that this was because they were first given the expectation that they would perform better.

According to the psychobiological model of endurance performance, *any* influence that causes an athlete to expect better performance has the potential to result in better performance. There is even evidence that exercise itself works partly as a placebo—that the fitter a person expects to get from an exercise program, the fitter he really does get. This would explain why it is often said that what distinguishes great coaches from other coaches is not their training system but rather their ability to get athletes to believe in their training system.

It has been suggested also that the phenomenon of peaking—of achieving breakthrough performances at the very end of a period of progressive training—is largely expectation-based. For example, a 2010 study done by Cory Baumann of Georgia State University and Thomas Wetter of the University of Wisconsin–Stevens Point and published in the *International Journal of Exercise Science* found that college cross country runners did their best racing in championship meets at the end of a competitive season, despite showing no improvement in fitness tests done periodically throughout the season.

All in all, high expectations for improvement and success are among the more powerful coping skills an endurance athlete can possess. As the saying goes, if you think you can, you're right. And if you think you can't (even if you say you can), you're also right. Thomas Voeckler understood this, and thus pursued every source of higher expectations that was available to him, whether it was a supportive audience, a success experience, or something else entirely. Consequently, while his second yellow jersey campaign unfolded much like the first, it ended quite differently.

Actually, it started somewhat differently as well. After stage 8, Thomas stood at 19th place in the General Classification, only 89 seconds behind race leader Thor Hushovd. Not since 2004 had Thomas been so close to the top so far into the Tour. Stage 9 was a "medium mountain" stage. On the day's first climb, Thomas initiated a break and was joined by five others. By the time the group reached the base of the second climb, they had increased their advantage on the peloton to 3.5 minutes.

Then they got lucky. On the descent of the Category II Col du Pas de Peyrol, several riders in the main field wiped out at high speed on the rain-slicked road. The men at the front of the peloton called a cease-fire to allow riders caught behind the wreckage to catch up. This bit of sportsmanship allowed Thomas's group to extend their lead to more than 8 minutes. The peloton chased hard over the last couple of climbs, but at the finish line, which Thomas reached 5 seconds behind stage winner Luis-León Sánchez, the gap was still close to 4 minutes. Thomas moved into the overall race lead, 1:49 ahead of Sanchez and 2:26 ahead of the nearest "serious" G.C. contender, Cadel Evans.

Afterward, Thomas told reporters, "The last time I wore it, it was said they let me take the yellow jersey. But this time I went out looking for it."

Translation: *Last time I did not expect to wear the yellow jersey. This time I did.*

Yet despite what Thomas had achieved in 2004, and despite the consistently high level of performance he had sustained since that breakthrough, nobody besides him really expected him to match, let alone exceed, the gritty transcendence of his first streak in yellow. After all, this time around his time buffer was not nearly as large. What's more, the race was already in the mountains, where the best riders—men like Cadel Evans and Andy Schleck—produce their best efforts. Yet on the morning of stage 18, the Queen Stage of the 2011 Tour de France, Thomas was still 66 seconds ahead of Schleck and 2:36 ahead of Evans. He had indeed equaled his feat of seven years earlier, enthralling the cycling world all over again, bringing fans old and new to the brink of coronary infarction repeatedly with his often-down-but-never-out racing.

Stage 18 was a 200-km race over three beyond-category climbs ending in a summit finish. We saw this very stage from the perspective of Cadel Evans in Chapter 6. Thomas's experience of that epic ride was very different, even though he pedaled in the eventual Tour winner's shadow throughout it.

Recall that Andy Schleck made a bold early solo move on the forbidding Col d'Izoard, which tops out at 7,743 feet. No one dared to follow him with so much climbing still ahead. By the time he reached the valley between the Col d'Izoard and the final climb of the day, the seemingly interminable 22.8-km ascent of the Col du Galibier, Schleck had completely erased his deficit to Thomas in the G.C. and become the virtual leader of the Tour de France. Schleck hit the lower slopes hard, and when the chase group arrived at the base, the

Luxembourgian was already 3 minutes and 50 seconds up the road. Thomas would have to complete the ascent at least 75 seconds faster than the defending champion of the Tour de France to hold on to the yellow jersey.

Evans had equal motivation to chase Schleck and more strength to do it, so he set the pace. There were no attacks and few changes in tempo. Evans just put himself at the front of the group and rode the legs off almost everyone behind him. Thomas settled into the Australian's wake for the most excruciating hour he had ever spent on a bicycle. Behind him, more accomplished cyclists flew away like dead leaves from a trundling wheelbarrow.

The real drama, however, was happening inside the few who hung on. Thomas's struggle looked and felt less like "racing" and more like dangling from a roof edge by the fingertips. It was an inexorable draining of energy, life, and spirit made agonizing by the unrelenting steadiness of the work, the utter impossibility of even momentarily giving in to the urgent need to relax, if only by 1 percent.

When Evans passed under the banner marking 2 km to the summit, only five men remained in his group, Thomas last among them. Schleck had passed under the same banner 2:56 earlier. In the preceding 21 km, the chasers had whittled only 54 seconds off Schleck's lead. Thomas needed to take back an additional 19 seconds in the last 2 km. It seemed impossible. His only remaining hope was his teammate Pierre Rolland, who had also survived, barely.

Embracing his painful duty, Rolland stood up and clawed his way ahead of Evans. Thomas followed close behind, urging his teammate on like a sadistic dogsled musher. But Rolland's martyr's mission sputtered out quickly and he returned to the caboose. Evans reclaimed the front and began a hard push to the finish. Thomas took second wheel and hung on, almost blinded by pain. Rolland and Damiano Cunego cracked in quick succession, leaving only Frank Schleck and Ivan Basso in contact with Evans and Thomas. It was down to the four best climbers in the world plus an average climber with invisible wings.

At the 1-km banner, Thomas was 2:35 behind Andy Schleck—back in the yellow jersey by 1 second. His legs were infernos of pain. Each gasping stint of upright pedaling lasted only six or seven breaths before he had to sit for a nominal reprieve that offered only the slightest diminution of agony. Three hundred meters from the line, Frank Schleck attacked and sprinted away to claim second place in the stage. Evans and Basso went after him. Thomas could not. Within sight of the end, his body had begun to shut down. He stood one last time and pedaled with his face tilted toward the heavens, tongue out and lolling slackly on his chin.

Thomas crossed the finish line 2 minutes and 21 seconds behind Andy Schleck, retaining the *maillot jaune* by 15 seconds—after more than 6 hours of riding. In photos taken at this instant, Thomas's face expresses unsurpassable joy mixed with unspeakable suffering. This face is the distilled essence of Thomas Voeckler's unique achievement as a yellow jersey wearer in the Tour de France: an ineffable, almost Pyrrhic triumph that includes elements of success and failure yet transcends both.

A report posted later that day on cyclingnews.com bore the headline "Astonishing Voeckler Still in Yellow." Thomas was described within the report as having pulled off a "miracle Tour."

It would have taken something more than a miracle, however, for Thomas to have escaped stage 19 with the *maillot jaune* still on his back. Hollow-legged from the start, he turned himself inside out on the Category I Col du Télégraphe and the beyond-category Col du Galibier just to reach the base of the Tour's most storied climb, Alpe d'Huez, in contact with the Schleck brothers, Evans, Basso, and Contador. He lost time to all of these men and ended the day in fourth place in the General Classification, 2:10 behind new leader Andy Schleck.

But Thomas had one more surprise in store. The last competitive stage of the Tour, stage 20, was a 42.5-km individual time trial. Thomas had never been a great time trialist. In the corresponding stage from the 2010 Tour, he had finished 128th and given up more than 9 minutes to the stage winner. If Thomas put in a similar performance this time, he would drop out of the top 10 in the final overall standings. He did not want that. Indeed, he now wanted to hold onto his fourth-place position as badly as he'd previously wanted to keep the yellow jersey. So motivated, Thomas rode the greatest time trial of his career, finishing in 13th place and losing only 2 minutes and 14 seconds to the stage winner, Tony Martin. It was more than enough to protect his position in the G.C.

It's worth emphasizing that Thomas Voeckler was no longer wearing the yellow jersey when he turned in this stunning performance. It was never really about the yellow jersey. It was about the potential that existed inside him all along—potential that required only matching expectations in order to produce something very, very special.

CHAPTER ELEVEN

PASSION
KNOWS NO AGE

ON THE 21ST DAY of the second month of his 44th year on earth, Ned Overend woke up just before sunrise in a room at the Aston Wailea Resort on the island of Maui. He ate a quick breakfast of oatmeal, a banana, and coffee, gathered his gear together, and made his way down to the beach. By nine o'clock Ned had finished setting up his transition area, put air in the tires of his Specialized S-Works mountain bike, and completed a 10-minute swim in the bath-like waters of the South Pacific. The sky was cloudless and the air warm, inching toward hot.

An amplified male voice pierced the morning quiet, calling all athletes to the start line of the 1998 XTERRA World Championship.

Ned joined 185 other competitors on a patch of powdery sand at the water's edge, finding a place up front amid a knot of professional racers. Mike Pigg, the defending champion of this off-road triathlon, looked relaxed and ready. Wes Hobson, one of the world's best short-course triathletes, raised his arms overhead to stretch his shoulders. Jimmy Riccitello, winner of the inaugural XTERRA in 1996, stared into the water, choosing his line. Michael Tobin, almost unbeatable in duathlons (run-bike-run races), made a small adjustment to the fit of his goggles. Ned sidled up beside the last of these men, conspicuous for his cycling shorts (the others wore Speedos) and bushy moustache, best remembered as the winner of the first-ever cross-country mountain biking world championship back in 1990.

Endurance athletes who compete in multi-hour events typically hit their peak between the ages of 30 and 35. Most of the pros on the beach that day fell within this range. Tobin was the youngest of the male contenders at 31. Pigg and Hobson had both recently celebrated their 34th birthdays. Riccitello was a boyish-looking 35.

The outlier, again, was Ned. At 43, Ned was not just older than the pros around him; he was more than five years past the age of the oldest person ever to win a world championship in any major endurance sport.

A gun cracked. The competitors high-stepped into the surf and dived forward. Ned stroked as hard as he could for the first 50 yards, bent on hitching a ride in the second pack. A relatively inexperienced swimmer, he had little hope of latching onto the first group, where Pigg, Hobson, and Riccitello were sure to be.

Glenn Wachtell, a local lifeguard, led the field toward a pill-shaped orange buoy marking the first of two hard right turns on the triangular course. Hobson was close behind him in the fourth position. At 250 meters, Ned had already fallen 23 seconds behind the leaders, but that was pretty good by his standards. Ned had finished third in the inaugural XTERRA and second in 1997, and the swim had been his undoing in both races. But he'd worked hard in the pool over the past several months, and lately things had started to click. He'd felt comfortable and efficient in his practice swims since arriving on Maui, and he could tell already that he was swimming better than he had in past XTERRAs.

A lead group of 15 athletes swam parallel to the shore through choppy waters toward the second buoy and then cut back toward the beach. The full circuit was 750 meters. The racers would swim it twice with a short beach run between loops. Ned reached the shore a little more than a minute behind the first echelon. Determined to shave time by all possible means, he sprinted between the swim exit and the reentry point while looking ahead to see if he might catch up to a faster group of swimmers. Not watching where he was putting his feet, he stumbled on a small rise in the sand and nearly fell. Back in the water, Ned was able to latch onto the feet of fellow pro Sasha Kreuke and stroked in his wake through much of the second loop.

Wes Hobson completed the swim still in fourth place and first among the major contenders. The race clock showed 14:58 as he charged through a gauntlet of cheering spectators into a grass transition area, where he crammed on his helmet, grabbed his mountain bike, and started the bike leg. Pigg entered transition 12 seconds behind Hobson, and Riccitello another 22 seconds back. Ned left the water in 43rd place, 2 minutes and 17 seconds after Hobson but more than 40 seconds closer to the lead than he'd been the year before.

Ned took a bit more time to gear up than some of the younger athletes had, donning a red sleeveless top with his name emblazoned on the back, a matching helmet and gloves, and sunglasses. The 30-kilometer bike course started with a short, paved section. It was crucial for Ned to get around as many racers as possible before the trail narrowed and passing became more difficult. By far the most skilled off-road rider in the field, he overtook no fewer than 36 superior swimmers and moved up to fifth place in the first 4 miles. Behind him, the next-best mountain biker, Michael Tobin, suffered a tire puncture and lost even more time than the 25 seconds he'd already given up to Ned in the swim.

Hobson was first to reach Heartbreak Hill, a 1,200-foot, 1-mile climb on the lower slopes of the otherworldly Haleakala Volcano, long dormant but radiating a magma-like heat on this day nevertheless. He shifted down to his smallest gear and attacked the rutted, rock-strewn hill at a high cadence in an effort to avoid stalling out, but his rear wheel caught a patch of loose dirt and spun. Unable to unclip from his pedals quickly enough, he fell in seeming slow motion onto his right side. The next man through, Riccitello, experienced a similar problem but managed to dismount and run his bike forward.

So steep and technical was the climb that even Ned bogged down at the same treacherous point. But he did not meet the same fate. Without a hint of panic, he executed a modified track stand, whipping his handlebar—and with it his front wheel—from side to side to hold his balance until he was able to find a good line and pedal his way out. A small crowd of spectators and photographers who had come here from the beach applauded the nifty maneuver. (I know because I was one of them.)

Near the summit of Heartbreak, Ned—whose climbing prowess had earned him the nickname Deadly Nedly—caught Pigg and moved into third place. As he whizzed past Pigg's left shoulder, Ned looked back, gently taunting the only man he'd never beaten at this event with a brief, silent stare.

The next target ahead on the trail was Jimmy Riccitello. Ned set his sights on the Texan's back while screaming along a straight, undulating descent. Both men were gaining on Hobson, who ran into trouble in another loose-dirt section of the course known as Bubba's Revenge, where he was compelled to unclip his right shoe and propel himself forward scooter-style for several frustrating meters. Minutes later, Hobson made a hairpin turn that afforded him an opportunity to check on the whereabouts of his chasers. They were right behind him.

The trail began to climb again. Ned passed Riccitello before Riccitello could catch Hobson. Still ascending, Ned pulled up right behind Hobson, relaxed briefly, and then swung to the left and surged into the lead. Ned had not yet recovered from the effort, however, when he came upon an abrupt uptick in the angle of the ascent that caught him off guard. He began to hyperventilate and was forced to dismount. He walked the bike upward in a doubled-over posture with his head hanging limply toward the dirt. Hobson was still close behind and, seeing Ned's compromised state, he seized the opportunity, churning the pedals furiously in a bid to knock Ned back to second place. But just before he pulled even, the trail flattened out and Ned remounted his bike and pulled away.

232

The new leader of the race soon came upon the second and last big climb on the course—a 1-mile, 1,420-foot soul-crusher that became known as Ned's Climb after the first XTERRA. At its base, Ned passed an aid station manned by a handful of teenagers sweating through matching blue T-shirts. He called out for water, gulped it, and then got down to the business of showing why the hill had been named after him. He pushed a big gear, putting his whole body into each downstroke with a piston-like rhythm.

At the top of the climb, Ned made a sharp right turn onto a narrow, rattling descent walled in on either side by thick vegetation. He holstered his lungs and loaded up his technical skills and derring-do. Ned kept his eyes focused well ahead on the trail, looking out for rocks that could flatten a tire as well as "compression dips"—shallow concavities where his front tire might abruptly sink, sending him somersaulting over the handlebar. Aiming to ride as lightly as possible over the uneven surface, he coasted out of the saddle with his legs almost fully straightened and his elbows locked, balancing his weight evenly between the two tires. His body absorbed a beating nevertheless, even with front and rear shock absorbers to soften the jolts.

On gentler sections of the long plunge toward the beach, Ned settled back onto the seat and pedaled hard. It was not enough for him to merely have *a* lead when he started to run. He needed as big a lead as possible. Last year, Ned had been first off the bike only to be run down by Pigg, and at least two of the other men chasing him today—Hobson and Tobin—were capable of running even faster than the defending champion.

The bike leg concluded with a right turn onto a short spur of trail that led to a green timing mat set in front of a changing tent. The race clock positioned beside the mat showed 1:43:18 as Ned executed a flying dismount and dumped his bike to the ground for a volunteer to haul away. A second volunteer handed Ned a plastic bag containing his running shoes and a sun visor. He ducked into the tent and sat on a folding chair to suit up for the final leg of the contest: an 11-kilometer obstacle-filled footrace.

Ned felt every single one of his 43 years as he exited the tent on the far side and broke into a bandy-legged run down a shaded trail toward Makena Beach. Even on fresh legs, Ned ran like a gorilla, arms hanging low and knuckles turned forward, but just now his fatigued stride looked especially simian.

At the beach, he made a right turn and followed markers that guided him through soft, dry sand. He felt like a sleeper fleeing a ghost in a nightmare, barely moving for all his effort. To his left, vacationers frolicked in the balmy water, oblivious to Ned's quest for a world championship title.

Out of sight behind him, Wes Hobson hit transition at 1:47:01 on the race clock with Jimmy Riccitello at his heels. If Ned ran well, it would be tough for either man to close the gap, but if Ned faltered—a real possibility given the heat and how hard he had pushed himself so far—the 11 kilometers of running ahead of the younger chasers offered ample opportunity to hunt him down.

Ned was prepared to make any sacrifice to prevent this from happening. In a television interview filmed the day before the race, he had said, "If the crabs are picking the meat off me on Makena Beach because I've blown up, that's okay. It's win or lose." It's possible he meant "win or die."

A 30-foot section of volleyball-size rocks that cut across the strand broke Ned's rhythm, slowing him to a hurried walk as he chose each foot placement with care. Once he'd gotten beyond the obstacle, he was back in loose sand, his shoes sinking almost out of sight with each landing. Ned felt grateful for the training excursions he'd made recently to Taos, New Mexico, to slog through sand dunes in 95-degree heat.

A bright yellow banner marked the next turn. Ned tacked right and plunged into a forest. He soon came upon a downed tree and hurdled it. As he drew his knees toward his chest, his left hamstring seized up. The burst of pain was followed immediately by a bolt of panic. Muscle cramps were on the short list of disasters that could turn the tables in favor of the whippersnappers behind him. Ned landed and resumed running, the twinge slowly working itself out as he pressed on.

Moments later, he came around a blind corner and nearly ran into a low branch reaching across the trail. He crouched to duck under it and the hamstring cramped again. Despair welled up in him. Ned swallowed it back and kept moving, forcing himself to run normally despite the pain. The muscle loosened up a bit but remained tender. If it cramped a third time, his race would probably be over.

Ned came out of the woods and turned left onto a gravel path. A moped-mounted cameraman and driver awaited him there and began to roll alongside him.

"What kind of lead I got?" Ned asked them.

"Four minutes," the cameraman told him.

Ned could hardly believe it. Perhaps, he thought, he *shouldn't* believe it. Unofficial time gap information was notoriously unreliable. But Ned couldn't help himself. Excitement sent him scudding ahead like a kite in a sudden wind blast. Perhaps the smarter move would have been to gear down to protect his damaged hamstring, but Ned had always raced from his heart, and he wasn't about to do otherwise now.

The gravel path dumped Ned onto Poolenalena Beach. An ebbing tide had left a wide strip of hard-packed wet sand that he was able to glide across efficiently. His hamstring was holding up, but now fatigue was weighing him down. He'd been redlining all morning long, initially to minimize time lost in the water, then to maximize time gained on the bike, and now to preserve his hard-earned lead on foot. In fact, his lead continued to grow as his closest chaser, the much larger Hobson, struggled to run through the loose sand and scramble over the rock formations and under the tree branches Ned had already negotiated.

At the north end of Poolenalena Beach, Ned was directed onto the Wailea Point Path. Its stone surface was more conducive to fast running than anything he had trod upon to this point. He opened up his stride, dropping his pace to well under 6 minutes per mile for the final charge toward the finish line back at Aston Wailea. When he came around a bend in the path, Ned could see the finish line banner in the near distance.

The race wasn't over yet. Fiendishly, the path was interrupted by one last short stretch of beach running. Ned crossed it with a ragged stride and a heaving chest, craning his neck twice to see if Hobson or Pigg or Riccitello or Tobin or even a fast-closing Peter Reid, winner of the Ironman World Championship a week before (and just 29 years old), was visible. The beach was empty.

Ned transitioned from sand to stone to grass in the span of 50 meters, guided by boundaries of white police tape stretched between wooden stakes. On either side of the stakes stood cheering spectators, whose shrill racket was drowned out by the race announcer's amplified baritone. As he barreled through the finishing chute, Ned extended his left arm and slapped hands with a few dozen strangers, smiling boyishly. He broke the tape at 2:24:16, exactly four and a half minutes ahead of Wes Hobson, to set a new course record and become the oldest world champion endurance athlete ever.

BEFORE HE DIED in 1996 at 100 years of age, comedian George Burns said, "If you ask me what is the most important key to longevity, I would have to say it is avoiding worry, stress, and tension. And if you didn't ask me, I'd still have to say it."

Science suggests Burns knew what he was talking about. Aging and longevity are influenced by a variety of factors, including genes and lifestyle, but research has proven that psychology has the greatest influence. Specifically, people who have a positive attitude and who don't sweat the small stuff tend to age slower and live longer.

Among the first scientists to document this connection was Stephen Jewett, a psychiatrist at New York Medical College. In 1973, *The Gerontologist* published Jewett's seminal paper, "Longevity and the Longevity Syndrome." In it, he shared what he had learned from observing 79 men and women between the ages of 87 and 103. He noted several common personality traits, including "freedom from anxiety," "optimism and a sense of humor," and a tendency to "see life as a great adventure."

Subsequent research has buttressed and extended Jewett's findings. Today there is general agreement among psychologists that four key personality traits that largely overlap with Jewett's—openness, conscientiousness, extraversion, and low neuroticism—are strongly predictive of long life and health in old age. A 2007 study performed by researchers at the University of Edinburgh and published in *Psychosomatic Medicine*, for example, found that people who scored low on a measure of neuroticism (a tendency toward fear and anxiety) were far less likely to die of cardiovascular disease over a 21-year period than were worriers.

Scientists are still trying to figure out why the four key personality traits slow the aging process. Researchers with dualistic leanings, who incline toward thinking of mind and body as separate, have generally looked for behavioral links between individual personality traits and particular healthy behaviors. Some such links have been identified. Conscientious men and women are less likely to abuse alcohol, while extraverted individuals are more likely to exercise.

Scientists who come at the same problem from a psychobiological perspective, where mind and body are viewed as interpenetrating and the concept of personality is replaced by that of coping style, have focused on emotion. This approach has been more fruitful, and it is now clear that emotion plays a far more significant role than behavior does in mediating the anti-aging effects of personality.

It is natural to think of emotions as mental experiences, but they are also body states. Coping styles are expressed largely through emotion, and emotion is expressed largely through body states. Neurotic persons, for example, spend a lot of time in a state of stress. The stress state involves (among other things) the release of cortisol, a hormone that, over time, inflicts a great deal of wear and tear on the body. Chronically elevated cortisol levels are known to cause everything from weight gain to brain atrophy. Neurotic people exhibit high cortisol levels and, perhaps for this reason, also face an increased risk of developing Alzheimer's disease and other chronic diseases.

The four key anti-aging personality traits not only combat many potential killers but also put the brakes on aging-related declines in physical fitness. In a 2012 study published in the *International Journal of Behavioral Medicine*, Magdalena Tolea and colleagues at the University of Missouri discovered that older men and women with neurotic personalities had weaker muscles compared to laid-back types of the same age. Differences in exercise habits accounted for only a small portion of this discrepancy.

Even more relevant to the interests of endurance athletes are the results of a 2013 study performed by researchers affiliated with the National Institute on Aging and published in *PLOS ONE*. More than 600 men and women as old as 96 completed a walking test that was used to assess their aerobic capacity (VO_2max). Those who scored low for neuroticism and high for extraversion, openness, and conscientiousness had a significantly greater aerobic capacity compared to their peers with less positive personality traits.

The aging process begins to sap muscle strength and aerobic capacity around 35 years of age in most people. Not surprisingly, as already noted, the peak performance years of endurance athletes also come to an end at this point in life. No athlete is exempt from the phenomenon of "the last PR," but there is a great deal of individual variation in the time course of aging-related athletic decline. Some athletes fall off their peak early and decline rapidly, while others sustain their highest level of performance much longer, and when at last they begin to slow down, they do so gradually.

What do these slower-aging athletes have that others lack? The studies I described above would lead us to expect that the secret lies in their coping style. Real-world evidence strongly supports this hunch. The most successful endurance athletes over the age of 40 are so similar in personality it's almost uncanny. What we see in all of these men and women is a limitless passion for sport and for the athletic lifestyle that stems from a positive, life-embracing personality (i.e., a non-neurotic, open, extraverted, conscientious style of coping with life).

A case in point is Haile Gebrselassie. From age 21 to 36, Gebrselassie set 27 world records in distance-running events. By the time he set the last of these records, most of his old rivals were retired. But "Geb" kept on racing, and racing well. In 2012, at age 39, he won the Great Manchester Run 10K in 27:39, beating 27-year-old marathon world record holder Patrick Makau. The next year, he won the Vienna Half Marathon in 1:01:14 and set an over-40 world record of 46:59 for 10 miles.

Gebrselassie's love of running is as legendary as his talent. "A day without running is not a good day," he told Paul Gittings in a 2013 appearance on CNN. Later in the same interview, Geb said, "What I'm thinking now is that I want to break all the masters records— over forty, over fifty, over sixty." These are the words of a man whose appetite for testing his limits as a runner is truly inexhaustible. While Gebrselassie understands that getting slower is inevitable, no amount of slowing can ruin running for him. He wants to do the most he can with what he has as long as he lives. Indeed, more than once, he has vowed to keep running until the day he dies.

While running is Haile Gebrselassie's singular calling, his passion for running is merely a special manifestation of an all-around zeal for life. His days at home in Addis Ababa are jam-packed with business undertakings (he's a very successful entrepreneur), appearances at community and political events, interviews, sponsor obligations, family time, festive meals, and, of course, a couple of runs. One senses that if Geb hadn't found running, he would have found something else to anchor it all. He may want to run until he dies, but he wants to live forever.

If Gebrselassie is known for smiling at all times except when he is racing, Natascha Badmann, whom we encountered in earlier chapters, is known for smiling even in competition. (Type her name into the search box at Google Images and you will see what I mean.) Badmann does not smile because she wins, although she won a lot in her prime years between 1998 and 2005, when she collected six Iron-man world champion titles. Rather, she wins because she smiles—or because of the passion behind the smile.

In her 20s, Badmann was an overweight and depressed single mother who loathed exercise. But a new boyfriend (whom she eventually married) convinced her to try a little jogging and cycling. In short order, the experiment led to a total rebirth. Badmann became a completely new person, one who loved her body and what she could do with it, and who brought a profound gratitude into her sports participation that made failure seem nothing to fear and success an almost inevitable outcome of a total embrace of the process.

In a 2004 interview, Badmann said, "I got into triathlon to become a happy and healthy person. I want to do it for the rest of my life."

Three years after making this comment, Badmann was on her way toward winning a seventh Ironman World Championship and becoming the event's oldest winner (she was 39) when she crashed her bike, suffering serious injuries. It would have been a good time to change her mind about doing triathlon for the rest of her life, but she did not. Instead of hanging it up, Badmann worked her way back to health, and then back to fitness, and then back to the top of the sport. In 2012, at age 45, she won Ironman South Africa, becoming the oldest Ironman winner in history. Six months later, she finished sixth in the women's competition at the Ironman World Championship in Hawaii.

The sport of cycling has its ageless wonders too, and they fit the same personality mold as Gebrselassie and Badmann. There's no better example than Jens Voigt, a fan favorite from Germany who retired from professional cycling one day after his 43rd birthday. Voigt's last competitive event—which took place on September 18, 2014, the very day of his retirement—was an attempt to break the one-hour time trial world record. The fact that he would even try such a thing says a lot about him. The existing mark had been set by a 30-year-old and had stood for almost a decade. The fact that Voigt succeeded says even more. He covered a distance of 51.115 kilometers on a track in Switzerland to smash the old standard.

Three weeks earlier, Voigt had participated in his last team road race, the seven-stage USA Pro Challenge in Colorado. He rode the same way he had ridden throughout his career: aggressively, fearlessly, and with unbridled enthusiasm. In stage 4, the inveterate breakaway specialist got himself into one last breakaway, along with 11 other members of the 115-man field. Forty kilometers from the finish line, on a steep climb, Voigt attacked from within the breakaway. No one could match the hoary German's acceleration. Tunneling deep into his "pain cave," as he called it, Voigt built a lead of 90 seconds over his former coconspirators, whose average age was 25.

Voigt had won the same stage of the same event in the same fashion back in 2012, at age 40. This time, however, it was not to be. A hard-chasing peloton swallowed up the shattered breakaway and then came after Voigt. With 10 km to go, his lead was 60 seconds. With 5 km to go, despite no letup from the leader, the gap was down to 35 seconds. Virtually everyone watching the spectacle wanted to see the swashbuckling veteran pull it off. Scores of spectators among the thousands lining the multi-circuit course hollered, "Go, Jensie!" Many of them sported T-shirts imprinted with Voigt's signature line, "Shut up, legs!" Twitter was ablaze with prayers for those legs. Voigt fed off the love, opening himself up to his suffering as few others could, and as he himself had done so many times before without ever dulling the edge of his passion, but it was no use. At 2 km to the finish, his lead was 20 seconds. Within sight of the finish line, the peloton engulfed him, still fighting, like a mad swimmer in a hurricane.

It was a heartbreaker for fans of Jens Voigt. But not for Voigt himself.

"Maybe, in a bizarre way, it was fitting it ended like this," he said to velonews.com reporter Neal Rogers after the race. "This is the story of my life—from twenty, thirty, even forty breakaways, maybe one works. This was the typical breakaway: You give it all, and you get caught. It was a perfect example of my career—you put it all on the line; you're taking risks [of] looking stupid."

The attitude expressed in these words—a harmonious blend of "damn the torpedoes" and "easy come, easy go"—goes a long way toward explaining why Voigt was the most beloved rider on the professional tour, and why he performed at such a high level for so many years.

Jens Voigt and Natascha Badmann and Haile Gebrselassie and other super-positive high-performing older athletes—including Ned Overend—offer anecdotal corroboration of the scientific evidence that a positive personality preserves endurance performance by decelerating the physical aging process. The problem is that there is very little we can do about our overall coping style. Athletes who are naturally neurotic or withdrawn may admire the likes of Voigt, Badmann, and Gebrselassie, but can they emulate them?

Actually, they can—in a sense. While people with a positive personality type are predisposed to develop passionate interests (in sports as well as in any number of other things), passions are not the exclusive domain of such people. Men and women with other coping styles are also capable of falling in love with pursuits that fit them. And when they do, these passions yield the same anti-aging benefits that a positive personality does.

Research by psychologists including Robert Vallerand—who defined passion in a 2012 paper published in *Psychology of Well-Being* as "a strong inclination toward a self-defining activity that people like (or even love), find important, and in which they invest time and energy on a regular basis"—has demonstrated that passion enhances psychological well-being in ways that are sort of like a personality makeover. People who have a strong passion for an activity are known to spend less time in age-accelerating emotional states such as anxiety, just as naturally positive people do. Indeed, Natascha Badmann may be a better example of the transformative power of passion than of innate positivity. The way she describes her pre-athlete self, there can be little doubt that she would have scored quite low on tests of openness, conscientiousness, extraversion, and non-neuroticism before she discovered triathlon, which became a passion that changed her profoundly and permanently.

There is no better role model for this passion-led approach to endurance sports (and no greater poster boy for its rewards) than Ned Overend. Ned started out as a runner, competing in cross country and track throughout his high school years in Marin County, California, and continuing with cross country through his first two years of college. At age 20, he quit running to chase another interest: motocross. After college, Ned's then-roommate got him hooked on the new sport of triathlon. Triathlon steered Ned back toward running, but because he now lived in the heart of the Rockies, he focused on mountain running. When he got injured and couldn't run for a while, he started cycling to stay fit and improved so quickly that he soon turned pro. Around this time, mountain biking became popular. The motocrosser in Ned was drawn to it. He traded skinny tires for knobby ones and won seven national championships and a world championship as a cross-country mountain bike racer.

It wasn't that Ned couldn't find something he really liked. He just liked variety, and he recognized that his hunger to train and compete was greatest when he tried new things and pursued diverse goals. Even when he concentrated for some time on a particular goal, he chased it in a measured and balanced way that kept his body and mind fresh. Throughout his mountain biking career, for example, Ned spent his winters tramping around his home in Durango, Colorado, on snowshoes and cross-country skis while his bike gathered dust. These alternative activities gave his "cycling muscles" a break, and the changeup kept him mentally engaged in his fitness through the off-season. He wouldn't start training seriously on the bike again until he missed it.

Even during the racing season, Ned did not push his body as hard as some of his rivals did. "I like to do my training short and sweet," he explained to me in a 1998 interview for *Triathlete*. "I don't mind training hard, but I don't tend to do a lot of long training. I get out there and I don't dick around. I get it done and I go home and work on other things I've got stacked up." In other words, Ned never trained beyond his enthusiasm.

After Ned and his wife, Pam, had their first child in 1987, he cut back on his travel and racing. Spending time with his family made him a happier person, and being a happier person made him a better athlete. Even so, Ned inevitably got itchy to go to new places as an athlete. In 1996, he retired from mountain biking and turned his attention to the emerging sport of off-road triathlon. Two years later, he was the sport's world champion.

VARIETY AND BALANCE WERE not the only factors that kept Ned Overend hungry as an athlete. Winning and improving did too. Underneath his easygoing demeanor beat the heart of a fierce competitor. One of the reasons Ned quit triathlon in the early 1980s was that he had limited success in the sport. One of the reasons he retired from mountain biking in 1996 was that he failed to make the U.S. Olympic Team. And one of the reasons he found himself back on the start line of the XTERRA World Championship in 1999 was that he believed he could win again, and perhaps even improve, despite being yet another year past 40.

To succeed, Ned would have to defeat not only the usual suspects such as Mike Tobin and Jimmy Riccitello but also rising stars like three-time and defending duathlon world champion Olivier Bernhard (age 31), up-and-coming pro triathlete Kerry Classen (27), and off-road triathlon specialist Mike Vine (26).

In 1998, the swim course had been accidentally mismeasured to Ned's advantage, being slightly shorter than advertised. The following year, however, the problem was corrected, giving Ned more space to lose time in the water. He came out of the Pacific 3:03 behind the leader, Classen, and only 2 seconds ahead of the notoriously hydrophobic duathlete Tobin.

If there was one discipline in which the 44-year-old Ned could not have expected much improvement, it was mountain biking, which had been his main focus throughout his late 20s and 30s. Sure enough, he covered the brutal 30-km bike leg almost 4 minutes slower than he had the year before. Even so, he outpaced Tobin by 4 minutes and started the run with as big a lead as he'd had the previous year. Tobin chased Overend like an assassin over the sand and rocks and roots, cutting the gap by 2:28, but he needed another 1:36. Ned won again.

In 2000, Ned attempted what seemed impossible: winning a third consecutive XTERRA World Championship title at 45. Turned out it *was* impossible. He finished fifth. "Today wasn't the day for me," he said afterward. "I figured about 20 minutes into the bike that I wasn't climbing well enough to catch the leaders."

A fourth-place finish at the 2001 XTERRA series finale confirmed for Ned that his days of winning the event were behind him. So, naturally, he moved on to other challenges. He did not cherry-pick, seeking out weak competition that he could dominate despite his advanced years. Quite the opposite, in fact. Still hungry to win against the best, Ned sought out premier events that played to his strengths, like really hilly road bike races.

On September 11, 2004, three weeks after he turned 49, Ned won the Colorado State Road Cycling Championship, a race he had last won more than 15 years earlier, in 1987.

In 2011, he returned to another race he had conquered long ago: the Iron Horse Classic, a mountainous 47-mile road race in Ned's hometown of Durango that he'd won in 1983, 1986, 1987, and 1992. The race became a two-man battle on a lung-busting ascent of Coal Bank Pass, which tops out over 10,000 feet. At the base of the climb, 19-year-old Howard Grotts attacked. Ned, then 55, was able to follow him initially, but as the air thinned he began to struggle and Grotts opened a 10-second gap. Approaching the summit, Ned rallied and caught the leader, and then left him behind on the subsequent descent. He maintained his advantage on the final climb up Molas Pass to the finish line and the win. Grotts held on for third.

Ned continues to redefine what is possible for older endurance athletes. Of course, what is possible for him might not be possible for everyone. But the wisdom of going where joy and happiness leads is undeniable, as is the time-defying power of trusting the instincts that guide an athlete—any athlete—toward the methods, goals, and athletic lifestyle that best fuel the fire inside. Science merely confirms what living examples like Ned Overend prove: If your passion endures, so will you.

CHAPTER TWELVE

IS IT WORTH IT?

STEVE PREFONTAINE HATED RUNNING in the cold. He reminded his University of Oregon teammates of this fact more than once during a stiff-legged warm-up jog on the Fox Den Country Club golf course in Knoxville, Tennessee. The other Ducks, being well accustomed to his pre-race grumbling (a ritual in all weathers), made no effort to brighten their leader's outlook. Besides, he was right: It was damn cold—a good 20 degrees below normal for the Monday before Thanksgiving. Visible puffs of CO_2 vapor issued from the runners' mouths on every fifth foot strike. Chill gusts from the northeast tousled Pre's trademark side-parted blond mop as he shuffled along over crunchy Bermuda grass, waiting until the last possible moment to remove his thick sweat suit and hooded windbreaker.

At 11 o'clock sharp, a shot rang out and the 1971 NCAA Cross Country Championship began. Two hundred eighty-seven runners charged ahead onto the 6-mile race route. Pre now wore only a thin cotton T-shirt and his scanty school uniform. In typical fashion, he sprinted straight to the head of the field, but was closely marked by a brace of confident men thirsting for the glory of knocking off the Golden Boy of American Running, who at just 20 years of age had already won three NCAA championship titles and three Amateur Athletic Union national championship races, set three American records, and appeared on the cover of *Sports Illustrated*. Among the challengers were future 800-meter Olympic gold medalist Dave Wottle of Bowling Green, 1968 Olympian Marty Liquori of Villanova, and defending NCAA 6-mile champion Garry Bjorklund of Minnesota.

Bjorklund was the boldest of these men in his defiance of Pre's claim to the front, throwing the aggressive early pace right back at him, even half-stepping him at times. Insistent on controlling every race from start to finish, Pre retaliated by pressing harder, to which Bjorklund responded in kind. And so it went. The co-leaders completed the first mile in 4:24, a reckless pace on any course, let alone a rollercoaster like this one.

Already, with 5 miles left to go, Pre felt awful. His legs were filled with sand, his mind with doubts. Most troubling was Bjorklund's comparative ease, the way he seemed to bound over the same grassy hummocks that Pre smacked into like brick walls.

Soon, Pre slipped from dictating the pace to sharing it to being dragged along by Bjorklund. A pitched battle was taking place inside Pre's mind. His suffering was an obsession, blotting out all else save for a narrow cone of frontal vision. He knew he could not survive another 20 minutes of this purgatory. He craved desperately to ease up, let Bjorklund go, and spare himself further misery. But something wouldn't let him.

In the third mile, Pre and Bjorklund pulled away from the pack along with two others: Mike Stack of North Dakota State and Dan Murphy of Washington State. Pre continued to give up in his head while plunging onward with his body. Bjorklund perceived Pre's crisis and at the halfway point of the race he surged ahead of the others. The breach came almost as a relief to Pre, who continued to run hard but no longer had to endure the torment of trying to keep up with the antagonist in the maroon-and-gold uniform of Minnesota.

Bjorklund stretched his lead to five or six strides and then stalled, redlining. Hope flooded back into the hard-breathing chaser, taking the edge off his agony. Pre raised his effort level a quarter-notch and began to close the gap. At 4 miles, the rivals were back together. Pre still yearned to let up, but the same deep compulsion that had stayed his hand earlier in the race now goaded him into testing Bjorklund with little surges. A slight lag in Bjorklund's reactions told all. Pre knew he had his challenger against the ropes. After cresting an especially tough hill, he surged again, this time sustaining the move. Bjorklund had no answer.

As Pre pulled away, he indulged in a bit of showboating with his stride, pumping his arms a little harder than necessary, lifting his knees a centimeter or two higher than would have been most efficient. The ostentation soon dissipated, though, leaving behind the primal grace of Pre's distinctive natural style. From the waist up he was a rodeo cowboy, arms loose and flailing. From the waist down, he was a bullet train, legs rolling as smoothly as steel wheels on rails.

A mile from the finish, the course turned sharply, sending runners back the way they'd come on a parallel track. Pre's lead on Bjorklund was up to 30 yards and still growing, fear of capture now fueling the refusal to relent. A minute or so after he'd made the turn, Pre came face to face with Tennessee's Doug Brown, still on his way out. Brown was struck by the blend of suffering and determination in the soon-to-be winner's countenance—an image he would never forget. Pre looked both worse and better than any man behind him.

Pre made a final turn onto the home straight and fixed his eyes on a wind-rattled banner hovering 15 feet above the fairway ahead of him. Head lolling, he coasted the last few strides and reined up to a semiconscious stagger at the line. A pair of race officials rushed to steady him. Bjorklund finished 7 seconds later.

The next day, Pre described the race in his diary. "It was a very hard race from the word go with a combination of great runners and a tough course," he wrote. "I had my problems winning. I felt several times like giving into the pain and letting Gary [sic] win but I just couldn't. I just kept driving myself harder and harder, longer and longer."

This frank confession of psychological vulnerability, of unsteadiness in the face of suffering, would have surprised Steve's legions of worshipful fans across America, known as "Pre's People." Through his sadomasochistic racing style and his brash public comments, Pre had built a reputation as the toughest of racers, a fearless gladiator for whom the mastery of effort came easily. "The only good race pace is a suicide pace," he said in typical fashion before one contest, "and today looks like a good day to die."

Such swaggering declarations had given some fans the impression that Pre actually enjoyed suffering. Nothing could have been further from the truth. He faced moments of crisis in almost every race, and on occasion his weaker side held sway. "I wasn't competitive," he lamented after a losing effort in Europe. "We were neck and neck with 50 yards left and I suddenly thought, 'Oh, hell, I don't want this bad enough. I don't care. Take it.'"

Even in training, Pre often struggled to meet the mental challenge of intense exertion. "Sometimes I wonder if pushing myself to the limits is really worth the pain I have to pay," he confided to his diary following a tough track workout in October 1971. "All I can say is it better be."

That fundamental question—*Is it worth it?*—recurred again and again in Pre's speech and writing. It betrayed a natural fear and loathing of the ineluctable unpleasantness of running hard. And yet Pre kept putting himself in situations where this question was bound to come up—because he feared and loathed the thought of being defeated by that unpleasantness even more. Pre's sister Linda said of him, "He feels the same pains and fears that we all do." What made him different, she added, was that, "despite his pain and fear, he said, in essence, 'Bring it on!'"

Pre was tough—there's no doubt about it—but his toughness did not consist in any kind of superhuman imperviousness to pain or fear. Instead it took the form of a steadfast refusal to accept in himself the wimp that exists in all of us. Exercising mental fitness was a daily battle for him, but a battle he chose. "How tough, in fact, is Steve Prefontaine?" he asked himself in an interview for *Track & Field News*. "When he's ready, very tough. When he's not ready, not very."

IS IT WORTH IT?

Being ready meant being able to answer in the affirmative that all-important question: *Is it worth it?* Pre recognized that how hard he was willing to try in a race depended on what the race meant to him. Although he seldom lost, Pre learned very early in his running career that winning was not the reward that made all the fear and pain worthwhile. Rather, it was self-discovery.

"Why run is a question often asked," he wrote in a high school essay. "Why go out there every afternoon and beat out your brains? . . . What is the logic of punishing yourself each day, of striving to become better, more efficient, tougher?" He went on to answer his own question. "The value in it is what you learn about yourself. In this sort of situation all kinds of qualities come out—things that you may not have seen in yourself before."

Through running, Pre discovered not only who he was but also who and what he wanted to be. And what he wanted to be, he let everyone know, was *tough*. For Pre, toughness, or guts, was more than jockish machismo. It was a high principle. He despised the common race tactic of "sitting and kicking," or drafting behind the race leader until the final stretch and then sprinting past him. Pre chastised himself on the rare occasion when he failed to make a race "honest" from start to finish, and more than once he publicly lambasted a runner who defeated him with this "gutless" strategy.

In January 1975, Pre was invited along with 19 other elite runners to undergo psychological and physiological testing at the Cooper Institute for Aerobic Research in Dallas. In the psychological test, Pre baffled his interviewers by stating that he raced not necessarily to win but to see "who has the most guts." He was then subjected to a VO_2 max test. This test is like a solo race on a treadmill except that it's open-ended. As such, it's a purer test of toughness than a normal race. The runner continues at ever-increasing intensity *until he cannot take the suffering any longer* and quits voluntarily. Pre scored an 84.4, surpassing all of the other runners in his cohort. To this day, Pre's result remains among the best ever recorded by any runner.

In actual races, having the most guts does not guarantee victory; often it is the best tactics (such as sitting and kicking) that prove decisive. Tactical racing exasperated Pre not only because he felt it sullied the purity of competition but also because he considered it unfair to spectators. Pre felt deeply accountable to the people who came out to see him race, and this feeling intensified his motivation to give his very best effort every time he stepped onto the track.

A few days before a January 1972 indoor track race, Pre penned another of his confessional diary entries. "I'm getting nervous for this weekend," he wrote. "The pressure is beginning to mount. What do I do? The only thing I can do is wait it out and when the gun goes off, run like hell, run to win, run for yourself, your family, the people that have come from all around to watch you give them a show that they will remember for ever and ever."

As the last line of this passage intimates, Pre viewed himself as a performer, or an artist. An artist is motivated by the thrill of discovering and transforming himself through his craft, by an urgent need to share with others something very particular that's inside him, and by the desire to have an effect on others. Pre shared the same nexus of motivations. He wanted to explore himself through running, to personify the principle of toughness, and to make an impression on people.

"Some people create with words or with music or with a brush and paints," he told Don Chapman, a classmate at the University of Oregon and a sportswriter for the school newspaper. "I like to make something beautiful when I run. I like to make people stop and say, 'I've never seen anyone run like that before.' It's more than just a race, it's a style. It's doing something better than anyone else. It's being creative."

If Pre was indeed an artist, his masterpiece was the final of the 1972 Olympic 5000 meters, not because it was his best race but because it was his most beautiful, the race that most fully captured Pre's essence, his strengths and his flaws.

Before that historic contest, Pre said, "If I lose forcing the pace all the way, well, at least I can live with myself." Everything he stood for was contained in this remark. Pre's goal was not to win. His goal was to give his absolute best effort, for his own sake, for the sake of those watching, and for the sake of the race itself.

When the time came, however, Pre did *not* force the pace all the way. Instead he sat in the middle of the 13-man field as the Soviet Union's Nikola Sviridov led through a slow 4:25 first mile. Had the moment proved too great for the 21-year-old? Had the admonitions he'd received not to serve as a windbreaker for his competitors gotten to him? These questions are still debated. Whatever the reason, Pre waited until the start of the last mile to seize control of the race. But when he did, he took the thing by the throat, flinging himself off the front at a 60-seconds-per-lap pace that, incredibly, he sustained all the way to the finish line.

The only problem: So did three other runners. Twice within the closing lap, a visibly disintegrating Pre dragged himself to within inches of retaking the lead he'd lost two laps earlier. The last of these efforts was almost without precedent in championship racing. Watch a thousand other races and you will not find another in which a runner makes an obvious last-ditch bid for the lead in the bell lap and fails—*and then makes another*. Pre did. But he did so at the cost of imploding on the homestretch, losing the bronze medal to Ian Stewart of Great Britain mere steps from the tape. He had vowed beforehand to make it a "pure guts race," and he had. It just wasn't the pure guts race he had planned. Such is art.

As soon as it was over, Pre took off his shoes and scuttled to a hiding place in the bowels of the Olympic stadium. He wanted to be alone. But Blaine Newnham, a sportswriter for the *Eugene Register-Guard*, found him. Newnham was the Howard Cosell to Pre's Muhammad Ali—the journalist who knew him best and who coaxed out his most revealing statements. A couple of days before the race, Pre had told Newnham, "Everybody is expecting so much from me. I just want to get the dang thing over with. . . . Maybe I'm too young to handle all of this." He was petrified, yet he overcame his terror to "give them a show that they will remember for ever and ever," a show that another newspaper journalist would describe as "one of the greatest, most wildly exciting distance races in history." When Newnham discovered a heartbroken Pre deep inside the Olympic stadium, he was overcome by the pathos of the beautiful catastrophe he had just witnessed. Instead of digging for sound bites, the reporter set aside his notepad and talked the hurting young man back up off the floor.

"Did you run for third or second?" Blaine asked. "No, you ran to win, you took the lead with a mile to go, you ran your butt off, and you finished fourth. Now how bad is that?"

"Well, it wasn't that bad," Pre allowed.

As their conversation was wrapping up, Great Britain's Dave Bedford, who had been in the race with Pre, sauntered into the room. Suddenly his old self, Pre called out, "I'll see you in Montreal, Bedford—and I'll kick your butt!"

Steve Prefontaine would not get his chance for redemption at the 1976 Olympics in Montreal. Late at night on May 29, 1975, he was killed in a single-car accident near his home in Eugene after leaving a beer-fueled party that followed yet another victory at Hayward Field, Pre's home track in Eugene, where his legend was born, and where he had left an indelible imprint on so many. Pre was conscious for several minutes as he lay trapped between his capsized MG convertible and the road. No one so full of life could have accepted dying so young. But at least he died knowing he'd left it all out there.

THE QUESTION THAT EACH athlete faces in the crucial moments of a race—*How bad do you want it?*—is fundamentally a question of motivation. A number of factors influence how close a fire walker gets to the wall of his or her ultimate physical limit, but motivation exerts the strongest influence. Lurking behind the question of how badly an athlete wants to do his or her best is a deeper question—the one Pre kept coming back to: *Is it worth it?* The intensity of an athlete's motivation to achieve the best performance he or she can is determined largely by the value placed on it. Athletes push through extremely high levels of perceived effort in races because they anticipate being *rewarded*. In most cases this reward is neither utilitarian (e.g., money) nor sensorial (e.g., a delicious celebratory meal) but personal. Some sort of meaning is attached to doing one's best. That is its value. And the meaning is different for each athlete.

Neuroscientists have learned a lot within the past decade about how the perception of value motivates people. Oscar Bartra of the University of Pennsylvania and other researchers have even identified a *brain valuation system*, which is seated in the ventromedial prefrontal cortex and the ventral striatum. These areas of the brain become intensely active whenever a person is presented with or thinks about something he or she values. The more a thing is valued, the more active the BVS becomes and the more a person is willing to work—or suffer—to obtain it. The BVS overlaps with another system, the *brain reward circuit,* in such a way that merely anticipating a reward offers a hint of the same pleasure (triggered by release of the neurotransmitter dopamine) a person gets from actually experiencing it.

This ability to taste the pleasure of a reward before it is attained enables highly motivated athletes to tolerate a higher level of perceived effort than they could tolerate otherwise. Activating the brain reward circuit through the BVS is like dunking one foot in cool water to distract attention from the pain of standing on hot coals with the other foot. All that is required to exploit this capacity for affective parallel processing is a reward that is sufficiently valued and hence motivating. But that's the tricky part. For while scientists have found that these brain systems work the same way in all healthy individuals, they have also found that the things people value are highly individual, especially where abstract rewards—such as those associated with the personal meaning an athlete attaches to trying his or her best—are concerned.

Look inside any great endurance athlete and you will discover a powerful personal motivation to try hard that is linked to the special meaning the sport has for him or her. Catherine Ndereba, a four-time winner of the Boston Marathon in the early 2000s and a devout Christian, interpreted her racing as the fulfillment of God's purpose for her life and routinely conversed with her creator during races. This practice was as much a part of her formula for success—and as true to her basic character—as Pre's bravado and showmanship were of his. Ndereba's faith was also an effective coping skill. Brain imaging studies indicate that prayer alters brain function in ways that reduce pain perception, so it may well reduce perceived effort in prayerful athletes like Ndereba.

Steve Prefontaine had different motivators. Like other athletes, he feared and loathed the stress and discomfort of racing. Also like other athletes, he faced up to these unpleasant feelings by endowing his sport with personal meaning, a source of motivation that made all of the suffering "worth it." But he did so in his own way, by interpreting running as an opportunity to discover and become his best self, and to give his best to others, through the relentless pursuit of toughness, or guts—a kind of courage.

Recreational athletes are every bit as capable as elite athletes of finding personal meaning in their sport and of using this meaning to motivate exceptional effort. But talent itself is motivating, a reality that gives the most gifted athletes an advantage in facing the question, *How bad do you want it?* Research psychologists have shown through a variety of experiments that people put more effort into sports, academics, and other activities when they perceive themselves as being good at them. Rare is the pupil who studies hardest in her least favorite subject, and rare too the athlete who samples five sports and settles on the one in which he experiences the least success.

Natural ability weighs heavily in endurance athletes' calculations of how much effort their sport is worth to them. Undoubtedly, a lack of world-class genes discourages many athletes from pursuing their ultimate physical limit with all they've got. Nevertheless, real-world evidence suggests that a dearth of talent is not an insuperable barrier to "wanting it" as much as an Olympic champion.

Consider John Bingham, better known as the Penguin, who is widely regarded as a kind of anti–Steve Prefontaine, the yin to Pre's yang. Pre famously said, "To give anything less than your best is to sacrifice the gift." Twenty years later, John Bingham countered, "When you're hurting, slow down." Both men have inspired legions of runners, but they've done so in very different ways. Many a runner has a Pre poster on a wall, and many a runner has a Penguin book on a bookshelf. But few runners have a Pre poster on a wall *and* a Penguin book on a bookshelf.

John Bingham grew up in a working-class Italian family in Chicago in the 1950s. Like most of his friends, he dreamed of becoming a professional athlete. The only thing that stopped him from fulfilling his dream was an extraordinary lack of athletic talent.

John's first love was baseball, but his tenure on the diamond was brief. He gave up the sport at age nine after failing to make the cut at Little League tryouts. In junior high, John went out for the basketball team, but he sat on the bench almost the entire season. When the coach finally let him onto the court to attempt a game-winning shot in the last minute of a nail-biter, he tossed an air ball and was carried off the court on the shoulders of the opposing team. So ended his basketball career.

After being discharged from the Army in 1976, John became completely sedentary. He also became a smoker and a heavy drinker. By the time he was 40, John weighed 240 pounds and felt as bad as he looked. He made several attempts to get back in shape, but was thwarted each time by flagging motivation. Then one day John fell into conversation with the fittest guy he knew, a colleague on the faculty of the Oberlin College Conservatory of Music and an avid cyclist. John came away from the exchange feeling fired up in a way he'd never been. He bought an ancient, steel-framed Peugeot 10-speed bike at a local yard sale. After a few rides, John began to see what his colleague saw in cycling. The more he rode, the fitter he became, and the fitter he became, the more he rode, working his way up to 62 miles in a single jaunt.

John's work required a fair amount of travel. Hating the hassle of trying to maintain his cycling habit on work-related trips, he took up running as a way to work out when he couldn't ride. He quickly discovered that running when you're overweight and out of shape is harder than cycling in the same condition. John's first run lasted only a few minutes. But he stuck with it, running as far as he could each time he laced up his trainers. It took him almost six months to build up to 3 miles.

A week after he crossed the 3-mile threshold, John was talked into doing a race. At that point he had no business attempting anything more challenging than a 5K fun run, but he agreed to participate in a duathlon that consisted of *two* 5-km runs separated by a 25-km bike leg. On the morning of the competition, John happened to walk by a table laden with trophies that were to be distributed to the top finishers in the various age and gender categories. Intoxicated by his recent gains in fitness, John spontaneously changed his goal from finishing the race to claiming one of those awards. He came up short, finishing dead last.

Hungry for redemption, John stepped up his training and found another race—an easier one without a bike segment. Despite trying as hard as he could, he finished last again. "I realized that if I was going to stay in the sport of running, I was going to have to find a reason other than winning," he wrote later.

In fact, John had already found another reason to run: enjoyment. Despite the vast disparity between his ambitions and his talent, John derived great satisfaction from the experience of racing. Just crossing the finish line made him feel good about himself, even if most of the other competitors had already gone home by the time he got there. John began to race frequently and went so far as to change jobs and move halfway across the country to make his life more accommodating to his training and racing. He had become an athlete after all and felt as fulfilled in his sport as any pro racer, minus the fame and fortune.

Actually, fame and fortune came too. A gifted storyteller, John began to post humorous accounts of his athletic adventures on a popular online message board for runners. In stark contrast to other posters, he embraced being slow, even adopting the nom de plume "the Penguin" in reference to his waddling stride. A writer who had contributed to *Runner's World* took a liking to John's stories and passed them along to Amby Burfoot, the magazine's editor. Burfoot saw in John an ideal voice for the new generation of runners, who were heavier, slower, and less competitive than previous generations. The first installment of the "Penguin Chronicles" appeared in the publication's May 1996 issue. Readers swooned and the column— originally scheduled to run for eight months—was made permanent.

A succession of books followed, bearing titles such as *The Courage to Start* and *No Need for Speed*. Running clubs and event directors from Seattle to Miami flew John in for speaking engagements, where he repeated the same message again and again: *You don't have to be fast to be a runner*. By the early 2000s, the Penguin was arguably the most celebrated American runner since Pre, far better known than the country's current crop of Olympians. Tens of thousands of women and men credited him with inspiring them to get off the couch and get moving.

They called themselves Penguins, the counterpart to Pre's People. Once intimidated by the more hard-core faction of the running community, these joggers now stood proudly apart from them. "Running isn't the be-all and end-all of our existence," the Penguin wrote. "Our lives and happiness don't revolve around the last run or next personal record."

John's best marathon time was 4:35. He once told a reporter that he could run a sub-four-hour marathon if he wanted to. "But I don't want to," he said. "I have no interest. The price for me to run a sub-four marathon would be so high it's not worth it."

It's not worth it. Echoes of Steve Prefontaine—except John was making the opposite choice. Or was he? In his fourth book, *An Accidental Athlete*, John made a startling confession.

"In spite of all my talk about the joy of the journey," he admitted, "at some level I'm a closet competitor. I enjoy passing people. I enjoy beating someone."

It turned out that, despite avowals to the contrary, John had never fully given up the desire to see how fast he could be. Like many athletes who lack special talent, he'd assumed initially that there was no point in trying as hard as he could. But he couldn't get rid of the feeling that the whole reason endurance sports existed was to provide a forum for redefining personal limits, and that the thrill of this pursuit was what drew anyone, talented or not, to endurance racing, even if one preferred not to admit it.

"Some runners tell me they don't feel competitive, even in races," John wrote. "I don't believe it." He went on to encourage runners of all ability levels to chase the goal of getting faster—not for its own sake but for the sake of the transformative experience that comes with trying as hard as you possibly can. He confided to his readers that the races in which he had pushed himself the hardest and suffered the most were among the most meaningful moments of his life. And the moment that stood out from all others, he said, occurred one year at the Sunburst 10K in South Bend, Indiana.

John's plan for this event was to run cautiously through the first half and then go for broke. At 5 miles, when he was going for broke, he was passed by a runner who appeared to be about John's age. His competitive instincts kicked in. John sped up and nosed ahead of his challenger, who quickly passed him back. John refused to let him get away. It hurt like hell, but he fully embraced his suffering, never losing hold of the conviction that the thing he was chasing was worth the agony he was heaping upon himself.

As he came toward the finish line, having at last shaken his challenger, John saw the race clock and realized he had a chance to break

51 minutes—a huge PR. He pushed even harder, hurt even more, and crossed the line at 51:03.

Euphoric, John turned around to shake hands with the man who, by his description, "helped me find something deep inside me that I had never known existed . . . a strength, a determination, and a willingness to suffer that I never knew I had."

Exactly. Every athlete who has pushed beyond his or her known limits of endurance in the quest for improvement understands these sentiments. There is no experience quite like that of driving yourself to the point of wanting to give up and then not giving up. In that moment of "raw reality," as Mark Allen has called it, when something inside you asks, *How bad do you want it?*, an inner curtain is drawn open, revealing a part of you that is not seen except in moments of crisis. And when your answer is to keep pushing, you come away from the trial with the kind of self-knowledge and self-respect that can't be bought.

In these encounters with raw reality, athletes find not only *reasons* to keep pushing but also *ways* to keep pushing—motivations (why) and coping skills (how) that they can go back to and build on the next time they are tempted to slow down or quit. And both the why and the how are to some degree personal, specific to the individual athlete.

MENTAL FITNESS, LIKE MOTIVATION, comes in many flavors. There is no such thing as a single ideal coping style that athletes converge on as they mature. While certain skills and traits—such as resilience—are essential to greatness in endurance sports and are therefore possessed in some measure by all of the best athletes, optimal mental fitness is an individual thing. In much the same way that optimal running form is different for each runner for the simple reason that each runner has a unique body, optimal mental fitness is specific to each athlete because each athlete has a one-of-a-kind self.

An athlete's personal formula for peak mental fitness is always consistent with the nature of his or her singular being.

In the preceding chapters we focused on coping skills that are more or less universal. Together we looked at core components of mental fitness that elite endurance athletes have used to overcome particular challenges. Jenny Barringer overcame competitive self-sabotage by bracing herself. Greg LeMond exploited the power of time-based goals to master the art of interpreting his effort perceptions and to overcome the lingering effects of a near-fatal accident to ride the race of his life. Siri Lindley overcame a pattern of choking by letting go of her dreams and learning to race in the flow of the moment. Willie Stewart used the acquired coping skill of adaptability to activate the hardwired coping skill of neuroplasticity and overcome the loss of an arm via the workaround effect. Cadel Evans overcame repeated failure by developing resilience, the one missing piece in his formula for greatness. Joseph Sullivan overcame having the "wrong body" for his sport via "bulletin boarding"—using spoken and unspoken challenges to his athletic ego as motivators. Paula Newby-Fraser overcame the fear-based misstep of overtraining by learning to trust her body and its intuitions. Ryan Vail overcame competitors with superior talent through the group effect—that is, by taking advantage of the performance-enhancing power of teamwork. Thomas Voeckler used the audience effect and the success effect to raise his expectations and get closer to his ultimate physical limit than most athletes are able to. And Ned Overend overcame the limitations of age by nurturing his passion for sport.

Elite athletes do not have a monopoly on these coping skills and traits. They are accessible to all. The stories and the science shared in the preceding chapters are intended to serve as a kind of path that any athlete can follow to develop these same abilities. But a complete and generic roadmap for the cultivation of maximum mental fitness does not exist, because again, there are many ways of exercising "mind over muscle" that work brilliantly for some athletes and not at all for others, based on who they are at the deepest level.

Perhaps the reason Pre remains so beloved today is that he was so wholly himself. His behaviors in and around races were never arbitrary or conforming but always expressed a cohesive, original self. (Who else would have run a victory lap wearing a T-shirt imprinted with a red octagon and the words "Stop Pre"?) But these quintessentially Pre behaviors were more than self-expression. They were also coping skills that aided his performance.

Although he was almost unbeatable at home, Pre failed to win on the international stage, leading some commentators to suggest that he should change his racing style of leading early only to be passed in the bell lap by runners using a sit-and-kick strategy. Pre was not deaf to these criticisms, but neither did he change his style. Front running suited him because it fit his personality—specifically, the part of his personality that craved control. "I feel more comfortable when I'm in control," he said. "You can slow the race down or speed it up." Indeed, studies have shown that athletes generally experience a lower level of perceived effort when they are allowed to control the intensity of exercise than they do when the same level of intensity is imposed externally.

Yet some athletes feel more comfortable as counterpunchers. Mo Farah, for example, won five world championships and two Olympic gold medals at 5000 and 10000 meters with a racing style that involved patiently working his way up through the field and assuming the lead only at the very end.

Pre's penchant for bellyaching before races was also a part of his distinctive recipe for handling the stress and discomfort of competing. His Oregon teammate Steve Bence told biographer Tom Jordan, "Before any race, Pre would always say how he didn't feel good and didn't want to run. No matter where the race was or how important it was, he was saying, 'Aw, I wish I wasn't running. I don't think I'm going to run well.' Then he'd go out and run like heck." All of this negative talk probably served to relieve some of the pressure Pre felt before races. He let himself off the hook to a degree by articulating a preemptive excuse for failure so that he could calm down and save his mental energy for when it was needed. Psychologists refer to this coping mechanism as "defensive pessimism."

There are other ways to deal with pre-race nerves—ways that might work better for athletes with a different sort of personality than Pre's. Psychological experiments have demonstrated that when people tell themselves they are excited rather than nervous before a challenge such as speaking in public or taking a math test, they perform better. This technique has not yet been tested in an exercise context, but it's reasonable to assume that it would work just as well before an endurance race because anxiety is known to increase perceived effort.

Steve Prefontaine arrived at his unique formula for mental fitness by first developing a strong sense of self and then being true to that identity. His distinctive style was a simple—but seldom easy—matter of being himself. Being oneself is in fact the only way that any athlete can evolve his or her individual formula for peak mental fitness. But this is not as automatic as it sounds. Athletes often hold back from being themselves. Another runner who shared Pre's instinct for pre-race complaining, for example, might have kept mum for fear of being judged a malingerer.

Being oneself also requires a certain amount of comfort with uncertainty. None of us are born knowing who we are. We become who we are by facing new challenges and coping with them. Pre embraced the uncertainty of pushing beyond past limits.

"I've never been here before," he said after a race in his freshman year at Oregon. "It was unexplored territory. It's strange. You find yourself in a spot in time you've never hit before and you don't know if you can finish. But I'm always exploring myself. I haven't reached the threshold of unconsciousness yet. Maybe I never will."

The path between you and the best you can be is unexplored territory. You are on your own, to some extent, to discover not only what motivates you to "leave it all out there" but also your special formula for maximum mental fitness. This is what it means to become your own sports psychologist. To approach your sport as an ongoing fire walk, aiming to move closer and closer to the unreachable wall that represents your ultimate physical limit, is to embark on a journey of transformation in which you become more and more the athlete— and the person—you want to be as you tackle the obstacles that hinder your progress. This journey is the greatest gift that endurance sports have to offer, and all you have to do to receive it is to wholly embrace the challenge of seeing how far you can go.

To be sure, not all athletes can afford to train for several hours a day. In many cases, an athlete must possess enough talent to make a go of racing professionally to justify that sort of investment. But there's a difference between time commitment and effort commitment. The race is the same distance for every athlete. When the gun goes off, the slowest competitor has as much reason as the fastest to give his or her best effort until the finish line is reached. And every athlete, regardless of how much time he or she chooses to devote to training, has the opportunity to work on developing the mental fitness that is needed to try harder and more effectively on race day. Talent may set an athlete's ultimate physical limit, but it does not determine how close to that limit an athlete is able to get. As John Bingham wrote, "I've seen runners at a 12-minute pace who I believe have more heart, more race sense, and more sheer guts than some of the world's fastest runners."

We've all seen these athletes. They are living proof that talent does not dictate one's capacity to acquire mental fitness, and that striving toward one's personal maximum of mental fitness is always "worth it." The same journey of self-becoming undertaken by Steve Prefontaine and the other master sports psychologists we've learned from in this book is available to all athletes who accept the challenge of the fire walk that leads toward full realization of inner potential.

SELECTED BIBLIOGRAPHY

INTRODUCTION

Cona, G., A. Cavazzana, A. Paoli, G. Marcolin, A. Grainer, and P. S. Bisiacchi. "It's a Matter of Mind! Cognitive Functioning Predicts the Athletic Performance in Ultra-Marathon Runners." *PLOS ONE* 10, no. 7 (July 2015): e0132943.

Pageaux, B., R. Lepers, K. C. Dietz, and S. M. Marcora. "Response Inhibition Impairs Subsequent Self-Paced Endurance Performance." *European Journal of Applied Physiology* 114, no. 5 (May 2014): 1095–1105.

Wall, B. A., G. Watson, J. J. Peiffer, C. R. Abbiss, R. Siegel, and P. B. Laursen. "Current Hydration Guidelines Are Erroneous: Dehydration Does Not Impair Exercise Performance in the Heat." *British Journal of Sports Medicine* 49, no. 16 (August 2015): 1077–1083.

Walsh, V. "Is Sport the Brain's Biggest Challenge?" *Current Biology* 24, no. 18 (2014): R859–R860.

CHAPTER 1

Havenar, J. and M. Lochbaum. "Differences in Participation Motives of First-Time Marathon Finishers and Pre-race Dropouts." *Journal of Sport Behavior* 30, no. 3 (September 2007): 270.

Marcora, S. M., W. Staiano, and V. Manning. "Mental Fatigue Impairs Physical Performance in Humans." *Journal of Applied Physiology* 106, no 3 (March 2009): 857–864.

Smith, R. E. "Effects of Coping Skills Training on Generalized Self-Efficacy and Locus of Control." *Journal of Personality and Social Psychology* 56, no. 2 (February 1989): 228–233.

CHAPTER 2

Baden, D. A., T. L. McLean, R. Tucker, T. D. Noakes, and A. St. Clair Gibson. "Effect of Anticipation During Unknown or Unexpected Exercise Duration on Rating of Perceived Exertion, Affect, and Physiological Function." *British Journal of Sports Medicine* 39, no. 10 (October 2005): 742–746.

Galak, J., and T. Meyvis. "The Pain Was Greater if It Will Happen Again: The Effect of Anticipated Continuation of Retrospective Discomfort." *Journal of Experimental Psychology: General* 140, no. 1 (February 2011): 63–75.

Ivanova, E., D. Jensen, J. Cassoff, F. Gu, and B. Knäuper. "Acceptance and Commitment Therapy Improves Exercise Tolerance in Sedentary Women." *Medicine and Science in Sports and Exercise* 47, no. 6 (June 2015): 1251–1258.

Smirmaul, B. P., J. L. Dantas, F. Y. Nakamura, and G. Pereira. "The Psychobiological Model: A New Explanation to Intensity Regulation and (In)Tolerance in Endurance Exercise." *Revista Brasileira de Educação Física e Esporte* 27, no. 2 (April–June 2013): 333–340.

CHAPTER 3

Allen, E. J., P. M. Dechow, D. G. Pope, and G. Wu. "Reference-Dependent Preferences: Evidence from Runners." Working Paper No. 20343, National Bureau of Economic Research (July 2014), doi: 10.3386/w20343.

Bar-Eli, M., G. Tenenbaum, J. S. Pie, Y. Btesh, and A. Almog. "Effect of Goal Difficulty, Goal Specificity and Duration of Practice Time Intervals on Muscular Endurance Performance." *Journal of Sports Science* 15, no. 2 (April 1997): 125–135.

Wittekind, A. L., D. Micklewright, and R. Beneke. "Teleoanticipation in All-Out Short-Duration Cycling." *British Journal of Sports Medicine* 45, no. 2 (February 2011): 114–119.

CHAPTER 4

Beilock, S. *Choke: What the Secrets of the Brain Reveal About Getting It Right When You Have To.* New York: Atria, 2011.

Blanchfield, A. W., J. Hardy, H. M. De Morree, W. Staiano, and S. M. Marcora. "Talking Yourself out of Exhaustion: The Effects of Self-Talk on Endurance Performance." *Medicine and Science in Sports and Exercise* 45, no. 5 (2014): 998–1007.

Renfree, A., J. West, M. Corbett, C. Rhoden, and A. St. Clair Gibson. "Complex Interplay Between Determinants of Pacing and Performance During 20-km Cycle Time Trials." *International Journal of Sports Physiology and Performance* 7, no. 2 (June 2012): 121–129.

Schücker, L., N. Hagemann, B. Strauss, and K. Völker. "The Effect of Attentional Focus on Running Economy." *Journal of Sports Science* 27, no. 12 (October 2009): 1241–1248.

Williams, E. L., H. S. Jones, S. Andy Sparks, D. C. Marchant, A. W. Midgley, and L. R. McNaughton. "Competitor Presence Reduces Internal Attentional Focus and Improves 16.1km Cycling Time Trial Performance." *Journal of Science and Medicine in Sport* 18, no. 4 (July 2015): 486–491.

Zachry, T., G. Wulf, J. Mercer, and N. Bezodis. "Increased Movement Accuracy and Reduced EMG Activity as the Result of Adopting an External Focus of Attention." *Brain Research Bulletin* 67, no. 4 (October 2005): 304–309.

CHAPTER 5

Furst, D. M., T. Ferr, and N. Megginson. "Motivation of Disabled Athletes to Participate in Triathlons." *Psychological Report* 72, no. 2 (April 1993): 403–406.

Haudum, A., J. Birklbauer, R. Sieghartsleitner, C. Gonaus, and E. Müller. "Blood Lactate Response, Oxygen Consumption, and Muscle Activity During Treadmill Running with Constraint." *Perceptual and Motor Skills* 119, no. 1 (August 2014): 20–37.

Valliant, P. M., I. Bezzubyk, L. Daley, and M. E. Asu. "Psychological Impact of Sport on Disabled Athletes." *Psychological Report* 56, no. 3 (June 1985): 923–929.

CHAPTER 6

Aarts, H., K. I. Ruys, H. Veling, R. A. Renes, J. H. de Groot, A. M. van Nunen, and S. Geertjes. "The Art of Anger: Reward Context Turns Avoidance Responses to Anger-Related Objects into Approach." *Psychological Science* 21, no. 10 (October 2010): 1406–1410.

Collins, D., and A. MacNamara. "The Rocky Road to the Top: Why Talent Needs Trauma." *Sports Medicine* 42, no. 11 (November 2012): 907–914.

Janssen, S. A., P. Spinhoven, and J. F. Brosschot. "Experimentally Induced Anger, Cardiovascular Reactivity, and Pain Sensitivity." *Journal of Psychosomatic Research* 51, no. 3 (September 2001): 479–485.

Sarkar, M., D. Fletcher, and D. J. Brown. "What Doesn't Kill Me . . . : Adversity-Related Experiences Are Vital in the Development of Superior Olympic Performance." *Journal of Science and Medicine in Sport* 18, no. 4 (July 2015): 475–479, doi: 10.1016/j.jsams.2014.06.010.

Seery, M. D., R. J. Leo, S. P. Lupien, C. L. Kondrak, and J. L. Almonte. "An Upside to Adversity? Moderate Cumulative Lifetime Adversity Is Associated with Resilient Responses in the Face of Controlled Stressors." *Psychological Science* 24, no. 7 (July 2013): 1181–1189.

Sekiguchi, A., M. Sugiura, Y. Taki, Y. Kotozaki, R. Nouchi, H. Takeuchi, T. Araki, S. Hanawa, S. Nakagawa, C. M. Miyauchi, A. Sakuma, and R. Kawashima. "Brain Structural Changes as Vulnerability Factors and Acquired Signs of Post-earthquake Stress." *Molecular Psychiatry* 18, no. 5 (May 2013): 618–623.

Wicks, R. J. *Bounce: Living the Resilient Life*. Oxford: Oxford University Press, 2009.

CHAPTER 7

Barrett, R. S., and J. M. Manning. "Relationships Between Rigging Set-Up, Anthropometry, Physical Capacity, Rowing Kinematics and Rowing Performance." *Sports Biomechanics* 3, no. 2 (July 2004): 221–235.

Dimakopolou, E., A. J. Blazevich, S. Kaloupsis, V. Diafas, and V. Bachev. "Prediction of Stroking Characteristics of Elite Rowers from Anthropometric Variables." *Serbian Journal of Sports Sciences* 1 (2007): 91–97.

CHAPTER 8

Halson, S. L., M. W. Bridge, R. Meeusen, B. Busschaert, M. Gleeson, D. A. Jones, and A. E. Jeukendrup. "Time Course of Performance Changes and Fatigue Markers During Intensified Training in Trained Cyclists." *Journal of Applied Physiology* 93, no. 3 (September 2002): 947–956.

CHAPTER 9

Cohen, E. E., R. Ejsmond-Frey, N. Knight, and R. J. Dunbar. "Rowers' High: Behavioural Synchrony Is Correlated with Elevated Pain Thresholds." *Biology Letters* 6, no. 1 (February 2010): 106–108.

Epstein, S. *The Sports Gene: Inside the Science of Extraordinary Performance*. New York: Current, 2013.

Finn, A. *Running with the Kenyans: Discovering the Secrets of the Fastest People on Earth*. New York: Ballantine Books, 2013.

Waytz, A., K. M. Hoffman, and S. A. Tawalter. "Superhumanization Bias in Whites' Perceptions of Blacks." *Social Psychological and Personality Science* 6 (October 2014): 352–359.

CHAPTER 10

Andreacci, J. L., L. M. LeMura, S. L. Cohen, E. A. Urbansky, S. A. Chelland, and S. P. von Duvillard. "The Effects of Frequency of Encouragement on Performance During Maximal Exercise Testing." *Journal of Sports Science* 20, no. 4 (April 2002): 345–352.

Bateson, M., L. Callow, J. R. Holmes, M. L. Redmond Roche, and D. Nettle. "Do Images of 'Watching Eyes' Induce Behaviour That Is More Pro-Social or More Normative? A Field Experiment on Littering." *PLOS ONE* 8, no. 12 (December 2013): e82055.

Baumann, C. W., and T. J. Wetter. "Aerobic and Anaerobic Changes in Collegiate Male Runners Across a Cross-County Season." *International Journal of Exercise Science* 3, no. 4 (2010): 9.

Blanchfield, A., J. Hardy, and S. Marcora. "Non-conscious Visual Cues Related to Affect and Action Alter Perception of Effort and Endurance Performance." *Frontiers in Human Neuroscience* 11, no. 8 (December 2014): 967.

Boutcher, S. H., L. A. Fleischer-Curtain, and S. D. Gines. "The Effect of

Self-Presentation on Perceived Exertion." *Journal of Sport and Exercise Psychology* 10, no. 3 (September 1988): 270.

Rhea, M. R., D. M. Landers, B. A. Alvar, and S. M. Arent. "The Effects of Competition and the Presence of an Audience on Weight Lifting Performance." *Journal of Strength and Conditioning Research* 17, no. 2 (May 2003): 303–306.

Van de Rijt, S., M. Kang, M. Restivo, and A. Patil. "Field Experiments of Success-Breeds-Success Dynamics." *Proceedings of the National Academy of Sciences* 111, no. 19 (May 2014): 6934–6939.

Weger, U. W., and S. Loughnan. "Mobilizing Unused Resources: Using the Placebo Concept to Enhance Cognitive Performance." *Quarterly Journal of Experimental Psychology* (Hove) 66, no. 1 (2013): 23–28.

CHAPTER 11

Jewett, S. "Longevity and the Longevity Syndrome." *The Gerontologist* 13, no. 1 (1973): 91–99.

Shipley, B. A., A. Weiss, G. Der, M. D. Taylor, and I. J. Deary. "Neuroticism, Extraversion, and Mortality in the UK Health and Lifestyle Survey: A 21-Year Prospective Cohort Study." *Psychosomatic Medicine* 69, no. 9 (December 2007): 923–931.

Terracciano, A., J. A. Schrack, A. R. Sutin, W. Chan, E. M. Simonsick, and L. Ferrucci. "Personality, Metabolic Rate and Aerobic Capacity." *PLOS ONE* 8, no. 1 (2013): e54746.

Tolea, M. I., A. Terracciano, E. M. Simonsick, E. J. Metter, P. T. Costa Jr., and L. Ferrucci. "Associations Between Personality Traits, Physical Activity Level, and Muscle Strength." *Journal of Research in Personality* 46, no. 3 (June 2012): 264–270.

Vallerand, R. J. "The Role of Passion in Sustainable Psychological Well-Being." *Psychological Well-Being* 2, no. 1 (2012), doi: 10.1186/2211-1522-2-1.

CHAPTER 12

Bartra, O., J. T. McGuire, and J. W. Kable. "The Valuation System: A Coordinate-Based Meta-Analysis of BOLD fMRI Experiments Examining Neural Correlates of Subjective Value." *Neuroimage* 1, no. 75 (August 2013): 412–427.

Brooks, A. W. "Get Excited: Reappraising Pre-performance Anxiety as Excitement." *Journal of Experimental Psychology: General* 143, no. 3 (June 2014): 1144–1158.

Dezutter, J., A. Wachholtz, and J. Corveleyn. "Prayer and Pain: The Mediating Role of Positive Re-Appraisal." *Journal of Behavioral Medicine* 34, no. 6 (December 2011): 542–549.

Lander, P. J., R. J. Butterly, and A. M. Edwards. "Self-Paced Exercise Is Less Physically Challenging Than Enforced Constant Pace Exercise of the Same Intensity: Influence of Complex Central Metabolic Control." *British Journal of Sports Medicine* 43, no. 10 (October 2009): 789–795.

Schunk, D. H. "Self-Efficacy, Motivation, and Performance." *Journal of Applied Sport Psychology* 7, no. 2 (1995): 112–137.

INDEX

272

Behavioral synchrony, 196, 197, 204
Beijing Olympics, 17, 40, 152, 153, 205
Beilock, Sian, 86, 87
Belete, Mimi, 53, 54
Bence, Steve: on Prefontaine, 263
Benson, Juli, 52
Berardelli, Claudio, 24
Berlin Marathon, 18
Bernaudeau, Jean-René, 216, 217
Bernhard, Olivier, 244
Bingham, John ("Penguin"), 257–258, 265;
    racing by, 258–259, 260–261; running
    by, 258, 259–260; training by, 258–259
Biology Letters, 196
Birmingham, Collis, 199
Bizzarri, Angela, 31, 42, 43, 44
Bjorklund, Garry, 248, 249
Blades, Pat, 58–59
BMC Racing Team, 138, 139, 140, 142, 146;
    Evans and, 125, 130
Body measurements: performance and,
    156; stroke patterns and, 153
Boland, Patrick, 118
Bookwalter, Brent, 142
Boonen, Tom, 212
Boston Marathon, 19, 203, 204, 221, 256
Bounce: Living the Resilient Life (Wicks),
    136
Boutcher, Stephen, 221
Bovim, Ingvill, 55
Brain, 25, 47, 87–88; challenging, 8–9;
    electrical activity of, 99; fatigue for,
    26; function, 99, 256; mind and, 24;
    muscle and, 27; performance and, 27;
    plasticity of, 116; rhythms, 99
Brain-imaging studies, 133, 256
Brain Research Bulletin, 88
Brain revolution, 8, 10, 12
Brain Training for Runners (Fitzgerald), 8
Brain valuation system (BVS), 255
Brehm, Jack, 69
Brioches la Boulangère team, 212, 214,
    215, 217
British Journal of Sports Medicine, 67
Brook, Chris, 110
Brown, Doug, 249

Bruhn, John, 196
Bulletin boarding, 159, 262
Burfoot, Amby: Bingham and, 259
Burghardt, Marcus, 139, 140, 142, 143
Burla, Serena, 117, 120; psychological
    changes for, 118–119
Burns, George: on longevity, 236
Burroughs, Heather: Barringer and, 42
Burton, Jeff, 1–2
Butts, Kendall, 111
Bydgoszcz 2013: 189–190, 205

Carfrae, Mirinda, 102, 187
Carlson, Timothy, 102
Casar, Sandy, 210, 214
Catalina Marathon, 123
Cave, Leanda, 103–104
Challenged Athletes Foundation, 112, 114
Challenges, 2, 8–9, 51, 66, 113, 120; coping
    with, 28–29; facing, 36, 264; muddling
    through, 13; overcoming, 14, 262;
    psychological, 11; responding to, 30, 35
Chapman, Don, 252
Chavanel, Sylvain, 214, 216–217
Cheating, 61, 62, 66
Cherop, Philemon, 191
Cheruiyot, Pasca, 44
Cheruiyot, Robert, 19
Chicago Marathon, 17, 18, 19–23, 24, 29,
    31, 205
Choke (Beilock), 86, 88
Choking, 32, 35, 41, 85, 87, 89–90, 100, 262;
    defining, 86; self-consciousness and, 99
Circuit de la Sarthe, 222
Classen, Kerry, 244
Close to Flying (Evans), 138
Coburn, Emma, 45
Cohen, Nathan, 153, 160, 161; Olympics
    and, 155, 156; rowing by, 150, 151, 152,
    154, 155, 162–168
Collins, Dave, 132, 135
Competition, 28, 36–37, 156, 195; adversity
    in, 141; challenges of, 132; high-stakes,
    87; level of, 221; purity of, 252
Competitor Radio Show, 90
Confidence issues, 33, 35, 36, 39–40, 48

London Olympics, 149, 156, 164, 220
Longevity, influences on, 236
Los Angeles Times, on LeMond, 62
Loughnan, Stephen, 223
Lucas, Bill, 164
Lydiard, Arthur, 203

Maadi Cup, 151
Macel, Teresa, 94
Macharinyang, Hosea, 191
Mack, Bobby, 190, 198, 199, 200, 201, 202, 206–207
MacLaren, Jim, 112
MacNamara, Aine, 132, 135
Mahoney, Dick, 203
Makau, Patrick, 239
Maloy, Elizabeth, 31
Mammoth Track Club, 204
Mancebo, Francisco, 214
Marcora, Samuele, 7, 11, 25, 26, 101, 223; psychobiological model of, 47, 69; spectator support and, 221; study by, 220
Marie, Thierry, 72
Marino, Amanda, 44
Marlborough Express, The, 162
Marlborough Rowing Association, 152
Martin, Tony, 146, 228
Maslow, Abraham, 87
McKaig, Alissa, 31, 32–33, 34; confidence issues and, 35, 36
McKeon, Sean, 39, 41, 51
McLaughlin, Allie, 41, 44
McMahon, Brigitte, 94
McNaughton, Lars, 89
Medhin, Teklemariam, 200, 207
Medicine and Science in Sports and Exercise, 49, 101
Meet of Champions, 2, 4
Meltdowns, 44–45, 46, 50, 51, 85, 99, 177, 178
Mental barriers, 11, 13
Mental capacity, 52, 102, 115, 243
Mental fitness, 24, 28, 29, 34, 50, 99, 115, 120, 250; components of, 262; coping style and, 30; developing, 12, 13, 14, 30,

35–36, 37, 116, 265; maximizing, 36–37, 261–262, 264, 265; training and, 35, 36
Merckx, Axel, 212
Merga, Deriba, 20
Merga, Imane, 201, 207
Meyer, Elana, 70, 71
Meyer, Greg, 204
Meyvis, Tom, 50
Mind: body and, 25; brain and, 24; muscle and, 8, 11, 12, 27, 262; performance and, 8, 9
Miyazuka, Hideya, 169
Moinard, Amaël, 143
Monfort, Maxime, 143
Montreal Olympics, 254
Moreau, Christophe, 216
Moss, Julie, 108, 112
Motivation, 11, 47, 137, 138, 159, 226, 228, 252, 254–255, 261; fodder for, 159; increasing, 136, 221; source of, 256
Motivational intensity, theory of, 69
Mouthon, Isabelle, 178
Movement patterns, 88, 158
Movement-related cortical potential (MRCP), 47
Mückel, Ute, 174, 175
Multisport, 4
Munich World Cup, 162
Murphy, Dan, 248
Muscle: brain and, 27; endurance racing and, 9, 69; mind and, 8, 11, 12, 27, 262

National Institute of Aging, 238
NBC Sports, 172, 177, 184, 185
NCAA Championships, 117–118, 181
NCAA Cross Country Championships, 39, 40, 41, 46, 50, 51, 53, 205, 247
Ndereba, Catherine, 256
Ndiku, Jonathan, 191, 199
Neuroplasticity, 117, 118, 119, 138, 159, 160; coping skill of, 262; workaround effect and, 157–158
Neuropsychology, 14, 159
Neuroticism, 237–238, 243
Neurotransmitters, 99, 255
New York City Marathon, 17, 119, 221

ABOUT THE AUTHOR

MATT FITZGERALD is an acclaimed endurance-sports writer and authority. His many previous books include the best-selling *Racing Weight; RUN: The Mind-Body Method of Running by Feel; Brain Training for Runners*; and *Diet Cults*. His book *Iron War* was long-listed for the 2012 William Hill Sports Book of the Year. Matt is a regular contributor to *Men's Fitness, Men's Health,*  *Outside, Runner's World, Bicycling, Running Times, Women's Running,* and other sports and fitness publications. He lives and trains in California.